What peopl

Medicine ot

I am in awe of Imelda Almqvis ...tainly making a powerful contribution to our ...ommunity through her books and workshops. If there was one teacher's work on the topic of "imagination" that I would choose to read it would be anything written by Imelda. Her passion, her wealth of knowledge, and ability as a story teller is unparalleled. Medicine of the Imagination is such an important book for our time as we must harness our imaginations as well as fearlessly explore our shadow to bring harmony back into our lives. This "inner activism" also brings healing and balancing to our world.
Sandra Ingerman, MA, award winning author of 12 books including *Walking in Light* and *The Book of Ceremony: Shamanic Wisdom for Invoking the Sacred in Everyday Life*

Imelda Almqvist is one of the most creative people I have ever met. A talented artist, writer, teacher and she lives in the heart of the creative imagination. Her medicine is her creativity! Not only is she a gift with her outpouring of creative expression, now she is teaching us how to tap into our own creative genius...
Michael Stone, Consultant, Teacher, Author, Radio Host and Producer of The Shift Network's Global Shamanism Summits, www.welloflight.com

When you meet teachers so full of knowledge usually they are dead, so you can only read their books! When you can work with someone like Imelda in person, you should grab the opportunity!
Katharine Lucy Haworth, shamanic practitioner, UK

For me, "imagination" is well symbolized by a flame. In that sense, Imelda Almqvist's book is a torch, a spark, a lightning

flash, a glowing hearth. She presents a spiral of embers leading into the heart of what fuels our creativity... and, conversely, the shadow-energies that can thwart it. But light and shadow exist together - a bright danse macabre - and we need to engage both to fully access our own creative depths. Step-by-step, with clear exercises in each chapter, Almqvist leads her reader into and through this dance, so we can each step into our own true creative heart-places. What an accomplishment! I love this book!
Renna Shesso, shamanic practitioner/teacher, author of *Math for Mystics* and *Planets for Pagans: Sacred Sites, Ancient Lore, and Magical Stargazing*

I like Imelda's style, it's intimate and witty, enabling me to begin to know her as a person as I read her books; I feel connected with her and so gain more from her words. Medicine of the Imagination is about getting intimate with the natural and spirit worlds, and Life, the Universe and Everything. She has vast experience and shares it in this book through her light style and deep words to explore life's interconnectedness through lenses of architecture, literature, theatre, music, art, mythology, and science. She shows us how they all weave with each other so nothing stands alone. It's mind-opening.
Elen Sentier, author of *The Celtic Chakras*, *Merlin*, and *Elen of the Ways*

In her new book, Imelda Almqvist puts us in touch with transcendence. She takes us on a tour of the deeper part of human experience – illness, ethics, evil, compassion and death – and gives us "simple" exercises with which to explore how these constructs and experiences reside within us. I diligently followed several of these "simple" directions and had a profound "AHA moment," finally truly "getting" how we are creating ourselves in each moment through our interactions with everything that comes our way, whether from inside or outside of us. We

are shapers of intention and the life force which follows that intention second by second – every perception, every thought, every action we experience or make is a creation which shapes and influences the events that follow. Imelda's book is a vehicle for understanding our true power. She shares a teaching from her son: "Everything is medicine!" She has given us a template that shows us how to use our lives to dance with all of that medicine with awareness and in the best possible way.
Susan Rossi, Open Channel Astrology. U.S.

After 25 years as a therapist I took a sabbatical and embarked on a Diploma in oil painting. Somehow it unlocked my imagination in such a way that I was led to Shamanism, and it's changing my life. Along this path I found Imelda, and I count that a blessing. Never has the world needed a call for us to reconnect with our true nature than now, and our creativity is the key to it that all too often has been lost in the hamster wheel of modern life. Imagination is our route to the divine, and in this wonderful book Imelda guides us toward how we can utilise it to heal ourselves, and the planet. It is truly a book for our time.
Trevor Silvester, Founder of Cognitive Hypnotherapy, author of six books including *Grow! Personal Development for Parents*

When most people hear the word "imagination," they think of children playing or adults daydreaming when they should be working. In other words, a waste of time. But properly harnessed and focused, imagination is one of humanity's oldest and most powerful tools for healing and growth. If we can imagine a world in which people fly into space and walk on the Moon, then we can also imagine a world in which we treat each other with compassion, accept our own inner darkness, and work together for a better future for everyone. This is no daydream, nor is it a waste of time. It is vital spiritual work that is more urgent than ever. Imelda Almqvist is offering us a powerful toolbox with

which to do this work. I suggest we take her up on that offer.
Laura Perry, author of *Ariadne's Thread, Labrys and Horns*, and the magical Witch Lit novel *The Bed*

In this current offering, Imelda takes us into the depths of the human imagination; a powerful aspect of our humanity, which may allow for our creating chaos or peace. This divine gift may hold a prescription for our growth, medicines for our wellbeing or a formula for destruction. Imelda escorts us deep into Wonderland, where magic and medicine is unearthed as we tunnel deeply into understanding the expansive possibilities of our imagination.
Dr. Janet Elizabeth Gale, Msc. D, author of *The Rush Hour Shaman: Shamanic Practices for Urban Living*, Shamanic Practitioner and Teacher, www.sulishealing.com

Who better than Imelda Almqvist to remind us that without the imagination, nothing could possibly be real?
Todd Wiggins, author of *Zeitgeist*

Human life is changing. We conduct much of our activity and communication a digital space. Yet, my work with people and organisations points to a yearning for human connection, for spirituality and for deeper meaning. Look no further than this thought provoking and intelligently written book to discover what is possible, in yourself and in your connections with others.
Professor Almuth McDowall, Birkbeck University of London

We are living in times where we need a different approach to health, health care and medicine. Imelda has been steadily providing such an empowering focus in her previous books, and Medicine of the Imagination continues this pioneering approach. When more of us are able to dwell in possibility, we will begin to realise the potential of truly creating a world that we wish to live

within, and that we wish our children and grandchildren inherit. If you are asking yourself how you can make a difference in your life, in your community and in your world, then this book is a great start.
Prune Harris, Founder of Imaginal Health, www.imaginalhealth.com

Imelda has given us a gem of a thought-provoking guide here. As responsible shamanic practitioners and healers, these are the issues we are grappling with daily. Each chapter invites you to explore and re-imagine what it means to be a practitioner of ancient methods in a modern context and ends with practical self-reflection exercises. Imelda shares the accumulated wisdom of her experiences of teaching and healing, and while clearly defining her own historical context and influences, you are invited into the dialogue to define, and hopefully refine, your own. As Socrates said, "The unexamined life is not worth living". Thank you, Imelda for jump starting this essential dialogue and providing a steering light as we unravel our subterranean influences and choose to consciously re-imagine the best possible for ourselves and the worlds, evolving and moving forward.
Chetna Lawless, Co-founder and Etheric Director of the Laughing Rainbow Mystery School, Composer of Metamorphoseme: an active meditation with the Elements

Imelda Almqvist has a deeply curious, free roving mind and in her new book Medicine of the Imagination she is showing us how she explores, so we can do it too. There is an open-ended generosity in the essence of Imelda's writing that in the reading of it, we can gift back to ourselves. Totally infectious! There is plenty of dark and plenty of light in these pages to satisfy the owl or the eagle (or both) in us all. In this current paradigm, how easy it is to lose ourselves in human miasma and forget our richness, our heritage and spiritual potential. This is writing

to inspire treasure seekers, it's a book for those who want to cherish and help our world bring a new dream into being.
Jill Hunter, healer, London UK

Imelda's work is beyond necessary at this time. It empowers us to reach beyond our limitations and guides us gently into a higher octave of our lives. Having the privilege of attending her workshops, I am blown away by the presence of truth, passion and love that comes through this woman. And now here is the third installation of what is to become an integral part of everyone's library - a book that reminds us of the power and responsibility of living our lives intently; to be present, stand in truth and engage with life with the full force of your imagination and dedication. I am super excited to see this work circling the globe and liberating people everywhere!
Manca Geberl, art therapist in training, Ljubljana

Imelda's brave new book steps into the world to stir the cauldron of care and volition in each of us. If you are feeling the need for inspiration, or simply long to feel the drumming of the beat of a fellow imaginative peace-bringer in this world, then this book might give you comfort and potent seeds for thought and activity at just the right moment. Prepare to be impassioned by possibility!
Carol Day, visionary and educator, author of *Wheel* and *Drum*

Medicine of the Imagination: Dwelling in Possibility

(A Passionate plea for Right Use of the Human Imagination)

Medicine of the Imagination: Dwelling in Possibility

(A Passionate plea for Right Use of the Human Imagination)

Imelda Almqvist

Winchester, UK
Washington, USA

JOHN HUNT PUBLISHING

First published by Moon Books, 2020
Moon Books is an imprint of John Hunt Publishing Ltd., No. 3 East Street, Alresford
Hampshire SO24 9EE, UK
office@jhpbooks.net
www.johnhuntpublishing.com
www.moon-books.net

For distributor details and how to order please visit the 'Ordering' section on our website.

Text copyright: Imelda Almqvist 2019

ISBN: 978 1 78904 432 4
978 1 78904 433 1 (ebook)
Library of Congress Control Number: 2019948326

All rights reserved. Except for brief quotations in critical articles or reviews, no part of this book may be reproduced in any manner without prior written permission from the publishers.

The rights of Imelda Almqvist as author have been asserted in accordance with the Copyright, Designs and Patents Act 1988.

A CIP catalogue record for this book is available from the British Library.

Design: Stuart Davies

UK: Printed and bound by CPI Group (UK) Ltd, Croydon, CR0 4YY
US: Printed and bound by Thomson-Shore, 7300 West Joy Road, Dexter, MI 48130

We operate a distinctive and ethical publishing philosophy in all areas of our business, from our global network of authors to production and worldwide distribution.

Contents

Foreword by Anita Sullivan

In July the sun is hot.
Is it shining? No, it's not.
From "A Song of the Weather" by Flanders and Swann

In some way, this stanza from a wry little 1960's song about the relentlessly rainy weather in Britain, both presents and sums up the paradox hidden in the book you are about to enter. Namely, the imagination is a kind of sun for us, a spacious and powerful energy capacity that comes with being human – one we can dip into freely to fuel every significant activity of our lives, from building sand castles on the beach to planning a suicide bombing. The human imagination glows and throbs with possibility, every day for every living human on the planet.

But there is the second verse of the song! In order to fully benefit from our gift, we must follow its operating instructions. To gain access to imagination's heat and light, we must regularly climb through clouds to meet with the sun on his/her own territory, and there carry out due diligence to prove that we fully understand the deeply reciprocal nature of this phenomenon. Yes, the sun of imagination may be reliably and perpetually hot, but its heat and light remain potentially dangerous to us until we have learned to honor the code through which it can emerge and function on our behalf.

This might sound like a whimsical, paradoxical metaphor, but in fact it describes an actual problem. A crisis, even. If we allow the word "Imagination" to fade from the dictionary of our minds, then we are also allowing it to disappear from our very selves, our physical and spiritual substance. In this current era of immense social and environmental change, if we willingly neglect or suppress our imaginations, do we risk losing control over what we have come to understand as essential human behavior?

Imelda Almqvist felt the potential of the human imagination to be so vital that she was compelled to write a manual in its defense, a book that she calls "a passionate plea for right use of the human imagination." Why such urgency about something most people take for granted, like consciousness, or light, or language? What, exactly does imagination do for us that we are in danger of losing?

You would think there could never be a practical approach to a problem so abstract that most people don't see it as a problem at all. Yet "failure of imagination" is a term that has crept into public discussions in recent years. Employers are seeing imagination as a financial asset – inching its way towards a qualification – for hiring new employees, even in careers where the tradition has always rewarded kind of bland "team player" mentality that frowns on innovative thinking. I once saw, in a fourth-floor meeting room at the Smithsonian's Museum of American History, scrawled on the white board leftover from a previous meeting, "Thinking Weakens the Team." I believe the words were not meant to be ironic. The meeting director might as well have written "Abandon Imagination, All Who Enter Here." More recently, however, I saw a sign on the classroom door of a municipal day-care facility. It said, "Imaginarium." And just this month I've been hearing this phrase as part of a public advertising slogan: "'Creative Planning': 'Wealth Management' redefined."

For a variety of reasons, Imelda has found herself uniquely qualified to take on philosophically unwieldy subjects and wrestle them into a state of solid usefulness, without the least bit of "dumbing down." She has a gift for bringing order out of chaos simply by re-imagining (!) the usual distinctions between the two. Through her years as a practicing healer in the shamanic tradition, as a creator of sacred art, and as a teacher for whom teaching and learning beautifully overlap like roof tiles – and most of all, as a person who listens to and notices *what is needed that she can do* – she simply does what she can. Each time (this is the third book in the series, and not the last) "what she can" turns out to be a thing that is wildly appropriate, and scrupulously essential.

Again, how does anyone get their arms and head around the human Imagination (shall I capitalize it now)? Imelda takes a kind of circular approach: Standing in the swiftly-flowing stream in her wading boots, she baits the hook of inquiry with the word "Imagination," and casts her line upon the waters. Each time, rotating slightly, she pulls in a different fish. She pulls in empathy and compassion; followed closely by their shadows, narcissism and psychopathy. She pulls in natural moral law, ethics; followed by evil. She pulls in the power of collective unconsciousness, dreaming, creativity; followed by Wetiko – a Native-American term for a collective virus that drives people "to consume, like cannibals, the life force of others – human and non-human – for private purpose or profit....without giving back something from their own lives."

The title of the book includes the word "medicine." This implies there is an illness that wants curing.

It soon becomes clear to Imelda and the readers, that Imagination is both the cure and the disease. Surprised? Probably not. This isn't the first-time we humans find ourselves swinging on that particular hinge.

Yet the purpose of this book is to offer fresh perspectives on the nature of Imagination in all its aspects. *"An imagination is that idea which is beyond human senses, and yet is clear in the human mind."* Almost everything we do, all day long, requires constant infusions of imagination (How do I get my car keys off the dashboard when I just locked myself out of the car?) Essentially, the author wishes us to claim Imagination once again as our birthright. But wait! I left out a word. We wish to claim *healthy* Imagination. And to do this, we must also re-acquaint ourselves with its shadow side.

Carefully, with thorough documentation, Imelda opens the full Pandora's box of the human Imagination. Inside, all jumbled together, are raw powers that can be used to create both healthy and unhealthy behaviors. Like perpetual children, we gleefully exercise our skill for believing two diametrically opposite ideas at the same time. This capacity for double-think can be taken as either pathological delusion, or as an essential skill of a healthy imagination. "We cannot create what we cannot imagine," she points out. But the collective imagination can be so powerful, she continues, that what began as a story, can gradually become real. For example, "heaven exists, because so many Christians have imagined it."

Medicine of the Imagination: Dwelling in Possibility might be seen, then, as a test run for the endurance and stunning vitality of the human imagination at this particular time in history. Humans, as a species, have been good at surviving, but our contract says that's no longer enough – we must, all of us, commit to thriving.

This book, like the author's previous two, operates as a training manual. Like her book number two (Sacred Art) it includes practical exercises at the end of each chapter, some of the best I have seen (I must add). They offer a chance to pause and synthesize the material as it is presented. They can also reinforce or introduce ways to reconnect with the larger, collective imagination, which is really the fuel source for all human behavior.

Because her work as a shamanic healer, teacher, workshop leader, in a field that often operates along the shadowy boundary between religion and science, fantasy and reality, Imelda has practical experience with the unleashing of "abnormal" and pathological behaviors such as narcissism and psychopathy, some of which, if treated with alternative "medicines" such as storytelling, dreamwork, group ritual practices, can transform their dark strengths into healthy imaginings.

Humans need the imagination of shamanic practitioners more than ever, Imelda says, to diffuse some of the collective dark energies we have been stockpiling for millennia, and which are manifesting themselves now in very big ways as humanity moves into the beginning stages of the Sixth Extinction. It is becoming more likely every day that political solutions to this crisis are simply not going to be coming along in time, if at all. The only possible way through is for some kind of collective imagination to provide a wellspring of strength and nourishment for the planet so that Earth's ancient intelligence and beauty can largely survive and remain healthy enough to rebuild from what is still here.

This book insists that the Imagination is alive and well, but like the sun in the song, not shining quite in the places it is most needed. The book is not simply a wish for us to use our amazing gift for positive changes, but a detailed map for how we can, attentively and together, re-connect to the powerful muscle of our healthy human Imagination, breathing together alongside the even larger heartbeat of the Earth.

Anita Sullivan, author of *The Bird That Swallowed the Music Box*
Eugene, Oregon
February 2019

Chapter 1

"Medicina" or The Healing Art

Etymology of the word medicine

C. 1200, "medical treatment, cure, remedy," also used figuratively, of spiritual remedies, from Old French medecine (Modern French médicine) "medicine, art of healing, cure, treatment, potion," from Latin medicina "the healing art, medicine; a remedy," also used figuratively, perhaps originally ars medicina "the medical art," from fem. of medicinus (adj.) "of a doctor," from medicus "a physician" (from PIE root med-"take appropriate measures"); though OED finds evidence for this is wanting. Meaning "a medicinal potion or plaster" in English is mid-14c.[1]

What is Medicine?

Let's start by defining what medicine is and explore what this word means to different people (or peoples). The primary definition in western society (as the dominant culture perceives and portrays it) appears below. This describes the process that unfolds when we visit a medical doctor:

Medicine

- The science or practice of the diagnosis, treatment, and prevention of disease (in technical use often taken to exclude surgery).
- A drug or other preparation prescribed for the treatment or prevention of disease.

A (very) brief history of modern medicine

Below follows a very brief history of medicine because it shows how approaches to illness and disease have shifted from ancient times until the 21st century.[2]

There were early medical traditions in Babylon, China, Egypt and India. The people of Ancient Greece introduced the concepts medical diagnosis and prognosis. (They also gave us the word therapy). The Hippocratic Oath was written in Greece in the 5th century BCE and remains the inspiration (and foundation) of oaths sworn by medical doctors upon graduation from medical school. In the medieval period in Europe, surgical practices inherited from the ancient masters were improved. The systematic training of training of doctors started around the year 1220, in Italy. During the Renaissance period our understanding of anatomy improved, and the microscope was invented. (In comparison: most of the witch trials in Europe took placed during the 16th-18th century, also known as the Early Modern Period). In the 19th century the germ theory of disease was developed, and this led to cures for many infectious diseases. Military doctors made significant advances in the treatments of trauma and surgery. In the 19th century an increased awareness of hygiene led to sanitary measures being taken. Successful anaesthesia for surgery was first used in 1846. Before that, the few operations that were possible were carried out either with no pain relief or after a generous dose of opium and/or alcohol. In the 20th century advanced research centres opened and they are often connected to major (teaching) hospitals. The mid-20th century saw the discovery of new biological treatments, such as antibiotics. These advancements, along with developments in chemistry, genetics and radiography led to modern medicine as we know it. Medicine became heavily professionalised in the 20th century and this opened new career paths for women, initially as nurses (from the 1870s) and later as doctors (especially after 1970).

As we live in a society where the scientific mode of perceiving reality reigns supreme, many people forget that the medical profession (as we know it today) is still *relatively young.* For most of human history a different kind of medicine prevailed: folk medicine, bush medicine, herbalism and so forth. Medical doctors have existed for centuries, but most people could not afford their services or lived outside the reach of the medical practices of the day.

Other kinds of medicine

Folk Medicine

(Sometimes known as Traditional Medicine or Indigenous Medicine)

This is medicine using herbal and other remedies based on traditional beliefs. The World Health Organization (WHO) defines traditional medicine as *the sum total of the knowledge, skills, and practices based on the theories, beliefs, and experiences indigenous to different cultures, whether explicable or not, used in the maintenance of health as well as in the prevention, diagnosis, improvement or treatment of physical and mental illness.*[4]

It refers to a body of knowledge (developed over many generations) within various societies all over the world before the era of modern medicine. Until today there are parts of the world (here I am referring to some Asian and African countries) where most (rural) people still rely on traditional medicine for their primary health care[3].

Alternative Medicine

One interesting observation is that when adopted outside its traditional culture traditional medicine is often called alternative medicine! Some examples of such practices (that many of us in western society have experience of) are Ayurvedic medicine, homeopathy, naturopathy, reflexology and acupuncture. Core disciplines which study traditional medicine include herbalism, ethno-medicine, ethnobotany and medical anthropology.

This process of adoption reminds me a little of the process where the old gods of an earlier culture sometimes become the demons of the new conquering culture. It is all a matter of perspective...

The word "medicine" as used by Native American people

In the context of traditional Native American (First Nation) cultures, (please note that there were and still are many different tribes or nations spread over a vast area, they are not one culturally unified group of people!), the word medicine is often used in a very different way. We speak of "bear medicine" or "big medicine" (and yes, people from a different culture using those terms constitutes a form of *cultural appropriation* – we will return to that concept shortly). Medicine here refers to the power inherent in a person, object, location or event. Power objects or medicine objects have the power to influence our well-being. It is common, even in western culture, to wear a gemstone (say), Thor's hammer or a small carving of a bear as a pendant. I have a polar bear necklace I wear daily, carved by an Inuit artist in Greenland. I feel both empowered and protected when I wear this. I feel naked and vulnerable without it.

People can store up "medicine" (spiritual power) by leading a life of integrity, compassion and right action (actively seeking wisdom and doing diligent shadow work). Some medicine is inborn. I think we all know people who have a unique gift (for listening, calming others and lifting their spirits, speaking to children etc.) Those talents are a type of "medicine" because they heal and help others. Native American peoples teach that Great Spirit gave every person alive a unique gift or talent. One of our spiritual tasks then is to unlock that talent and use in service to others and our world. When we fail to do so, we fail ourselves on the level of soul and we also fail our communities. The same principle is true when we opt out of helping those others, who may face challenges or disadvantages in tapping into their gifts. Disabled people are *differently able* but how often does our culture create the right support and circumstances for those gifts to blossom?! The Paralympic Games are a wonderful celebration of this, but we need to extend similar opportunities to people who are not athletes, allowing them to star in their unique way.

> *Good medicine always gives you a sense of sacredness or sacred power. Good medicine is healing.*
> Jean Wolf [5]

Home remedies
Most families in the Western world make use of (at least some) home remedies. Those might be based on recipes handed down by grandparents or other family members. We also find many recipes and remedies on the internet today and there is a thriving industry in self-help books or "herbalism for beginners" type books.

Healing Modalities

We need to make a distinction between medicine and healing. As a shamanic teacher I offer courses in shamanic healing work. When I did my shamanic teacher training (in the US), I was warned not to use the word "medicine" in either course descriptions or the name of my website. In the US claiming that you practice *medicine* is legally reserved for medical professionals. For that reason alone, I have spent years staying clear of the word medicine. However, being based in Europe, I am not aware of such legislation and there are plenty of websites offering e.g. story medicine or other medicine that is non-medical in nature. Practitioners of shamanism offer *soul medicine*. My key point here is that older forms of medicine were used all over the world, including Europe, long before the medical profession claimed that word.

Story Medicine

The telling of stories is a crucial aspect of any healing process. After a shamanic healing session with clients we tell them The Healing Story (I was schooled in this practice by Sandra Ingerman[6]). Storytelling ignites the human imagination; it allows us to reframe events and discover the heroic aspects of our everyday lives. It can also provide fresh scripts and ideas, helping us break out of established ways of relating and perceiving the world.

Art Therapy

One healing modality I that myself trained in is Art Therapy, which is a form of psychotherapy that uses art media as its primary mode of expression and communication. Within this context, art is not used as diagnostic tool but as a medium to address emotional issues which may be confusing and distressing.

Art therapists work with children, young people, adults and the elderly. Clients may have a wide range of difficulties, disabilities or diagnoses. These include emotional, behavioural or mental health problems, learning or physical disabilities, life-limiting conditions, neurological conditions and physical illnesses. Art therapy is provided in groups or individually, depending on clients' needs. It is not a recreational activity, nor an art lesson, but the sessions can be enjoyable. Clients do not need to have any previous experience or expertise in art.[7]

Magic

The moment we discuss alternative remedies we tread a very fine line between tradition and "quacksalvers". This is an area of contention.

The most powerful medicine belonging to one society is easily viewed as poison or complete nonsense by another culture (and this works both ways!) When a powerful indigenous shaman travels with his or her medicine bundle – and this happens in modern times – custom officers will open the bundle and say: "It only contains some twigs and bones". Those custom officials have no idea what they are really looking at and that they should not be touching those things! No shaman puts those items in their check-in language, out of respect for their helping spirits and ancestors whose medicine and spiritual power is embodied in those objects. Yet by carrying them on our person we risk intrusion and violation of what we hold most sacred.

Holistic

The word holistic means treating a human being in their totality and looking at the way all parts interact and play their role in the full picture. It is the very opposite of the (so called) mechanic approach where a human body is viewed as a "machine" with parts that need fixing or replacing. This may just work for your car – it will not work for you!

In terms of etymology the words whole and holy are closely related. The room stem (*halig* in Old English) means holy, consecrated, sacred, godly or ecclesiastical. Essentially it means "whole, uninjured" so the key meaning of the world holy is *"that which must be preserved whole or intact, that cannot be transgressed or violated"*. This is something to bear in mind when thinking of standard medical procedures.

Medicine Woman or Man

A medicine woman or man is not a medical professional but a traditional spiritual healer using local remedies and working within the cosmology of a specific culture. The term belongs to the indigenous peoples of the Americas but (once again thanks to the phenomenon of cultural appropriation) is sometimes used in a wider sense as referring to traditional healers in other cultures, for instance Africa. In the ceremonial context of the First Nations people of North America the word medicine usually refers to spiritual healing and sacred objects. For many tribes their medicine was related to their gods and ancestors -meaning that it was sacred or holy and kept away from the prying eyes of outsiders at all cost. This means Western people taking such objects or displaying them in museums is an act of grave disrespect.

Cultural Appropriation

Using the term medicine man or woman has been criticized by Native Americans, just as using the terms shaman and shamanism has been questioned by the indigenous peoples of Siberia:

> *While non-Native anthropologists sometimes use the term "shaman" for Indigenous healers worldwide, including the Americas, "shaman" is the specific name for a spiritual mediator from the Tungusic peoples of Siberia and is not used in Native American or First Nations communities.*[8]

One further thing I wish to point out is that spiritual, ceremonial and healing knowledge has been passed from one generation to another for thousands of years. Training a gifted medicine person took (and still takes) many years (and severe ordeals or initiations) often longer than the training of medical doctors today.

Any earthly phenomenon known to human beings has a *shadow*, or negative (lower octave) expression. Finding words for spiritual matters and sacred process is tricky at the best of times. In this book I will try to honour different cultural perspectives, but I cannot walk away from the fact that certain words have made it into our vocabulary. For instance, the anthropologist Michael Harner[9] bundled together spiritual key principles practised by many indigenous peoples and reintroduced them in western culture as a phenomenon called *core shamanism*.

In modern western society we need to tread with extreme care around the issue of *cultural appropriation.* This phrase (which originates in sociology) refers a process where elements of one culture end up being adopted by members of another culture. In our times this process has acquired the specific meaning of Western people taking the traditions, ceremonies and sacred objects of indigenous/tribal peoples for their own use -without the consent of the elders and peoples of the original tribes. This might take the form of Western people holding sweat lodges, speaking of their totem animals, hosting vision quests or even offering Ayahuasca ceremonies or the ritual use of peyote mushrooms (all common examples in contemporary western culture). A detailed discussion of this issue falls outside the scope of this book, but I urge all readers to educate themselves about this.

I respect the opinions and feelings of the Siberian peoples but I cannot single-handedly wipe out decades of the word "shamanism" being used to denote specific spiritual practices in western culture. If I deliberately start using a different word, I will confuse the readers of my book. What I can do is apologising publicly:

> *I am sorry that the word shamanism was appropriated without your consent and blessing. I acknowledge that I myself am part of that problem (for powerful cultural reasons perhaps, but there is no doubt that I am).*

However, honouring the spirit of this book I also need to make the following point:

> *The positive expression (or higher octave) of cultural appropriation is mutual and respectful cultural exchange!*

This is how cultures, tribes, clans and societies have evolved since time began. This is a process of cross-fertilization and often it is how innovation occurs. Any culture that stays completely free from any influence of outsiders is at risk of becoming extremely stagnant. Researchers use the phrase *pure cultures free of foreign influence,* for this concept or ideal. Anthropologists speak of *primary innovations* (that emerge within a society and sometimes they are chance discoveries or accidents).[10]

They also speak about *diffusion*: a process where innovations move from one culture to another. Direct contact, among cultures, generally results in the most far-reaching changes, and cultures located on major trade routes tend to change more rapidly than do those in more isolated places. However, because no human society has ever been isolated for a long time, diffusion has always been an important factor in culture. This implies that completely"pure"cultures, free from *all* outside influences, have never existed.[10]

At the time of writing this book (2018) one story that grabbed global headlines was of John Allen Chau, an American missionary, who was killed by members of an isolated tribe (the Sentinelese) on a remote island, (North Sentinel Island) in the place where the Bay of Bengal meets the Andaman Sea. It is a well-known fact that the Sentinelese do not welcome outsiders and that they shoot arrows at invaders. This Neolithic tribe, thought to be at least 30,000 years old, have aggressively resisted contact with outsiders for many generations. Chau, who gave his diaries to the fisherman who ferried him across, had wanted to "declare Jesus" to the Sentinelese.[11] The Sentinelese have been described as "the most remote tribe in the world". During the 2004 Asian tsunami one tribe member was photographed firing arrows at a helicopter on a beach.

When we engage our imagination, we marvel at the fact that *the Stone Age is not over,* on this island today. Thinking of extinct animals and the threats posed by global warming, we could choose to feel gratitude and admiration for the fact that this tribe has preserved their ancestral way of life. The word missionary is rapidly becoming outdated. Today it is neither morally nor politically correct to convert other people to another, supposedly "superior", faith. The Sentinelese tribe may well be "the purest culture" that exists in our world today and the death of Chau is an object lesson for all of us when it comes to cultural purity and cultural exchange.

Witch Doctor

One rather offensive term, still in use, is witch doctor. Originally this refers to a healer capable of treating ailments and believed to be caused by witchcraft. In the developing world this term is still in use to differentiate traditional or spiritual healing from contemporary medicine (the medical profession).

My children sometimes affectionately call me a Witch Doctor. They know very well that Mum is not a medical doctor, but they do observe large numbers of people coming to our house for healing sessions (and courses in healing). Be that as it may, in western culture the term carries connotations of "black" magic and disreputable methods (if not an association of "complete nonsense") and it is best avoided unless a practitioner actively and positively self-identifies with this term (I know someone who does).

Core Shamanism

The following definition was taken from the website of the Foundation for Shamanic Studies, founded by Michael Harner[9]:

> *Core Shamanism consists of the universal, near-universal, and common features of shamanism, together with journeys to other worlds, a distinguishing feature of shamanism. As originated, researched, and developed by Michael Harner, the principles*

of Core Shamanism are not bound to any specific cultural group or perspective. Since the West overwhelmingly lost its shamanic knowledge centuries ago due to religious oppression, the Foundation's programs in Core Shamanism are particularly intended for Westerners to reacquire access to their rightful spiritual heritage through quality workshops and training courses.

Training in Core Shamanism includes teaching students to alter their consciousness through classic shamanic non-drug techniques such as sonic driving, especially in the form of repetitive drumming, so that they can discover their own hidden spiritual resources, transform their lives, and learn how to help others.

While non-Native anthropologists sometimes use the term "shaman" for Indigenous healers worldwide, including the Americas, please note that "shaman" is the specific name for a spiritual mediator or facilitator of the Ural-Altaic peoples. It comes to us from the Russian word sha'man and that word in turn comes from the Tungus language: saman.[12]

Words for shamans and Healers

Here are some words from cultures I myself have visited and I also thank some of my students, who have provided input based on their own diverse cultural backgrounds.

Vǫlva or völva (Old Norse spelling is *vǫlva*) is translated as Norse Witch by historian of religions Maria Kvilhaug[13]. The term refers to a seeress, prophetess or Sybil in Old Scandinavia. This word is sometimes translated as "shaman" but this remains subject to academic and cross-cultural debate.

Spákona or *spækona*: is a seer who specializes in prophecy

Seiðkona "seiðr-woman" or a *seiðmaðr* «seiðr-man»: female or male practitioner of seidr

Angakok – Inuit Shaman

Curandero/Curandera – Spanish word for (male/female) healer

Noaidi – Sami word for "the one who sees"

Sangoma – Zula word for healer or shaman (South Africa)
Turkey -Şaman

Based on the first comprehensive dictionary of Turkic languages, Dīwān Lughāt al-Turk, ("Compendium of the languages of the Turks") KAM (quam) is the word used for shaman meaning philosopher, seer, wiseman and doctor. In some old Turkish texts it was used for sorcerer magician, diviner and seer as well. Those are etymological aspect but to my knowledge we do not use KAM in our daily language, the word which covers all is ŞAMAN.
Kiymet Akcan Ozgur[14]

In this context it is worth mentioning that it is often claimed that there is no indigenous British word for shaman but author Elen Sentier, who comes from family practicing indigenous forms of shamanism, uses the word *Awenydd.* [15]

All witches [völur] are descended from Widening Wolf
All transsexual sorcerers [Seiðberendr] from the Tree of Intent
All sorcerers [Seiðmennir] from Black Head
(Hyndluljóð, st. Poetic Edda)
"Wed to the Wand" – the Völva, a Norse Witch[13]

(Please note: when it comes to finding a healer, it is always best to follow word-of-mouth recommendations. Failing that, consult a listing that is carefully vetted and subject to checks and quality control!)

Activity #1: Find Your Medicine!

I believe that most of us have moments where we find something, or are gifted something, that holds potent personal medicine. A colleague once gave me a raven feather from Arizona, which had been part of a ceremonial costume he had made dedicated to the Norse god Odin. Another colleague gave me a bear skull and its indwelling great bear spirit has become personal ally. Both feather and skull have a prominent place on my altar as power objects.

Having said that, the smallest things can be medicine objects if we open ourselves to their meaning: an autumn leave when we reach "that time of life" and say farewell to youth – the colours might show us the beauty of ageing and letting go. We may find a pebble shaped just like a breast when our soul needs nourishment (or when we are receiving treatment for breast cancer).

As you go about your business, keep an eye out. Also open yourself to gifts from others, without actively soliciting anything! Put some attention on giving someone else a medicine gift: are you willing to release something that needs to move on?! Does something very striking or symbolic come to attention? For instance: "I picked you some sage for you as you enter your wisdom years" – or you could give someone a seed packet for a flower or plant that holds personal symbolism. "May this quality or essence take root in your life and grow abundantly". Make some rosemary infusion for boosting memory. Put a sprig of fresh lavender on your pillow for sound sleep...

As you become ready and willing to receive, try to become equally willing to *release* and participate in this great dance. Power objects have an indwelling spirit, they have their own dreams about where they want to go and who they want to be with.

Do some research: what words are (or were) used in your ancestral line for spirit workers or healers? Please write those words in a notebook dedicated to the exercises in this book.

Chapter 2

Mapping the Imagination

To ask for a map is to say, "Tell me a story".
Peter Turchi[1]

The etymology of imagination
"Faculty of the mind which forms and manipulates images," mid-14c., ymaginacion, from Old French imaginacion "concept, mental picture; hallucination," from Latin imaginationem (nominative imaginatio) "imagination, a fancy," noun of action from past participle stem of imaginary "to form an image of, represent"), from imago "an image, a likeness," from stem of imitari "to copy, imitate" (from PIE root*aim-" to copy")[2]

What is our imagination?

According to the definition above the imagination is a faculty of the human mind which forms and manipulates images. Most people in Western culture might think of the human imagination as a slide show of images and the ability to use our will and intention to manipulate those images and create new combinations and concepts.

Some people (like me!) are said to have an overactive imagination. When I was a teenager my brothers would laugh at my inability to watch horror movies. For me there was no distinction between watching a nightmare and living one.

I just googled overactive imagination and the first search result was a site about the "fantasy prone personality", known as a disposition or personality trait in which a person experiences a lifelong extensive and deep involvement in fantasy.

American psychologists Sheryl C. Wilson and Theodore X.

Barber first identified FPP in 1981, said to apply to about 4% of the population:

> *A fantasy prone person is reported to spend a large portion of their time fantasizing, have vividly intense fantasies, have paranormal experiences, and have intense religious experiences. People with FPP are reported to spend over half of their time awake fantasizing or daydreaming and will often confuse or mix their fantasies with their real memories. They also report out-of-body experiences.*[3]

This is a cocktail of phenomena this book will unpick. Nothing on earth exists without its dark side or shadow manifestation. This *even goes for the human imagination,* at the root of all those things.

For now, I hasten to say that my imagination, having a lively and inquisitive mind, has always been one of my most precious assets. It has allowed me to make painting and writing my profession. It has also allowed me to do innovative work in the field of shamanism and pioneer innovative ways of working with ancient concepts.

The Fantasy Prone Person

I grew up in a family burdened with mental health histories, where both physical and emotional abuse were an everyday occurrence. My imagination allowed me to escape this rather harsh reality by escaping into other worlds, parallel realms.

For years I perceived my imagination as a realm that existed largely inside my own head. I greatly enjoyed the ability to manipulate images and ideas. In bed at night I would also manipulate numbers and play mind games with number sequences. Had anyone pushed me on this (no one did) I would have said that those images, ideas, stories and number sequences originated somewhere in my own brain. As an art student in Amsterdam, reading the books of Carl Jung and Sigmund

Freud introduced me to the notion that *my own psyche includes mysterious realms,* which Jung called The Unconscious and Freud the Id.

Perhaps Freud's single most enduring and important idea was that the human psyche (personality) has more than one aspect. Freud (1923) saw the psyche structured into three parts (i.e. tripartite), the id, ego and superego, all developing at different stages in our lives. These are systems, not parts of the brain, or in any way physical. According to Freud's model of the psyche, the id is the primitive and instinctual part of the mind that contains sexual and aggressive drives and hidden memories, the super-ego operates as a moral conscience, and the ego is the realistic part that mediates between the desires of the id and the super-ego.[4]

Where Freud explored our personal id (unconscious material), Jung moved in a different direction and became interested in the cosmic blueprints or patterns we find in the minds of all human beings. He called this The Collective Unconscious[5]. (Decades later the pioneer of family constellations work, Bert Hellinger, would speak of The Knowing Field[6] and the biologist and author Rupert Sheldrake[7] coined the term Morphogenetic Field in his hypothesis of morphic resonance).

The Collective Unconscious can be thought of as a universal library or taproot of human knowledge and experiences dating from the beginning of Time itself. It cannot be *learned,* it is innate in all human beings and often seeks expression through stories, mythology, art and symbolism. Today we might speak of a hologram (or even the internet) rather than a library!

Jung stated that the religious experience must be linked to the experience of the archetypes of the Collective Unconscious. This means that God or Goddess (experience of Divinity and The Divine) is lived as a psychic experience of the path that leads one to the realization of one's psychic wholeness[7]

(For teaching or public speaking purposes I often use the

world "cosmic blueprints" rather than archetypes, because it is not aligned with a specific school of thought).

The Difference between Fantasy and Imagination

To me the imagination is a much larger phenomenon and fantasy is only a small but specific way of using our powers of imagination. Imagination comes into play during empathy, reading social situations and etiquette correctly (social imagination), using metaphors and understanding symbolism, retelling stories but staying true to the original and so forth. Our imagination is the lens of perception through which we view the world and arrive at a personal take on "reality".

Fantasy, however, relates to the function of "making something up that doesn't exist", something far removed from what we consider "reality". There is a type of fiction called Fantasy, written for entertainment. No one believes these stories are true in any everyday sense but many people enjoy being immersed in a world of made-belief for a while. The same goes for certain films. We sometimes call this escapism.

Some sources link fantasy to all things supernatural. The implication is that the supernatural does not exist, therefore any tales or stories involving other worlds are "made up", for reasons of entertainment. I take issue with this because in my experience other realms are ultimately more "real" than everyday reality. The world we live in appears extremely solid but many of its phenomena are ultimately fleeting. Strong emotions come and go, political regimes come and go to – not unlike weather systems. We are born and one day we die. One human life-span is essentially just one blink of an eye when viewed on the truly vast time scales that apply to Earth (currently estimated to be just over 4.5 billion years old). Therefore, this world feels more "fleeting" to me than the worlds outside time and space that hold the memories of all things that ever happened on Earth, the souls of all dead people – as well as many realms and beings that never had a physical presence on Earth.

I believe that many writers (*any* artists) do their creative work from their innate shaman, (as it were), the natural born shaman[5] that goes so strong in all children and survives into adulthood somewhere deep within us. In Jung's terminology we could speak of this "inner shaman" as an archetype. The spirits come out to play even when "pure fantasy" is being written. Creative people positively plunder or raid world mythology and other global sources for ideas, story lines, other world locations and characters. I have conversations about this with my own children: the games they like playing always have a shaman, sage or mage in it. J.R.R. Tolkien's books The Hobbit and The Lord of the Rings were influenced and inspired by his academic fields of philology and early German (especially Old Norse) mythology and poetry.

For all of those reasons "pure fantasy" does not exist. Even fantasy will have some foothold in myths and legends, in stories about shamans or magicians (people with supernatural powers) and in writing done by other authors. None of those things exist in a cultural vacuum. Therefore, I hesitate to say that fantasy is "only made-up things". I think that we are dealing with a continuum here!

Intrepid Explorers of the Great Within

My own perception of the world took a whole new turn once I started training in shamanism. This education meant learning how to access other worlds actively, safely and return to everyday reality at will. It also meant learning how to communicate with spirits, as in inhabitants of other realms leading an existence of their own -not just characters from my own imagination.

The start of shamanic training felt like someone took a shotgun and blew off the very back of my head. There was no longer a distinct boundary between my personal imagination (inner world) and the vast realms of spirits (external to me) that I had always sensed and communicated with -but no one had ever drawn me the map. No one had ever explained proper protocol to me either.

Anyone who undertakes shamanic training soon comes face to face with another part of the human self: the ego. In shamanism we define the human ego as the part of us that is in service to our earthly needs and desires. At best it is a competent air traffic control manager. At worst it is a rabid dog that runs riot, high on egomania, barking at the people around us.

Shamanic training breaks our "egoic container" (meaning the way our ego holds our sense of self together and sets the priorities in our life). It forces us to release many fond and flattering ideas we have about ourselves, so the spirits can arrive and direct the process that really needs to unfold – a process that truly serves the highest good. *(That is: both our personal highest good and the highest good of the world and those around us!)* This involves the mammoth task of taking back years of projections and judgements we have blindly thrown at others. This is not unlike peeling an onion and fearing that we will ultimately find a void, an empty space, at the heart of things.

Many people start shamanic training and drop out. With others their inner observer watches it all but they do not make the full commitment that the spirits unfailingly demand. They hold on tight to the lives they had before and attempt to "sprinkle some shamanism on top". They pay lip service to shamanic concepts but stay in the comfort zone (they talk the talk without walking the walk). They will *not* do fearless shadow work and heal themselves before attempting to heal others – they continue to stage re-enactments of core trauma dramas.

Only people who truly live a spirit-led life are capable of bringing healing, spiritual guidance and leadership to others. We need such people - dismembered, initiated, rewired and re-membered by Spirit - very badly at this time of paradigm shift. When old structures fall apart, we need visionary people with practical skills – if we are to avoid lengthy periods of chaos.

My own first shamanic teacher (Simon Buxton) made me dig my own grave and he buried me alive for a night. All my personal demons (and the family skeletons!) came rattling and calling. I remain extremely grateful for this ordeal, this initiation.

As my relationship with my personal team of allies started evolving and deepening, I came to see how the boundary between my personal imagination, the Web of Life (or Web of Wyrd) and the world of spirit was far more fluid than I had ever realised before.

> *As above, so below, as within, so without, as the universe, so the soul…*
>
> Hermes Trismegistus[8]

I discovered that everything around me (the whole universe) can also be found *within me.* That Life is a Hall of Mirrors and that every single person I meet holds up a sacred mirror for me. I can choose to embrace all these people as teachers – and often their lessons are painful, but powerful. Other times they are hilarious. They are always life-affirming and divinely timed. The universe has a great sense of humour!

The well-spring of ideas I had considered "my private possession or collection" was really a gift from Spirit. It represents the spirits working through me, gifting me material. My artist's ego had to bite the bullet: I was less creative and inspired than I thought! I am, only and ultimately, the lucky recipient of a divinely guided creative flow moving through me.

My creations and offerings do not belong to me alone – they are in service to the world I live in, to Life itself and to my calling.

My imagination is the interface for this sacred encounter. It is the canvas where I write messages to the spirits and they reply (not unlike a message board). It is a beautiful place, a fertile place. It is the best country I have ever visited! It is also the place where healing and miracles (powerful "medicine") are found. That is the dimension I wish to explore in this book!

Activity#2: Map Your Imagination!

Go to a place where you can be undisturbed for a while. Read these instructions in full before starting the exercise. Close your eyes with a strong intention of walking around your own imagination. Then do just that. This may work through images or through other senses: you may feel things, hear things or smell something. Memories may float up.

Take regular deep breaths while doing this. Use your own breathing to ground and centre yourself. Now start exploring more actively:

- If your imagination presents you with a cupboard - open it!
- If you find yourself in a landscape – explore it!
- If you come face to face with a person from the past (or even a younger self!) – start a dialogue!

Please note that everything is possible in this realm: dead people can be resurrected, our child selves are found playing on the beach, the seasons can reverse etc.

Follow the process. Be willing to suspend all notions of disbelief. If critical thoughts float up – just let them be and let them go.

When things come to a natural end, or when you have experienced enough for today, please bring yourself back to the here and now. Open your eyes. Write some notes or make a sketch. *(You could consider doing this aloud and making a voice recording so you can listen to yourself later!)* Make note of good places or interesting things you saw in the distance. Return another day and explore further!

Chapter 3

We cannot create what we cannot imagine

I am enough of an artist to draw freely upon my imagination. Imagination is more important than knowledge. For knowledge is limited, whereas imagination encircles the world.
Albert Einstein[1]

Birth on Earth

No one is born into a vacuum. We are born into a family (and the web of connections gifts and imprints that make up the ancestral family field). We are all born into, what I will call, The Human Family: all of us together (alive, dead and not yet born).

Our birth places us in a set of circumstances that shapes us profoundly: our parents and siblings, other people around us, land and location, the trends and zeitgeist at that time (and how your unique family relates to all those things and defines itself). Other influences too come into play: do we face additional challenges such as disabilities or severe family karma? Are we born into warzone or do we carry a congenital disease? Do we have access to good health care and quality education -or not?

The list of "shaping influences" is endless. The wonderful thing about this is that it makes us all unique! My astrologer friend Susan Rossi emphasises how the configuration of the heavens at the time of our birth creates a unique "cosmogram" (or mirror) of our soul: you may meet people born on the same day as you -but in a different location. You may have an identical twin but one of you will have been born a bit before the other one. The configuration of the skies will move and shift even in the time it takes for a twin to arrive and twins will have similar but not identical natal charts. The same thing is true for people born at exactly the same time but in a slightly different location.

There will be small shifts and differences. *One natal chart can be a blueprint for many potential (different) lives and life choices.* Nothing is set in stone. Isn't it amazing how, by our sheer physicality, only one person can occupy one particular place on the Time-Space Continuum, at one time and that includes during birth?! It gives the phrase "we all have our place here on Earth" a whole new dimension of meaning!

We cannot live without those "shaping factors and forces". They are a deeply ingrained part of our humanity. I sometimes compare this to a pair of glasses: without them we would not see much (other than a blur) but as soon as we wear them, they impose a lens of perception and a frame of reference. This is the human condition: it has parameters. We need to constantly check our own assumptions and pay close attention when people around us challenge us or sincerely hold a completely different belief. Those encounters offer doorways on growth in consciousness. Watch the TED talk: How to let go of being a "good" person — and become a better person by Dolly Chugh (2018).[2] We can become deeply entrenched in the belief that "we are a good person", while in reality we sometimes do well and other times poorly.

Limiting Beliefs and Expansive Beliefs

If the (so called) New Age dawning has brought us one widespread useful thing, it may be the awareness that we all have deeply ingrained limiting beliefs.

Working as a shamanic practitioner and teacher allows me to witness people very close up as they work through major shifts. This privilege has demonstrated time after time that it is true that our beliefs shape our experiences and reality, in both positive and negative ways.

If we raise a child with kindness and proper support, it is more likely to become an adult holding the core belief that most people mean well. If a child is raised in an abusive family, it may well become an adult who never quite trusts other people or feels other people "are out to get him or her". We call that state of mind "paranoid" but it is not paranoia when for two decades this was your everyday reality!

It is said that we repeat the core patterns of our childhood until we become aware of them and consciously make changes. My own life proves this. Some patterns and assumptions date from the pre-verbal period in our life and those can be harder to excavate and dislodge because they became deeply ingrained before we had any means of putting words or concepts to the world around. Our world needs good psychotherapists, self-help groups and the profusion of helping professions Western society offers.

Let me use myself as an example. I grew up in a family where mental health histories exist on both sides of the family. Both my parents suffered severe abuse (physical, emotional, psychological) in their own families of origin (and so did my grandparents!) They were Roman Catholics and children started arriving in rapid succession. My parents did not have any awareness of engaging in therapy or healing before having children – which meant that they (unconsciously and unintentionally) recreated the dysfunctional patterns they themselves had grown up with (it was the only "reality" they knew!) I grew up as a "human boxing ball" with no concept of personal boundaries. I became an anxious and desperate people-pleaser because I lived in fear of suffering physical and emotional abuse the minute I "put one foot wrong". Unfortunately, such an attitude "invites abuse", it actively attracts people who engage on that frequency of interaction. Once I left home, I spent years changing and healing this inner programming. Two things changed my life completely: working The Twelve Step program to recover from co-dependency (CoDA)[3] and committing to shamanism as a spiritual path and way of life. Shamanic healing[4] is one of the most powerful interventions I know – it can literally turn lives around. Many clients have since told me that shamanic healing sessions we did turned their lives around.

Here is a "trigger warning": people who, like my younger self, experienced severe abuse in life may find some of the content of this book challenging. This may not be the right book for you at this time. Please read it when your life is stable enough for you to welcome challenges to previous-held perceptions.

Before I continue I want to state one thing early on and unequivocally: *The responsibility for abuse lies with the abusers (not the victims) at all times!*

This issue is tricky as research shows that every abuser was abused themselves – although that never excuses or justifies their behaviour. My younger self was devastated to see how certain issues and patterns kept recurring and repeating. Just "walking away" never solved anything because the issue would pop up with another person (or in a different set of circumstances) sooner or later. This forced me to reflect on the *profoundly unsettling (but unavoidable) conclusion that I myself somehow seemed to be creating the very scenarios I most wished to avoid and be free of!*

Eventually I learned that this repetition is always about pain coming into awareness – It indicates a serious issue that seeks healing. Every time this happens, the life crisis actually presents an opportunity for leaning and change!

Once I was able to view the process on that level, things started shifting because I could respond in ways different from the past. This soon attracted different situations and different people.

In my early twenties I made two life-changing personal decisions: one was that the early abuse which shaped my life *was not doing to define or limit my life.* That journey of recovery and reprogramming my own mind forced me to study healing modalities and develop healing skills.

The second decision was committing to a lifetime of self-reflection and self-improvement) to spare my own children the abuse and humiliation that coloured my own childhood. If this has made a significant difference to life quality of my own three children – I have met my greatest ambition in this lifetime!

Beliefs as Inner Saboteurs

One problem is that if we live from the belief that "everyone is out to get us", that very belief will shape (even poison) our interactions with others. Even in a situation with great potential for friendship or positive engagement, these beliefs will inevitably come into play and cleverly sabotage or distort things.

When you have suffered physical and emotional abuse, situations such as meeting new people in an unfamiliar setting can carry intolerable stress: anxiety, uncertainty, "knowing all will end badly as usual". On some level sabotaging the situation (that is to say: *actively creating the outcome you fear*) shortcuts this anxiety and it also confirms your worldview (I was right, you see!) At least you can walk away feeling you can *trust yourself,* which is empowering in a dysfunctional way.

For people dealing with severe trust issues, normal mainstream social interaction is unlikely to shift anything (it just offers repeats). Healing that requires a spiritual intervention offered in a profoundly healing space held by an experienced professional. Group therapy is one such example. The facilitator will create the right space and ensure certain boundaries are observed (boundaries that no one observes in everyday life, such as taking turns fairly and everyone having equal sharing time – not to mention clear confidentiality settings and a clear end-time for people to go home!) The facilitator will also keep a close eye and bring a professional understanding to the very patterns she/he knows are going to come into play. This process then offers opportunities for awareness and gentle correction (trying out a new way of being, in safely held space).

The processes used are sometimes referred to as *transference* and *counter-transference.* Essentially the transference is defined as a client's unconscious conflict that keeps repeating in everyday life. (In truth it does not only happen in therapy, it happens in all key relationships in the person's life!) Essentially a client (or student if you are a teacher) is going to project feelings (experienced with key figures and in early life experiences) onto the practitioner/therapist/teacher. Those feelings can be either negative or positive (or a mix). The counter-transference in turn refers to the feelings provoked or activated in the facilitator. Clients, patients and students can exert extreme pressure for the facilitator to engage in a "tango" (an old pattern with familiar steps). This is why psychotherapists have supervision – because it helps them spot and disentangle such issues. We need to master the art of making positive choices about how we act -rather than automatically and constantly reacting to others. Only awareness can stop blind collusion in this tango.

We cannot create what we cannot imagine

We need to become aware of the principles at work here:

- *We cannot create what we cannot imagine*
- *We will keep on (re-)creating what we have not healed*
- *We will (unconsciously) push others to collude with us in this process of "miscreation" (creating dysfunctional, hurtful or unhealthy reality)*
- *Just as we will defeat ourselves by creating the very scenarios that give us nightmares, the opposite is true as well: our own beliefs will limit our capacity to create.*

For instance: if we have difficulties putting financial value on what we do and services we offer, then we are creating a professional life of working long hours and still struggling to pay the bills. We are also creating a scenario of permanent exhaustion because on the energetic level our exchanges with other people are not balanced. This in turn can create resentment and drain us of joy. Doing (professionally speaking) what we are good at, ought to bring rewards in the form of respect from others and receiving the going market rates for our services (please note: not extortion but fair energy exchange!)

The opposite thing also occurs: some people are convinced of their own "worth" and they put a high price on their time and services *without having earned this*. They know their worth in potential (meaning that five years of hard graft would indeed get them there) but they take a shortcut, which fails and frustrates. Both extremes are dysfunctional.

A person who has never been happy may not even know how happiness feels or what "ingredients happiness is made of". Therefore, they will have difficulties creating it. Someone who has not grown up witnessing a balanced life will have difficulties creating balance. Here is where role models come in: when we do something very well, we offer others a template.

Our Golden Shadow

Taking things one step further I will now claim that there are many things that we collectively do not create because we are not even aware that they are possible. We may have lost them, or we may never have experienced them. One issue then is that we ourselves pose limits on our imagination, but we do not even realise this! (I first learned about the concept of the golden shadow from a book by Robert Johnson titled: Owning Your Own Shadow[5]).

When my younger self moved to London and entered a happy period of selling paintings, completing commissions and providing artwork for publishers, my own mother pointed out to me repeatedly that "this could never have happened if I had stayed in Amsterdam". She could have chosen to take wild joy and pride in the fact that her daughter was enjoying a degree of "success" in her chosen profession. – One core belief in my family of birth was that a life spent painting was going to be a life spent in dire poverty. Even when, (at age seventeen, when I applied for Art School and attended interviews with a homemade portfolio of self-taught drawings), I managed not to take on that family belief and subsequently show that a different outcome was possible, my parents refused to give me credit for that achievement. It was easier to credit the foreign city of London!

Even though I had broken free of one specific limiting belief, my parents tried very hard to slap a related limiting belief on me – as that was (apparently) more comfortable than re-examining their own beliefs around "art" and "success". (Please note that I do not blame them for this – I am just trying to illustrate a dynamic I managed to heal in my own life! Please also note that "success" is a very individual thing for which different people operate different definitions and yardsticks – hence the quotation marks).

Postscript in the final round of editing: moving to London forced me to switch languages and work in English and that fact has certainly contributed to my work gaining a global audience. Had I stayed in either Amsterdam or Stockholm, working and writing primarily in Dutch or Swedish – this could not have happened, at least not on the same scale.

What my parents did here is something *we all do to ourselves*! Our *golden shadow* means that we cannot always claim the talents, achievements and areas of life where we could shine. We often project this onto others instead (and admire them greatly!)

All of us may well have potential we never tap into during our lifetime on Earth. Our family systems, culture and education system wrap us in a very tight net of assumptions, expectations and obligations. Given enough time, we end up perceiving that net of human conditioning as "our own skin".

This is one of the reasons we now find a vast array of seminars "out there" offering us the chance to realise our full human potential. I believe in some of these offerings but not in all of them. Any social phenomenon will have a shadow and one such shadow here is that less scrupulous people see a way of earning money by selling gullible people pipe dreams. "Attend just one 2-hour tele-class and you will never again be plagued by limiting beliefs!" If only!! Limiting beliefs are more like Russian Matryoshka nested dolls: when you peel off one layer, the next one appears. There is no quick fix, only a life-long commitment to self-monitoring and (painfully, painstakingly) peeling off every layer as we become aware of it. It is hard work that continues until we die (and possibly beyond).

Activity #3: The Unbearable Lightness of Being

What would you create if there were no limits on what you could create?

This is a tricky question, but one well worth engaging in. Human beings are wired for security and the familiar. One extreme of this is that we end up building ourselves a golden cage. If enough time passes, even we give no thought to the person we might have been, the things we might have reached for.

Go to a place where you can undisturbed for some time:

If I were to die tomorrow, what are my regrets?
Do any of these regrets involve things I have not done or tried?

Write those things down. Next ask yourself: If I had two years left to live – is there any way I could do some of these things? You may need get creative and do them in an adapted form but still, there are always more possibilities than a human being perceives!

Had you always wanted to have children but did not? Offer yourself as a voluntary or honorary grandparent or mentor to a young person who needs the loving involvement of a responsible adult.

Did you never take a gap year? Can you take three months out to travel to the places you have always wanted to see?!

Are there people you know you harmed – find loving and creative ways of making amends to them. If doing this for the person concerned is not appropriate (they may be deceased, out of reach or your reappearance in their lives may affect them negatively) then do something for a person in need who is ready and willing to receive your specific offering. Use your imagination!

When all is done, observe how it feels when your psychic backpack gets lighter. This is what author Milan Kundera[6] called the unbearable lightness of being (as I interpret his beautiful words).

Chapter 4

Illness and Active Imagination

The person we choose to be ... automatically creates a dark double the person we choose not to be.
Thomas Moore[1]

One does not become enlightened by imagining figures of light, but by making the darkness conscious.
C. G. Jung[2]

The teachings of Gargoyle and Troll Child

My husband is going through a stressful period of reorganisation and redundancies at work. He said today: "You never fail to teach me something but the greatest lesson you have taught me recently is that every single thing that happens always brings a gift -but often we need to look pretty hard to find that gift. Sometimes we see the gift only years later -but it is there, hidden somewhere..." This has helped him switch from living in a state of fear (of losing his job) to living from a place of adventure: what is the gift, what is the learning, why have the spirits tailored this specific challenge for me? Might it be time to do something completely different altogether?! (His shift in attitude makes my life easier too!)

Yesterday I had a small operation under local anaesthetic. I decided to view this as a shamanic journey. As the doctor entered my body, I also "walked in" using the "x-ray eyes of the shaman". It was an incredible experience! I know that our human body is a gift from Mother Earth and that ultimately there is no distinction between the two. This is a key teaching in shamanism. However yesterday I ended up walking deep inside my own body and it was like walking around the root system underneath a forest, where all organisms are connected, and all the trees are communicating with each other through their roots. In that moment I knew that my own body literally IS the Earth and that death is an illusion because after death our body only returns to what it has been all along: of the earth, a unique constellation of particles gifted by – and on loan from – our Ultimate Mother: Mother Earth. There is incredible healing in accessing that deep knowing. For me it briefly dissolved the boundary between Life and Death, between Being and Not-being, between Time and Eternity. What a gift!

The procedure was a biopsy followed by the removal of a cyst hidden deep inside the tissue of my breast. In November 2017 I discovered a painful swelling on the underside of one breast. It turned out to be an infected cyst that soon became an abscess. I sought medical attention and my doctor put me on triple courses of antibiotics for several months. The cyst did not shift so eventually I was referred to a breast clinic and oncologist. It turned out to be harmless, but mammograms and scans showed another cyst deeper in the tissue that needed removing.

The X-ray eyes of the shaman

That is the medical story -but what unfolded for me was a very different process. Days after discovering the cyst I asked two shamanic teacher friends to scan me with the x-ray eyes of the shaman. Susan Rossi[3] reported back, using both the techniques of shamanic seeing *and* an astrology reading on the relevant section of my natal chart. Both methods showed the same thing and they were complementary, providing a full picture for me to work with. The cyst had appeared to her as a gatekeeper taking the form of a gargoyle. He flagged a long-standing issue of not operating healthy boundaries. This cyst appearing on the underside of the right-side breast indicated a strong issue of over-giving not being balanced by receiving enough in return.

The penny dropped instantly because I knew exactly what she was talking about. She had seen right through me! I had been under the illusion that this issue, this life-long imbalance in my life, could somehow wait or be ignored altogether. Not so!

Daily Dialogues with the Dis-Ease Spirit

Here it is helpful to remember that the word disease consists of the parts dis and ease: disease means: not at ease. The "dis" part refers to lack, want, discomfort, distress or trouble.

I took the antibiotics my doctor prescribed but also started an intense program of self-healing. When possible I took an hour out of my schedule at lunchtime -while my three children were in school -and started a daily dialogue with Gargoyle. In our first encounter, he told me to draw a picture of where the cyst sat on my own breast and to compare this with my natal chart. The cyst corresponded to my "Moon in Cancer": the place of mothering and nurturing issues. You can't make that up!

For three months (as this cyst showed no signs of clearing up, no matter what my doctor threw at it) this Inner Gatekeeper called Gargoyle took me on a journey into the deepest recesses with myself. One day Gargoyle introduced me to another being: Troll Child.

Troll Child

Troll Child appeared to me as a very cute troll toddler. He could have been drawn by John Bauer[4], the Swedish author and illustrator of the book *Bland Tomtar och Troll* (Among Gnomes and Trolls). Bauer will always be one of my favourite artists as his work is so quintessentially Scandinavian, his love for the forest so great.

The medical doctor had ordered hot long baths with Epsom salts to draw out the infection. I was in the bath when Troll Child appeared. I took him (I perceived him as a boy) in my arms and he started crying. He said: "From birth everyone has forced their psychic rubbish down my throat and it is making me so sick... I just can't do that any longer! I need to vomit it all out and have my tummy back to myself!"

I cried and kept rocking him. As a high-sensitive, intuitive and artistic child (vaguely knowing I was born into this family with the soul wish of making a difference), I became a sponge from birth: absorbing the negative vibrations in the hope of relieving others of pain by taking it upon myself. Until today believe this had some (limited) positive effect as my two brothers (both younger than me) got off more lightly. Ancestral healing work teaches that this is a dynamic in families: if one person carries a heavier burden – often others carry less. They will have more freedom to live the lives of their choice.

Such processes are extremely complex and layered. They affect and entangle multiple generations. It has taken me years to study those dynamics and develop powerful healing methods for addressing them. Undoubtedly that was one larger (cosmic) reason my soul chose this particular family. Spiritually speaking it forced me to find techniques for performing ancestral healing work.

Coming face to face with a magical innocent being representing the part of me that had taken on this awful burden was both horrifying and liberating. There was no way I was going to continue living with that! I told Troll Child that he didn't need to do that any longer -that I was now ready to set different boundaries and unhook myself from "karmic family theatre". Hearing that, he stopped crying, put his thumb in his mouth and fell asleep in my arms.

At the hospital, while the doctor performed the biopsy and took the lump out, I walked around my own body and tracked her movements. In doing so I met a troll family (they had many children and Troll Child was just one of them) playing with an egg. This "egg" was the cyst. They really liked playing with it and seeing the shock on their faces as the medical doctor made it disappear was funny!

Forensic lab work showed that the cyst was benign. What struck me was that I would never have known about this second cyst, if Gargoyle had not led me to Troll Child. Gargoyle was only the Gatekeeper, but if I do not play by the rules that Gargoyle sets for my own benefit, then more serious things can definitely manifest in my breast!

This is just one example from my own life where I used the process of *active imagination*, following the mystical principle that *the illness is the cure*. To stay well, we all need to become intrepid explorers, willing to face whatever is lurking in our own body and the unconscious regions of our own psyche.

Balancing inner sacred feminine and masculine

Why did Troll Child appear as a boy?! I am (and identify as) a woman and my baby self was a girl. It could be because I have three sons and holding their baby selves in my arms changed me forever. Their births made me a mum. I also am aware that in the healing of this issue within myself there were issues to be balanced around sacred feminine and sacred masculine.

In my family of birth there was a long-standing active imprint where a daughter sacrificed herself on behalf of her mother (or both her parents). This is called *"wegcijferen"* in Dutch: a type of maths where you take yourself out of the equation so other variables get all the space and attention. This needed balancing through me reclaiming the qualities of the sacred masculine within myself.

Part of the healing journey with Gargoyle and Troll Child was reclaiming for myself something only males are supposed to have in my family; the focus on self and the expectation that others will make sacrifices to support those career choices. I decided to give myself permission to be more "masculine" in the way I set boundaries and expect others to honour those boundaries. That includes the right to do work at the right level for a person with my education and skills.

After re-setting those boundaries, I am a happier person. I finally charge the going professional rate for my time and expertise.

To shift physical symptoms fully (so they need not return) we also need to address the emotional and spiritual dimensions. I highly recommend ancestral healing work and having a shamanic practitioner check on past life issues and personal/ collective karma. Surrendering to surgery without doing any of these things does not always produce the desired outcomes. *The situations and dynamics that caused the imbalance in the first place remain active.*

Activity #4: Dialogue with a Dis-Ease Spirit

Go to a place where you can be undisturbed for a while. If possible, do this exercise outside, sitting on the earth. Many people have some long-standing health or well-being issue. Put focus on something that continues to bother you and give you discomfort, stress or pain.

If you are in robust health, think of something non-physical: do you get headaches? Do you sometimes feel physically burdened by work or family commitments? When the stress level rises, where in your body do you feel that?

If this still produces no result – please revisit the last time you were actually ill... Does not matter if this was the flu or an upset stomach, minor surgery... a broken arm... Just time travel back to the time of that illness or injury.

Take some deep breaths and allow your awareness to drop down into your heart (away from the busy monkey brain). Then ask the dis-ease (*"not at ease")* spirit to appear to you in any way or form it chooses. Open yourself to whatever comes. (Perceiving does not necessarily mean seeing, you may hear/sense/feel/ smell/ feel touched by something...) When this arrives, greet it with gratitude and ask what the lesson or mirror is that it is holding up for you? However weird this appears – open yourself to it and pay close attention.

When your audience is over, express gratitude and return to waking reality. Write notes. What insights did you gain? Was there any sense of this being having your best interests at heart? Were you surprised? Did you feel moved? Next time you fall ill, will you use this technique?

Chapter 5

Medical care or Medicine of the Imagination

I believe that imagination is stronger than knowledge. That myth is more potent than history. That dreams are more powerful than facts. That hope always triumphs over experience. That laughter is the only cure for grief. And I believe that love is stronger than death.

Robert Fulghum[1]

Dilemma

The experience described in the previous chapter obviously poses an interesting dilemma: what is the relationship between medical care and medicine of the imagination? Some people are surprised to hear I even use mainstream medical care -am I not a "teacher of powerful shamanic healing methods and ancestral medicine traditions?!"

My personal philosophy is that both have their place. When my eldest son breaks his elbow by taking a fall in the school playground, as he once did, I am not going to solve that using healing techniques alone. He needs the medical intervention and a plaster cast. I will speed the healing process up using my "shaman mother" toolkit. I will also encourage and teach him to do so himself (meaning I do not act without his permission, but I do this together with him, involving him). After receiving the phone call from the school ("Mrs Almqvist, your son is on his way to hospital in an ambulance. There is a teacher with him. Please meet them in A&E!") I used my own x-ray eyes to scan the injury. By the time I got to A&E I had clear picture of what was happening in his elbow. This helped us ask the medical team the right questions about his treatment.

When a child has difficulty breathing and turns blue in the face, as our middle son once did as a toddler, you call the emergency services before attempting to administer medicine of the imagination. Riding the ambulance with him, as they gave him oxygen, I squeezed his hand and told him a magical story about what was happening. To take his mind away from panic mode but also so he later finds positives in the memory of that ride across south London with the sirens screeching over our head. Well darling, that was one occasion where all other cars on the road in London made way for you! (That is what he remembers ten years later).

Holistic and shamanic methods complimenting medical care

I am not advocating that we turn our back on the medical profession. I believe such advice can be harmful. I teach my students of shamanic healing to always work alongside (complement) medical treatment. If a client makes a positive decision to opt out of medical treatment, I will warn them of the risks and state clearly that I do not advice this but I will not withhold shamanic healing or other energy work.

However, I do believe that we must always track what is happening on the energetic level. Collectively we need to become more willing to engage with illness on the personal and symbolic level. Doing so can reduce the need for both treatment and conventional medication.

Developing a spiritual toolkit and honing your intuition before crisis strikes

By the time a fully-fledged health issue presents it is generally not the right moment to start learning a whole new way of perceiving our own body.

In this book I will make a strong argument for people learning some key principles of shamanism (or similar energy healing medicine techniques if they prefer). If one develops some fluency and confidence before any health issues strike, then it means one that one has an alternative lens of perception (or viewfinder) that can be used with a degree of trust in one's own spirit allies and intuition.

Once an acute crisis occurs the average person will be anxious and preoccupied. That generally is not the optimal time for learning a whole new way of perceiving the world and oneself. However, on occasion, I see people do this, spurred on by crisis they cast off old skins like a snake so new person emerges in a very short time-frame. This process will depend on personality type, energy level and the person's support system.

Your support system

If you prefer to follow the holistic route to the exclusion of all medical care, you will need a support system of people who truly understand what you are doing and why you are doing this so they can support you in a targeted way and really boost your confidence. Not people who later say: "I told you so" or "I never thought that would work..."

Shamanic practitioners need to be aware that their seeing may be clouded by emotions. No brain surgeon would operate on her own child or father -that would be left to the colleague they trust most. The same thing is true for holistic practitioners -they rely on second opinions and assistance from colleagues.

When accidents or incidents have occurred in far-flung locations I have sometimes administered "emergency energy medicine" to family members, but I would avoid this in a situation where a competent colleague is available.

I use shamanism all the time with my own children to boost their confidence just before exams[2] and helping them sort out friendship group issues etc. There is a difference between toolkit work (as described in my first book Natural Born Shamans[3]) and healing work. As a family member, we may just be part of the problem that needs addressing (or one of the forces holding someone back).

The bottom line is that we need to be willing to dance with *all* shadows, including our own, in this work… We need to release all notions of "the perfect parent" (who does not exist!) We all have a shadow and our children will inevitably encounter our shadow (just as we will theirs). In addition to that we stand together in the same ancestral field. Some things are not DIY jobs, they need to be done by others.

Activity #5: Meet Your Inner Doctor

I have mentioned Carl Jung's concept of archetypes which operate in the human psyche and explained that I prefer calling then cosmic blueprints.

Following the spiritual teaching that all that is around you can also be found within you, I now invite you to do a meditation to meet your Inner Doctor. Release all and any ideas how this person may appear to you: he/she/it, human form/animal form/any form and so forth. When you have made the connection, ask for guidance.

This may range from cutting out sugar to a warning to have some issue scanned or checked out medically. Follow the advice. Promise to pay close attention to any future guidance offered. Often spontaneous insights will be offered in dreams once you open yourself to guidance. Ancient people knew this and actively used a technique called Dream Incubation: intentional dreaming in a dream incubation chamber or temple.

Chapter 6

The Shaman's Map

Judge a man by his questions rather than by his answers.
Voltaire[1]

It is not the answer that enlightens, but the question.
Decouvertes[1]

Plato's Cave

Plato has Socrates describe a group of people who have lived chained to the wall of a cave for all of their lives, facing a blank wall. Those people watch shadows projected on the wall, from objects passing in front of a fire behind them, and they give names to these shadows. Those shadows are the prisoners' reality. Socrates explains how the philosopher is like a prisoner who is freed from the cave and comes to understand that the shadows on the wall are not reality at all, for he can perceive the true form of reality rather than the manufactured reality of the shadows seen by the prisoners. The inmates of this place do not even desire to leave their prison, for they know no better life. They manage to break their bonds one day and discover that their reality was not what they thought it was. They discovered the sun; which Plato uses as an analogy for the fire that man cannot see behind. Just like the fire that casts light on the walls of the cave, the human condition is forever bound to the impressions that are received through the senses. Even if these interpretations are an absurd misrepresentation of reality, we cannot somehow break free from the bonds of our human condition -just as the prisoners could not free themselves from their chains. If, however, we were to miraculously escape our bondage, we would find a world that we could not understand -the sun is incomprehensible for someone who has never seen it. In other words, we would encounter another

> *"realm," a place incomprehensible because, theoretically, it is the source of a higher reality than the one we have always known; it is the realm of pure Form, pure fact.*
> Wikipedia[2]

My art studio in London faces West (not North!) It has three windows that overlook the road we live on. At a certain time of year, the sun will set behind the old Victorian school building opposite our house, with its row of gargoyles, in such a way that the rays of the dying sun project the shadows of people walking up or down the road on the white wall of my studio. The grammar schoolgirl in me finds this fascinating because the universe suddenly places me in Plato's cave (a 21st century version of it!), arguably a reversed version! The people walking the pavement outside our house have no idea that their shadows are walking around my studio. They are certainly not confined to any cave. I, however, am joined by these mystery companions, if only very briefly, for the time it takes them to walk past our house!

The nested realms of the human imagination

Working with the infinite yet nested realms of the human imagination, Plato's Cave flags that larger question about perception and reality. What is the fabric of reality? How "real" is reality? Does reality consist of facts and tangible things or is our reality shaped largely by our own perception? How much escapes our perception? (How much is going on around us without us being aware of it).

The spirits often lead me on adventures and I receive answers (partial answers or pointers) through dreams. Per definition these questions cannot be answered fully or finally. All we can do is dance with these questions as our personal and collective consciousness evolves (and always being aware of our human-centred paradigm).

Collectively we do not wonder how spirits or indeed elementals feel about all the plastic pollution. In addition to causing the deaths of animals it seems foolish (dangerous!) not to realise that Newton's Third Law applies here too: for every action there is an equal reaction! We cannot behave like this and act surprised (shocked) at the Earth being forced to cleanse herself, by means of earthquakes, floods, storms and fires. (In other words: things we perceive as *disasters, natural catastrophes*).

People tell me that I ask good questions and I hope that this is true! I fill many private notebooks with questions... I pick the brains of people I admire as often as they will let me... I read ferociously.... I keep a dream diary.... Many of my art videos started with tricky questions I tried to answer for myself[2]. Making art videos is my personal way of home-schooling myself!

The insight that changed the course of my life was delivered by shamanism. There is a place where the boundary (or veil) between my personal imagination and the vastness of the spirit world dissolves. Here portals open and inhabitants of "worlds unseen" step forward. In shamanism we often speak of a veil between the worlds. *That same veil exists in our inner world or our psyche a well.* It is in that "mysterious shadow land" that life-changing work occurs.

I gained full use of my imagination only by releasing the notion that it was my personal imagination, a faculty tied to my physical body and belonging to me alone. The moment I let go of that notion, all limits dissolved. Today I see the human imagination as a very powerful muscle that needs regular exercise and using correctly... Just like all "muscles" in a human body, it weakens and even atrophies when it is not used fully. The moment this happens our world of perception grows very small (no matter what our physical powers or limitations are).

Is Reality "real"?!

A shamanic initiation can dissolve the boundaries between

external reality and internal reality. Some people would go as far as saying that "life is but a dream and what we perceive as reality are dreams projected onto a cosmic screen". Philosophers tell us that it is impossible to prove that we are not dreaming at any given time.

One course I teach is called The Shaman's Map. It offers an introduction to all basic key principles and concepts of core shamanism. It gives people a basic map, so they can start navigating other worlds safely.

The map is not the territory – this is one thing we must always bear in mind. Most maps show only a certain area, country or section. World maps exist of course, and night sky maps exist too. An interesting video doing the rounds that shows a map of the universe, as we understand it today: "The Most Detailed Map to Date of Our Place in the Universe.[3] It spans more than 500 million light-years and contains more than 100,000 galaxies. It looks a bit like a feather curling in on itself or perhaps a dust bunny spinning under your bed!

Core shamanism teaches that there are three worlds: a middle world (where everyday reality occurs), lower world and upper world. The upper world is sky world where we find many levels and humanoid teachers (say an "owl woman" or "mad professor"). We find crystalline cities and even schools dedicated to learning. We access it by going up (climb a tree, board a flying carpet, sit on the back of a bird… etc.) The lower world is deep in the earth. Its landscapes resemble earth: forests, mountains, rivers, caves. We travel there by means of moving down (dropping down a rabbit hole, dropping down a hollow tree trunk or, we may take a modern elevator!) The middle world is the zone where the events we perceive as everyday reality occur. As well as the material physical world that we experience as a human being on earth, there is an energetic parallel version where everything exists in energetic (not solid) form. Shamans use this world to find lost property, solve crimes and help the souls of dead people transition to other realms in the upper or lower world (psycho pomp work).

Essentially one could practice core shamanism for decades (as many people do) and always discover new places. The map is not the territory it is only representation of the territory for a specific purpose. We use political maps, geographical maps, sight-seeing maps for tourists (with the main attractions marked), nautical maps (that show stretches of oceans, lakes or rivers) and so forth. The same territory (let's say Great Britain) will look very different in all these maps. A tourist map of the City of London does not resemble a geographical map of the whole UK. An A-Z map of Central London barely resembles a map of the greater London area.

Cosmology

Cosmology

An account or theory about the origin of the universe

Different cultures have always had different cosmologies, shaped by creation stories, culture heroes (mythology) and generally also by beliefs about where people go after death. You could say that a cosmology shared by a community or tribe is a map (or a collection of maps) because it helps people orientate themselves in space and time.

The Northern peoples of Old Europe had a unique cosmology of their own and it does not really resemble the map of core shamanism too much. They believed that a world tree called Yggdrasil (most likely an ash or possibly a yew) acts as the spine of the universe, thus holding up and sheltering many worlds or realms. In a very real sense, you could say that *the world tree IS the map*! People often explore all these worlds by climbing up and down the tree and dropping down its roots where we find three wells and the Norns.

We commonly speak of the nine worlds of the Northern

Tradition but Norwegian scholar Maria Kvilhaug points out that twelve worlds are referred to in the ancient texts (the Eddas) and that the nine worlds we so often hear about refer to nine universes that existed before the present one (in the Vǫluspá) or else as the number of worlds in which goddess Hel rules – embodying mortality and not to be confused with the Christian concept of Hell as a realm of post-death punishment and eternal suffering. In addition, there are worlds in which Hel (mortality or death) does not rule and those are worlds of the immortals. (If this intrigues you, I highly recommend her book: The Seed of Yggdrasil[4]). There is some evidence that Anglo-Saxons believed in seven worlds, as Brian Branson points out in his book Lost Gods of England[5].

Another scholar, Geoffrey Ashe, wrote a wonderful book titled Dawn Before the Dawn[6] in which he investigates whether a possible prehistoric Golden Age might have existed[7]. This ancient society may have inspired the idea of "a sacred mountain to the north" at the very heart of their cosmology (rather than a world tree), the magical properties of the number seven (rather than nine) and all of this is linked to both the night sky and bear symbolism.[8]

A more detailed discussion falls outside the scope of this book but star constellation Ursa Major or Big (She) Bear has seven stars, often perceived a seven sages, seers or rishi, whose virtues are extolled at many places in Vedas and Hindu literature. The rishi may well be linked to the sacred number seven appearing in the cosmology of early cultures in the Altai mountain range (where Mongolia, the USSR and China meet). This was an ancient society and it gave us the notion of "a sacred mountain in the north", the magical properties of sacred number seven and bear cults and bear symbolism in sub-arctic regions.

In the Zohar[9], the chief text of the Jewish Kabbalah, there are four universes (or planes of existence) but the Lurianic system adds a fifth universe: Adam Kadmon, a kind of manifest

Godhead between the En Sof (The Absolute or Infinite) and the four lower worlds. I invite you to run your own searches and to check my own Cosmos webpage, it features paintings inspired by cosmology and ethnoastronomy.[10]

Planes of existence

Before we continue, here is a brief summary of my key points so far:

- Most religions and spiritual belief systems (but not all) teach that there is a continuation of consciousness after death
- This indicates that there are realms or planes of existence beyond the world we know and inhabit in a physical body here on Earth
- Different cultures have given different names to those worlds: the spirit world, astral realms, parallel worlds (a phrase from science), the other world (Celtic), The Afterlife (Christianity), Heaven and Hell (Christianity), The Other Side, The Dreamtime or Dreaming (Australian aboriginal), The Land of the Dead (which I personally perceive as a domain within the vast realm that is the spirit world), the Great Beyond etc. Some belief systems appear to place the other world in the future: The Future Life, The Next World, The World to Come…
- Many cultures have spiritual experts holding the office of sage/priest/shaman or spiritual director. These technicians of ecstasy (a term coined by Mircea Eliade) act as mediators between this world and the world of spirit: they seek guidance, communicate with spirits, deities and ancestors on behalf of the community, they perform ceremonies and divination work, they perform healing work on behalf of individuals and communities, they work to restore the balance between the worlds to ensure good crops, good

hunting, (even good weather and good deaths!) by doing all of these things they draw down blessings and good fertility on their communities. The tribe thrives only by virtue of a balanced relationship with the larger Web of Life.

- These shamans/sages/workers of magic undertake many journeys to the spirit world as part of their job. They map these other worlds and describe the inhabitants of these "worlds unseen" for their communities. Those stories contain messages about right living and right relationship. The shaman will follow the cosmology of the tribe but by making his or her journeys he/she will also add to the cosmology of the tribe. Truly great shamans are sometimes remembered and honoured as mythological figures after their death.
- Last but not least it is their job to initiate and train future shamans, so someone will be able to continue performing this holy office.

Belief system realms

The human imagination plays a key role in the way a collective cosmology is maintained and retold.

Even as a very young child the spirits would come and ask me to perform tasks in other worlds. Those tasks most commonly consisted of psycho pomp work: talking to and accompanying the souls of dead people. In some cases of the recent (and rather confused) dead the spirits felt that a young girl was a very unthreatening presence, still anchored in the world they had just left. I could sometimes "get through" where other beings could not. This generally involved the tricky matter of convincing a person that they were truly dead (and not just lost or dreaming).

To honour the cultural appropriation issue, let me clarify that I did this work two full decades before I even learned the words "shamanism" or "soul conductor". I only did what I was wired to do. The most neutral term is probably *spirit worker* and a more specific term for this type of work is *deathwalker* or *soul conductor*. At age seven I did not think: I am talking to spirits… ah, now let's borrow a term from indigenous Siberian peoples and call this activity shamanism. My family was Roman Catholic. The word shamanism was never mentioned in our house.

For me this illustrates one extremely important point: what the activity is called matters less than the fact that I was doing this (just as in other contexts and locations: other people were/are doing this) because it *needs to be done*. Some people have always done this (anthropological and folklore accounts suggests) in all cultures. It is our birth right. Some of us are called to be spirit workers and we respond. There is no cultural theft involved in that.

I started this book in my 51st year on the planet. That is nearly half a century of navigating worlds. Going on decades of traveling, observing, responding and keeping journals I will share some personal observations about the energetic nature and properties of these other worlds. I will warn you in advance that they "do things differently there": the rules are very different from "embodied existence" on Earth. I will emphasize again that these are my *personal* observations (other practitioners may perceive things differently).

Other World Observations

Our imagination is a key-tool in accessing other world realms

Cynical people will say: "There you see: it is all pure fantasy! This proves that it is all in your own mind!!" This is not the case, but the spirits will indeed communicate with us through our dreams, our imagination and our senses. Because we are still in a human body (the moment we leave it permanently is the moment we die!) we cannot fly free the way the souls of dead people can do. The physical systems that operate our body keep running. We breathe, our heart beats, blood pulses in our veins.

I observe that I do not leave my body and take off. It is more a case of the spirits tugging on the strings of my imagination, so my body comes with me as I step through the veil that separates the worlds. That allows me to have my senses in gear: while in the other world I can feel, hear, taste, smell -and this makes for a more vivid experience. What makes me different from the spirits I meet there is that I must return to the realm of everyday reality. I can't stay indefinitely. I also believe that there are places I cannot go until the day I die. They are too far-flung and the rules that govern them do not work for human bodies. We can go only some of the way.

Our imagination is not only a navigation-aid but it is involved in the actual co-creation of those realms

This principle is even harder to follow. In my early days of shamanism, I was concerned with questions such as: does this realm really exist? Why is my perception different from the experiences of others? This is called non-consensual reality.

Courtesy of my Roman Catholic upbringing I also chewed away on questions such as these: does Heaven really assist or it more of a children's picture book representation of the Afterlife? Surely people who practiced other religions (say Hindu people) are not going to end up in Heaven – there must be other places than Heaven that cater for the souls of the dead? But then what happens to people who do not believe in either Heaven or any gods/goddesses/pantheon/prime movers?

Over time I learned how groups of people believing the same thing are energetically involved in maintaining (or even creating energetic realms). Two millennia of people practicing Christianity and believing in Heaven would absolutely have created Heaven -assuming it didn't already exist. Heaven might not have existed before Jesus Christ walked the earth and shared his teachings. Remember that Jesus Christ was not a Christian!

Pre-Christian heathen peoples or tribes believed in different gods, pantheons and afterlife structures before Christ and before the Bible was written. This means that for the organising and conceptual principle of the human mind (governed by time-space continuum limits), there is point where Heaven came into existence.

The many generations following, sharing that belief and powering that manifestation through faith and imagination, would have expanded and solidified that celestial mansion (or manifestation). This is why we can safely say that Heaven exists – but it is not all there is – there are other and different lands of the dead. It could equally well be argued that God (the male and only Christian God) once personally created Heaven to receive the souls of the devout dead who lived according to his Ten Commandments. This soon becomes a chicken-and-egg conundrum, due to the human mind being restricted by the laws of the space-time continuum. The creativity of the universe is completely unlimited – much exists that we humans cannot even begin to conceive of. In Western culture we think in a linear way while most spiritual and religious phenomena are cyclical.

The bottom line is that for the purpose of reading this book it does not matter whether one male Christian God created Heaven or if devout believers co-created Heaven. So much energy and faith have by now been invested in the realm called Heaven – it exists! Energetically speaking it is a reality that can be accessed and worked with.

Creation Is Always Happening

After two millennia of the dominant religion serving up stories and images of this one male omnipotent God who created the world in seven days in western culture, we have lost track of the fact that Creation is always happening and that every human being is a contributor and co-creator in that process. Not only humans, but All That Is (all beings, even ones we perceive as non-sentient or non-animate) are involved in the collective creation of reality.

One of the key teachings of many indigenous elders (and non-Western traditions) is that Creation is an ever-unfolding sacred process. I believe that the world is not intended to be a Vale of Tears – but we human beings often make it so. Sickness and death as such do not need to lead to suffering (I am making a distinction here between feeling physical pain and profound existential suffering on the level of soul). Much suffering is caused by denial, lack of acceptance and trying to force our will on outcomes we cannot control. We can also do deep inner work on all of those things and change our attitude. What we cannot change, on an individual level, is the suffering that human beings inflict on each other: murder, rape, betrayal, sexual abuse and violence (to mention but a few). We have no control over natural disasters either, but we have lost the art of working with the elements and non-human forces involved in those disasters.

For as long as all of us collectively continue to buy into the "Vale of Tears" paradigm that too will remain a reality – because we are all feeding that outcome! (Every time we say: "Oh well, that is Life…" in this context, we reinforce this!) One of the things we need to do, individually and collectively is to master the right use of the human imagination so we can start creating the world we all dream of – not the world we are all dreaming into being from a trance-state or cultural and ancestral default settings (which is the world we see around us today).

Not only that, but we cannot create this better world without honouring our non-human co-creators, the divine forces that also sing in all non-human beings, even inanimate ones. We need to learn sit in council (or circle) with all parties and listen to all viewpoints before any far-reaching decision is made. Those parties involve the unborn children and our future descendants as well as land, mountains and the elements. What does the element of water say about polluted oceans choking on plastic? What does the element of air say about deforestation and toxic emissions? What do the spirits of place say about the building of a road?[11]

In Iceland a rock, known as Ófeigskirkja has been at the centre of a long battle to stop a road being built in an 8,000-year-old landscape just north of Reykjavik. Some people believe this to be the home of elves, or hidden folk. In the end a compromise was agreed with the elves, through the activism and spirit communication of a local seer. She reports that the elves moved their altar and pews out of this rock (which had been their chapel) and moved its sacred energy to another location. It is a well-known fact in Iceland that people pay a price for upsetting the elves (through mishaps, accidents or other misfortune). Even non-believers would rather play safe than risk incurring the wrath of the *huldufólk* (hidden folk).

PS: During the final edits of this book a river in New Zealand became the first in the world to be granted the same legal rights as a person![12]

What we do to others we literally do to ourselves and the human family and death doesn't solve that ...

What we do to others (including land, animals, water, trees...) we literally do to ourselves because it leaves an imprint on the Web of Life. Dying and "going to Heaven" does not solve the problem of the energetic trains we have set in motion. Unresolved issues and trauma pool in the family web (ancestral field or knowing family field) and will affect/burden others long after our personal death. As long as this continues, we are not completely free, not even after our personal death.

Karma and Samsara

This, I have come to believe, is what Eastern religions refer to as karma. Karma is not punishment but a larger cosmic responsibility for all our actions and energetic interactions involving others, (including animals, land, property and situations): All That Is, the whole Web of Life. When there are imbalances or unresolved issues, we must keep working on this (encountering key people and situations in different lifetimes on Earth) until we bring things into balance and release ourselves from what Eastern religions call the wheel of rebirth.

Buddhism calls this *samsara*: the never-ending cycle of death and rebirth. When a person dies their energy shape shifts into another form: "Depending on the actions performed in previous lives, rebirth could be as a human or animal or even ghosts, demi-gods, or gods. Being born as a human is seen by Buddhists as a rare opportunity to work towards escaping this cycle of samsara. The escape from samsara is called Nirvana or enlightenment." [13]

Ørlǫg

My home (Norse) cosmology calls this Ørlǫg: *Ørlǫg means primal layer and represents our personal choices. These choices directly affect our hamingja and our lives. It is the part of our soul that connects us to the web of wyrd. Our ørlǫg is the one thread in the web that we have direct contact with and also have direct control over. Our personal choices do determine who we become.* [14]

I often explain to my students that if we visualise all of Creation (the Web of Wyrd) as a great spider web – then (mixing metaphors) Ørlǫg is my "neck of the woods": the intersection where my choices and actions cross and interweave (at times entangle) with the fate lines of others. I sometimes perceive this as my own smaller web within the larger spider web. The Norns (Norse Fates) are forever weaving this web, meting out the destinies of all beings and cutting the threads of life for those who die. However, I am one of the spinners and weavers too! As a human being I have the gift of free will, meaning there is a lot I can create/manifest or block/destruct within the large destiny that the Norns are spinning for me. I would go as far as saying that all human beings have multiple possible destinies – but there is one highest outcome: that is the life where we live our soul purpose and meet our "cosmic appointments" with others. Shamanic teacher Betsy Bergstrom[15] calls those *destiny dates*!)

Heaven exists but not everyone goes straight to Heaven
Heaven exists – yes, but it remains a simplification. Many deaths are compromised (especially sudden, accidental or violent deaths) and those people do not fly straight up to Heaven. They often stay around in the parallel version of everyday reality – meaning that energetically speaking they are still with us. They may attach themselves to people ("possession"), buildings ("haunted houses") or land. They need compassionate and non-judgmental help -not demonizing or "exorcising"! Despite our belief in Heaven, everyday language indicates that we all know this on some *level.*

I can create something in the other world through using my intention and imagination
This is sometimes done by people who send out meditations or guided visualisations. Sometimes they may share an otherworld location they stumbled across – other times they may themselves create an otherworld temple or sanctuary. Once other people visit and invest energy in that too, it becomes a larger and more solid energetic reality.

Intentional mis-creation or harmful creations
This principle, unfortunately, can also be used by people of low frequency intention. The Nazis did this: they built energetic otherworld structures to support their campaigns in the everyday world. One piece of guidance I received from spirit recently was how much dismantling of that is still to be done – but also how neo-fascist movements plug into that. (Please note that involving yourself in any of this is not safe for beginners!)

Not all other world realms and inhabitants are safe

The notion that death (say a suicide or an execution) can solve a problem is an illusion. The problem is just shoved into the other world. People who were serial killers during their life on Earth will not miraculously become saints in their moment of death. Some people of "a low vibration" make attempts to influence events on Earth even after their personal death (possession).

Suicide

Over the years I have worked with many cases of suicide. Both in the sense of pulling people back from the brink (generally by staging a symbolic death and rebirth) [16], but I have also been asked by families to check on loved ones who took their own lives. In those cases, I have found them in a variety of locations and situations in the Afterlife *but in none of those situations had the primary issues causing suicide been resolved with immediate effect*. It is my observation that people carry those issues with them beyond death where once again, with compassionate assistance, they will need to work on balancing them. If anything, things are worse by then, because even more people are now entangled in a pattern of grave loss and grief (even guilt) that will affect even unborn future family members unless (and until) the issues are healed.

Free Will

I observe that the principle of honouring free will is wired deeply into our universe. I find that many spirits and celestial beings honour this principle absolutely. This may mean (for instance) that if you do not believe in angels you cut yourself off from the support of angels because they will honour your boundaries. (Then again, other people end up believing in angels only after some divine emergency or miraculous intervention occurs).

The Reverse Magic of Worrying

One related principle is that worrying serves little purpose. I once wrote a blog titled "the reverse magic of worrying" because it actively feeds and creates negative outcomes.[17] On the human level worrying is an understandable response to uncertain situations but on the spiritual-magical level it's not advisable.

Partnership and balance between the worlds

When there is sacred balance between the worlds, human beings operate in partnership with the spirits and this refers to a mutual arrangement, not a dictatorship! I have never set store by great magicians summoning evil spirits and getting them to do their bidding (as depicted in certain Grimoires). There is something wrong with this scenario and the principles it portrays (and I am not even going to mention the energetic consequences, assuming one managed to do this!) Some of my students of shamanism tell me that the one single most important thing I have ever taught them is that they may operate boundaries even in their interactions with spirits.

Greater Cosmic Journey

The Journey Continues. Heaven is not the final destination for Christians. After death souls go to different places, depending on their needs, beliefs and the events that shaped their life. A soul might conceivably go to Heaven and after a major rest remember other lifetimes and unfinished business – and then proceed to another realm where further learning or balancing can occur.

This also means that here on Earth we do not see the larger journey of a person's soul. We cannot comprehend, from our earthbound human perspective, why a soul would choose challenging life experiences such as a severe disability or a violent death in childhood. Once, when a person had died at a young age, I was told that his presence was needed elsewhere in the universe. That he was a comic wanderer.

Death and Separation

The type of question my students of Death and Dying then ask is: if a Christian person is very close friends with a Buddhist (say) – will they never meet again after death?! My observation is that the other world is very elastic and immediate – thinking of someone strongly will pull them towards you. There are many locations in the other world where people can hang out – just as they do on Earth. Heaven or Nirvana is not a "high security prison" or closed system. In the final reckoning it is a state of mind rather than a place. I see no reason they would not meet again and share experiences.

Spirits, Saints and Impostors

A related question is this one: if I do a journey or meditation and I meet (say) Jesus Christ (or Cleopatra… insert a famous name) is it really Jesus Christ? Based on decades of shamanic work and teaching I perceive this as very tricky.

On the one hand the (real) Jesus Christ once anchored an energetic field and vibration here on Earth. In the 21st century I often hear that referred to as Christ Consciousness. Outside Time people can still connect to that, merge with that and benefit from that. About this I have no doubt. If it existed on Earth, it will definitely have its counterpart in the other world.

> We know that heaven is real because just after Jesus' baptism "a voice from heaven said, "This is my beloved Son, with whom I am well pleased" (Matt 3:17) and it is known that God is in heaven and so heaven is a specific place where God resides as Jesus warned that "whoever denies me before men, I also will deny before my Father who is in heaven" (Matt 10:33)
>
> Jack Wellman in Christian Crier[18]

Having said that, the other world is very elastic and "shape-shifty". Spirits and gods can take any form they like (which is why the goddess Freyja – to use a common Pagan example - might appear in a different form to you compared to how I see her. Part of that is perception (the process of seeing works through our imagination) and the other part is personal relationship (she is likely to take a form that means something to *you*). It seems perfectly possible to me that a spirit could take the form of Christ (often a popular representation of Christ – after all it is doubtful that he had blue eyes and blond hair in real life!) but not be Christ. However, if a helping spirit does this in order to further Christ Consciousness – does the distinction matter?! Also, high frequency beings such as Christ (or Freyja) are multi-dimensional and able to be in many places at the same time. There is likely to be a seed or grain of Christ/Freyja essence in any appearance that serves a higher or cosmic good. To my mind these problems are not problems – they are distortions caused by earth-bound perception.

However, just as there are high vibration beings, there are also lower vibration beings that might just "try it on". I would fail in my duties as a spirit ambassador if I did not make my students (and readers) aware of this issue. Always use your discernment, even when journeying in other worlds!

Stepping Outside Time

The world of spirit is situated Outside Time (and probably wraps itself around Time like the proverbial snake biting its own tail). It does not "know time" the way time rules our human lives as an organising dimension. When we visit other realms, we step outside the earthbound time-space continuum. This explains why, in myths and fairy tales, we hear of people who accidentally stepped through a portal. When they return "five days later", 500 years have passed on earth. We also hear that if people eat or drink something in the other world (one example is Persephone eating the pomegranate seeds in the underworld with Hades) they can never again belong fully to only this world (earth world). From that moment on they will have a soul contract that makes them walk between the worlds (and this is a fair description of people who answer a calling to be shamans/ mediums/spirit workers).

All faiths, spiritual paths or belief systems are portals of the same temple

They may take us along different routes (some more scenic and winding than others) but they ultimately lead us back to our Divine Origin (however we perceive this) and luminous consciousness. I imagine that the ultimate initiation is releasing all and any sense of separation (and ego) and achieving true unity consciousness: oneness with the Divine. That implies releasing our attachment to any specific religion or path.

Activity #6: A Night Out at The Karmic Theatre

Please go to a place where you can be undisturbed for a while. Light a candle. Take some deep breaths. With every outbreath release your everyday concerns for the duration of this activity. Now take a moment to think of an issue that repeatedly plays out in your family (with a loved one, partner or very close friend).

Examples of this are: not feeling seen, feeling abandoned, feeling that no matter how much you do or offer it is never enough, feeling that any love you receive is conditional on you behaving a certain way etc.

Close your eyes and ask your compassionate ancestors to show you where this dynamic originates. Once again you may not *see,* but instead sense/hear or experience a deep inner knowing.

As you gain some clarity, perform a simple act of unhooking yourself (you may need to act this out with a small hand gesture: perhaps pulling out a hook and literally taking a step back).

Ask the compassionate ancestors to unravel this and fill the space thus created with love and blessings. Witness this process. When it is done, slowly bring yourself back. Open your eyes. Do you feel lighter or different? Tell someone you trust 100% about what you just did.

Congratulations: you unhooked yourself from one act in the karmic theatre!!

Chapter 7

Death and our Imagination

I watched the Poison Mother art video again yesterday, to help prepare for the arrival of the seeds of my poison plants, and got a big insight about the inner healing forces I see inside my chest. A little male warrior with a spear who wants to kill and remove everything AND a plant spirit woman who nourishes and replenishes. They merge to become a deep indigo bowl that contains a flame that either leaps or banks depending on the state of my cells as I perceive them. That little warrior is apoptosis, the cyclical death of cells. When apoptosis fails, what results is cancer, uncontrolled, harmful growth that hijacks other body processes. The plant mother is cellular growth and regeneration of sustaining body processes. It's not possible to be hijacking and nourishing at the same time -one or the other -so we need that apoptosis so that regeneration can take place. I know this is common scientific knowledge, but your Poison Mother work internalized it for me. I watched the video when you first released it, but I was more ready to RECEIVE it at this point. So, thank you thank you thank you! These videos are teachings that keep going deeper!!
Susan Rossi[1]

On a Southwest airline flight from Las Vegas to Salt Lake City (a one-hour flight) in 2000 a group of crew members and some passengers restrained and killed a passenger who turned violent, assaulted other passengers and tried to break into the cockpit. According to the autopsy-report 19-year old Jonathan Burton died of asphyxiation (he was pushed head-down on the floor and had multiple bruises and contusions).[2]

Shaman-sorcerers have the upper hand; as beings on their way to

dying, they have someone whispering in their ear that everything is ephemeral. The whisperer is Death, the infallible advisor, the only one who won't ever tell you a lie.
Don Juan Matus[3]

Death as our Ally

If our imagination fails us spectacularly in one area of our life, it surely is in our collective and personal relationship to Death. I have capitalized Death here to refer to Death as a cosmic force, the personification of an unshakeable principle, the great leveller, our ally and teacher! In this chapter I will use the word death (lower case d) to refer to the personal process of transition.

There have always been exceptions and gifted people: doulas, death midwives, compassionate priests who truly provide comfort when Death appears. However, by and large we are in denial about Death in Western culture and that messes up our lives, our traditions and the way we parent our children. In obituaries we see phrases such as "she lost her life after a long battle with cancer". I will examine the cancer part of that statement in Chapter 18. In this chapter we will look at the death part.

"Any option is better than death"

I recently stumbled across a video about a Russian Cryo Center that sells the prospect that a few decades from now cryogenically frozen people could be resurrected either in their own bodies or those of humanoid robots; or even have their minds uploaded to a computer. This clinic uses liquid nitrogen in which bodies are suspended, head down. The "bargain option" is to only have your head frozen. They will even put your pets on ice, for a fee. *Any option is better than death': Russian cryo center offers clients chance to be revived.*[4]

If they have their way, perhaps the word "death" will leave our vocabulary and instead we will say; "on ice for now"? This obviously raises the question whether this really is the future of science and the future of humanity or a colossal scam! One question occurs immediately: if you are only going to have your head preserved, whose body is it going to be mounted on to resurrect you? This question begs asking especially in a bleak future where everyone (presumably) has access to uber-advanced technology... Another obvious question is: are the people of the future really going to be eager to defrost and resurrect zombies from the year 2019?! One or two might just provide interesting material for medical or historical research but a whole army of frozen corpses?! What if over-population for them is even more of a global issue than it is right now? And I'd rather not think about the issue of lengthy power failures either.

On the opposite end of the scale the following video is currently doing the rounds on Facebook -What is the best way to face death? Author Kevin Toolis discusses the lessons we can learn from Ireland.[5] A different again, unflinching but ultimately refreshing, perspective, is offered by: "The Smoke Gets in Your Eyes: And Other Lessons from The Crematorium by Caitlin Doughty.[6]

In our culture we are in denial about Death. We pretend it does not exist, which is an illusion that is challenged in every waking moment. We push Death to the very fringes of our awareness and our culture. We leave it to experts and prefer not to look too closely. Many people now die in hospital and are taken straight to a funeral parlour after death. The washing and laying-out of the body is done by professionals, not by the loving hands of family members performing a holy office. Viewings also happen at the funeral parlour, subject to opening hours and a lot of make up being applied to make the corpse look "natural". Cars habitually hit animals (roadkill) and drive on, without giving this any further thought.

Death Cafes

There are some positive indications that Death is not going be "photo-shopped out of our collective awareness". We now have a thriving hospice culture: places where people spend their final days, surrounded by their families, receiving gentle palliative care (not brutal medical treatments).

Death Cafes are springing up all over the world. At a Death Cafe people, often strangers, gather to eat cake, drink tea and discuss death. The objective is to increase awareness of death with a view to helping people make the most of their finite lives.

There is a group-directed discussion of death with no agenda, objectives or themes. It is a discussion group rather than a grief support or counselling session. Death Cafes are offered on a non-profit basis, in an accessible space with proper confidentiality settings – and there is always food and drink, especially cake![7]

Death Cafes have spread quickly across Europe, North America and Australasia. As of today, we have offered 6262 Death Cafes in 56 countries since September 2011. If 10 people came to each one that would be 62620 participants. We've established both that there are people who are keen to talk about death and that many are passionate enough to organise their own Death Cafe. [7]

Rites of Passage

Individuals moving through key times of transition need Rites of Passage. There are many such transitions in an average human lifespan. Death is the final one, not the only one. Most other transitions and losses are, in a way, preparation for the final transition that is death. Rites of passage are about marking those occasions and communities supporting individuals through these transitions in sacred ways.

Rites of passage are often mentioned in anthropology books and texts I have read. Many people know that tribal peoples host puberty rites for teenagers, marking the point where a child becomes a young adult. What is perhaps less well known is that they have rites for many other moments as well; warriors coming home from battle (needing spiritual cleansing, transition and serious honouring for sacrifices made), older people becoming Elders of the Community and perhaps receiving a ceremonial name, menstruation huts where women gather at the time of Dark Moon, special rites to honour ancestors and seek their guidance and blessings. Always remembering that we all die one day and then we too join the Ancestors, Outside Time.

It is wonderful that these rites are documented. I just wish we would not only read about them but take the teaching to heart and act on the inspiration by offering those rites of passage to our own communities. Increasing numbers of people (my own colleagues and students proudly included in this) are rediscovering this and finding new ways of doing this.

Imelda Almqvist[8]

In shamanism today (in both indigenous and other forms of contemporary practice) the key mystery (revelation through initiation) is that Death is not the end. Death is a birth back into the realm of Spirit. People who know this (shamans as well as for instance people who have survived NDE's or Near Death Experiences) lose their fear of death. The great paradox is that *it is only once we release our fear of Death dissipates that we can live Life to the full.*

This is the reason why initiation is a key word in shamanism. Some modern words or terms that describe this process of initiation are spiritual crisis, dark night of the soul, awakening, nervous breakdown or "hitting bottom-rock so the only way forward is up".

Author Charlotte Du Cann[9] words it beautifully: *When you go down into the underworld part of you never returns. That is the deal. You eat the six seeds of the pomegranate and that action seals a certain bargain with life thereafter. It is a deal nobody signs if they think about it, and yet those who sign never regret it. If you don't go into the underworld you never find out what it means to go home. That is why no one regrets initiation, however it comes. It makes your upperworld life very hard thereafter, but your inner life becomes immeasurably rich. You have roots in the earth and you have a place to go when you die. Those things count for everything. They make you bold and free.*

We cannot edit Death out of our lives, even when we are young, healthy and ignorant. Our own body is in a constant process of cell-death and cell-generation. We die to our younger selves as we grow older. The baby, child and teenager I was, are no more (though they live on within me). I am currently parenting teenagers and eventually I may even be initiated into the mysteries of grandmotherhood. I sincerely hope that I will live long enough and remain mentally active enough to become a true Elder of the human family.

Great inspiration (and modelling) for our times is provided by the International Council of Thirteen Indigenous Grandmothers, who represent a global alliance of prayer, education and healing for Mother Earth, for seven generations to come. They are deeply concerned with the unprecedented destruction of Mother Earth and the destruction of indigenous ways of life. I invite you to read their mission statement on their website.[10]

I have used the expression lower octave – higher octave before. In a dualistic culture we need to constantly ask ourselves: where have we let things slide into their lower octave expression?

Old person past their sell-by-date -Elder of the Community and Wisdom Keeper

Death as an insult, something that "won't happen to me" -Death as an ally and teacher of meaning

Troubled, "difficult" or wayward child – heroic child that has chosen to carry and heal ancestral issues

Death as total obliteration – Death as the ultimate healing and a birth back into the spirit world

Self-serving spirituality or "cosmic ordering system" – life-

changing commitment to the challenges and gifts of a spiritual path

Preparation visits to the Land of the Dead

Contemporary shamanism offers something called death preparation work. It goes beyond what a psychotherapist or counsellor might do, such as dealing with unfinished (emotional) business, putting your affairs in order, leaving instructions for your own funeral or memorial service. Shamanic practitioners can take their clients on trips to other worlds. When your child is about to start school, you often take them on some visits, so they know where they are going (which reduces anxiety and helps them form mental pictures of their future). We can do the same thing for people who have a limited time to live. We can do some trial runs. It is even possible to start preparing a place for yourself in the afterlife.

Imagining Death

Our imagination is a vital tool in generating mental pictures of life after our own personal death. This work clarifies areas where action is needed. What am I going to do with my teaching notes for all the courses that I have painstakingly envisioned, researched and written? So much research and spirit-led creativity has gone into those! Yet I also hold the awareness that every era will produce its own spiritual teachers. My notes or my unique way of working may not have any relevance (say) fifty years from now. Then again, those notes mean a lot to me and I would like them to go to someone who will appreciate them, be it only as a historical document. If I were to die this year, I would give copies to some of my most trusted students.

A shamanic practitioner colleague of mine has already asked if my youngest son would like to have her drum from Siberia once she passes. He said yes. He was twelve years old when the question was asked so we don't know how he will feel the day this drum arrives in the hands of his (hopefully) *much* older self!

Having said that, he is wise enough to give it to the right person, if he then feels it is not his to keep. My colleague and my son both know that.

The "battle" with a terminal illness

When people die from cancer it is common to speak of their final years or months as "a battle with cancer". I understand this cultural reference, but the word battle does not sit right with me. This way of speaking is deeply ingrained in our language. Quoting from an article by cancer survivor Xeni Jardin[11], people will commonly say:

> *"You'll beat this."*
> *"You got this."*
> *"You'll win this battle."*
> *"Cancer isn't as tough as you."*
> *"You have a positive attitude and you're a fighter, so I know you'll get well soon."*
> *"You'll be fine."*

When we engage in "combat" with ourselves -we are at war with ourselves! Xeni Jardin[11] says: *Am I the invading army or the battleground? Am I the soldier or a hostage the soldiers are trying to liberate? All of the above? If the chemotherapy and radiation and surgery and drugs don't work, and I die, will people be disappointed in me for not "fighting" hard enough?*

Our imagination needs to be in gear when we speak to people dealing with cancer. Our imagination needs to be in gear when speaking to *anyone*, if we want to stand a chance of them feeling understood and supported. Let's not create wars where there might not be any.

Ego Death

For as long as we have a human body, we also have an ego.

This is a vital function that guards our best interests, not unlike a guard-dog. Without it we would not survive – we all need a healthy dose of it. However, the human ego can "grow too large for its doghouse" (as it were) and start running the show. At that point we cross over into the territories of Narcissism.

My own teachers of shamanism have all taught me that death is, ultimately, the death of the human ego. That is also why we (commonly) feel such immense fear of death. It is the human ego yelling like a toddler, throwing tantrums, stomping its foot at the prospect of not being the centre attention any longer.

One of the gifts that ancient shamanic practices can bestow is teaching people ways of reaching non-egoic states of consciousness, where a larger perspective kicks in. We no longer look at the world from the "me-me-me place" but we start seeing our own place in the larger scheme of things (in the Divine Plan, if you are religious-minded).

Looking at Death from that place (and I try to make this a regular practice) brings the following insights:

- My time on Earth is limited and I was privileged to have that time at all
- Living forever (or being resurrected through cryogenics) has no place in the larger scheme of things because the journey of my soul continues in non-material realms just as other souls are entitled to their time on Earth (and I don't want to maintain and unhealthy attachment to a dead body floating in a cryo tank as this will have an impact on my soul's journey after death)
- Mythology teaches us, in no uncertain terms, that immortality (on earth) is a curse, not a blessing. It would mean being imprisoned in an ever-aging and ever-more-decrepit body. It would also mean no more birth and babies – just a grotesquely aged world population no longer able to look after itself…

I much prefer to take a leaf out of our middle son's book (words spoken when he was three years old): there is a small house in Yellow (golden) Land where I lived long before I was born. That small house is there waiting for me to come home. There are animal friends in Yellow Land who look after that house for me while I am away.

And in the words of our youngest son Brendan (at age seven)[12]: *"... Mum, do you realise that if you were the only human being in the history of earth that DID manage to live forever, it would be a terrible fate indeed because everyone you ever knew would die. And one day the Sun itself will die by burning out and swallowing up the Earth and Moon. And all living things will long have moved to other realms and other universes. But Mum, if you managed to be immortal, you would be this sad little creature floating all alone in an empty universe. And you would feel a great cosmic loneliness you have no comprehension of today. And therefore Mummy, you should be VERY GRATEFUL FOR THE CERTAINTY THAT YOU ARE GOING TO DIE ONE DAY!!!"*

Death as the ultimate healing

Many spiritual traditions teach that the moment of our death is a prime opportunity for spiritual revelation –embraced at the right level of consciousness. This is another reason why dying well-prepared (and breaking free of the earthly bonds) is said to be so important.

In the moment of death, we step back Outside Time and Space. Assuming we manage to drop our attachments to earth-life (meaning that a soul connection to loved ones and loved places remains but the needy or self-seeking part of our attachment is released) then Death can be a moment of great revelation. We remember once again our timeless selves, who we were, before this incarnation. We can journey deep into the mysteries of the cosmos. Some traditions say that we can achieve enlightenment by dying the right way. This is a concept worth meditating on.

Hinduism believes in the rebirth and reincarnation of souls. The souls are immortal and imperishable. A soul is part of a *jiva,* the limited being, who is subject to the impurities of attachment, delusion and laws of karma. Death is therefore not a great calamity, not an end of all, but a natural process in the existence of a *jiva* as a separate entity, a resting period during which it recuperates, reassembles its resources, adjusts its course and returns to the earth to continue its journey. *In Hinduism, unless a soul is liberated, neither life nor after life are permanent. They are both part of a grand illusion: His state of mind at the time of death, that is what thoughts and what desires were predominant in his consciousness at the time of his death, decides in which direction the jiva will travel and in what form it will appear again.*[13]

Where do murderers (serial killers, school shooters, suicidal terrorists) go after death?

This is a question that we have probably all asked ourselves at least once. It is usually (and can only be) answered from within a specific religion or belief system:

Christians might believe that they burn in Hell for all eternity unless they ask for forgiveness and return to the embrace of Jesus (who died for the salvation of all our sins).

Atheists believe that dead-is-dead: they got away with it and that the end of it.

Buddhism teaches that there are three types of death: the end of life, exhaustion of merit, premature death. On the brink of death, good and evil karma will flash before a person's eyes.

The Chinese always say: "At the time of death, the ghosts that feel injustice will come and ask for one's life." Therefore, serial killers might see a procession of dead souls seeking justice, by means of karmic action.

In Islam murder is seen as a grave sin and death is viewed as the termination of earthly life and the beginning of the afterlife. The angel of death appears to extract a person's soul. After the burial, two angels come to test the dead on their faith. Wicked souls are thrown in hell or the underworld where they are punished until the Day of Judgment.

> *And whoever kills a believer intentionally, his punishment is Hell; he shall abide in it, and Allah will send His wrath on him and curse him and prepare for him a painful chastisement.*
> (Surah an-Nisā' 4:93)[14]

Judaism believes in an afterlife regards the preservation of human life as one of its supreme moral values and forbids doing anything that might shorten life. Euthanasia is murder, full stop. Injustice is addressed by divine agents in the afterlife.

> *The value of human life is infinite and beyond measure, so that any part of life – even if only an hour or a second – is of precisely the same worth as seventy years of it, just as any fraction of infinity, being indivisible, remains infinite.*
> Lord Jakobovits[15]

Activity #7: Write Your Own Obituary

Go to a place where you can be undisturbed for a while. Light a candle.

Rather than running from the notion of your own personal death, lean into this. Whisper to it. Embrace it briefly. What might it feel like, to take this step?

Use your imagination to envision a good death for yourself, the best death you can imagine. What are the key elements? Think of things such as the presence of loved ones, unfinished business or lack thereof, any legacy you left for others and so forth.

Now write your own obituary: describe the way you died, the key events in your life what gave your life meaning, who will survive whom and keep your memory alive.

Finally ask yourself one more question: what would you most like to receive from the living? (I have done this work with groups of both adults and children and the answer is usually: to be remembered, to keep my memory alive).

Return to everyday consciousness and take a long hard look at your own life: where do you need to make changes or shift focus? Have you made a will and left medical and/or spiritual directives for extreme circumstances? If not, start working on it. It will bring you peace of mind and more headspace for living life to the full…

Chapter 8

The Problem with Our Imagination

A good friend will help you move, but a true friend will help you move a body.
Steven J. Daniels[1]

... you're just as dangerous as the beings the rest of the people fear but you can't afford to be as honest abo[2]ut it...
Anne Bishop[2]

Sins of commission and sins of omission

The problem with our imagination is that its powers are vaster than most of us ever realise (or harness and direct). That is why it can also be used to create undesirable things and not just on a small scale or personal level. Limiting my own opportunities and joy in life is sad and tough. Dreaming up nasty scenarios for other people without being aware of the power of my imagination gets trickier.

An individual or group of people using their imagination to deliberately create thought forms, "hang-outs in the other world" or large energetic manifestations, (such as otherworld sanctuaries or temples), is exponentially trickier again.

Here is where using the imagination touches the realm of, so called, *black magic*. Both white and black magic heavily draw on the imagination. People practicing magic actively school, train and expand their imagination.

Growing up in a Roman Catholic family there was emphasis on "sins of commission and sins of omission". My own parents still went to confession with the village priest during their childhood – my brothers and I did not. However, I did grow up in a heavily religious atmosphere of "putting others before myself" (martyrdom as an ideal and virtue) and "never sinning, even in the privacy of my own head". The general idea was to atone for such sins: Lustful thoughts about the boy next door – twenty Hail Mary's. Shouting at your brother – say The Lord's Prayer ten times and so forth. I prayed often and fervently as a child. I was hyper aware of my own failings and failures. From a very young age I felt I needed to carry the suffering of the world on my shoulders. For years I dreamed of becoming a saint. My maternal grandmother encouraged such flights of fancy by talking to me about my namesake Saint Imelda, the famous child saint. Needless to say this childhood ambition failed completely!

This system (of controlling people by means of ideology and doctrine) fails in that it completely suppresses the human shadow. Recently I "confessed" some ugly thought to a wise compassionate friend, and she replied: *"Yes, that is your shadow speaking, but your shadow too has a voice and deserves to be heard! It is still a fragment of a larger personal truth and larger picture..."* The relief was immense! Even on a purely physical level I felt lighter after she said that.

I imagine someone saying this to my younger self! I would have felt validated and understood and I would still have done all the soul searching into why I felt triggered or annoyed enough to have ugly thoughts. However, to hammer into young children the notion that it is *a sin to have negative thoughts at all* is very damaging and this interferes with their ability to draw appropriate boundaries and to stand up for themselves. It creates people who desperately please others in dysfunctional ways, do not express anger (meaning that they feel the anger anyway but bottle it up to the point where it eventually expresses itself as a physical issue, illness or depression). It creates people who feel they need to be "nice" the whole time and often such people reach a ripe old age without knowing who they truly are, without expressing their authentic self in the world. Do you know any people who always have a nervous smile plastered on their face, or people who can never say 'no' and it ruins their life?! Check out a TED talk by Diana Wais titled Emotional laws are the answer for better relationships.[3]

Think no evil

I ended up with a compromise: for years I thought it was OK to entertain unpleasant thoughts and fantasies, for *as long as it all happened only in the privacy of my own head*. Once I started studying shamanism that assumption did not stand up to scrutiny. I am always in the process of creating my own reality. Not only that: all of us are always co-creating our collective reality. A mind full of negative thoughts and unexpressed anger is going to create low-vibration outcomes and manifestations.

Multiply this by many minds full of the same "litter" and you get the kind of outcomes we collectively perceive as "collective reality" or hard facts (such as polluted oceans, creative terrorists and egomaniac self-serving politicians").

Energetic structures

The next tier of this "wedding cake" is a group of people joining forces to deliberately create energetic structures. This powerful tool can be used for the greater good of all (if it concerns structures of protection and temples of light) but can equally well be used to the detriment of all (as the Nazis did).

If we do not harness and focus the power of our imagination, we will create confused outcomes a best. If we do not practice any form of spiritual hygiene and walk around with a mind full of psychic litter, we will actively litter the world with low vibration outcomes. (Then we all read the papers and say: what is the world coming to?) If we take no responsibility for part-creating those outcomes we cannot take back the power to change these outcomes either! We are more powerful than we think, than *we have been conditioned to believe.*

The Confirmation Bias

Another problem with the human imagination is that it is relatively easy to make something up and then find "evidence" to support the idea. Psychologists call this Confirmation Bias. At the time of writing this chapter (March 2018) there is a series of posts appearing on Facebook where people are discussing "Ascension symptoms".[4]

Ascension is explained as involving an acceleration of vibrational energy and an expansion of awareness that creates a shift in consciousness. When any life system raises its state of vibration from one energetic level (or realm of existence) to another (higher) state, it is said to be ascending. This could be compared to tuning a radio to a specific frequency.

This process is said to bring physical, emotional and spiritual symptoms as the person is rewired or "upgraded". The idea is that old patterns drop away as people embody more light. Such symptoms can vary from stomach and digestive issues, nausea, food intolerances, headaches, changes in perception, burst of energy or a complete lack of energy and so forth. Obviously, those same symptoms can have other plausible causes as well. We have pushed the eco-systems on Earth to the very limit. Acid rain pours down on us while we breathe polluted air and eat genetically modified foods.

Do I believe that shifts in consciousness are occurring? Yes, I do. Do I believe that human beings are all at different stages in terms of this process? Yes, I do. Do I personally call that process "Ascension" – no, because for me that has connotations of being lifted straight up into Heaven.

What I do believe is that the moment a group of people (be it self-identified as New Age or "Light Workers" or other) coins the concept of "Mass Ascension" and "ascension symptoms", people are going to find evidence that it exists. In other words: a lens of perception is created and if enough people subscribe to that specific lens, we have a phenomenon! If enough people find "evidence" that appears to fit in with this phenomenon (Confirmation Bias), then this will be taken that as proof that Ascension exists, and more people will join the movement.

One phrase for this phenomenon is Reality Tunnels:

> *Every kind of ignorance in the world all results from not realizing that our perceptions are gambles. We believe what we see and then we believe our interpretation of it, we don't even know we are making an interpretation most of the time. We think this is reality.*
> Robert Anton Wilson[5]

> *The idea does not necessarily imply that there is no objective truth; rather that our access to it is mediated through our senses, experience, conditioning, prior beliefs, and other non-objective factors. The implied individual world each person occupies is said to be their reality tunnel. The term can also apply to groups of people united by beliefs: we can speak of the fundamentalist Christian reality tunnel or the ontological naturalist reality tunnel.*
> Wikipedia[6]

Shamans have always undergone initiations and those initiations have rewired or rebooted them. When people engage with shamanism or embark on any other committed spiritual path, profound changes in perception will occur and it is inevitable that those will be accompanied by physical and emotional symptoms.

Another valid take on this is that if the rise in "ascension symptoms" means that more people are showing greater sensitivity to issues such as quality of drinking water, air pollution or how food products and meat are sourced, meaning that there is more pressure on companies and legislators to improve standards and safety checks – and then I am all for it!

"The Curse"

Yet another example of a large group of people collectively using their imagination to create (or rather demonise) something is the phenomenon of women collectively referring to their menstruation as "The Curse". This is a far cry from what this monthly event can be and has been for women in earlier times. Fertility ensures the survival of the tribe. Earlier peoples who lived under harsh conditions with a high mortality rate knew very well that the birth of a child is a gift for the whole community because it helps ensure the future and survival of that Tribe.

Before the Church Fathers deliberately imposed the patriarchal lens of perception that bodily functions where somehow "dirty" and related to "sin", women experienced the mysteries of Life and Death through menstruation, birth and death. I am not saying that this was always glorified and "easy". It is a well-known fact that in times and locations with poorer hygiene and no medical care (especially no Caesarean sections) a shocking percentage of women dies in childbirth. Women in developing countries are a staggering 300 times more likely to die in childbirth today.[7]

In all cultures and ages "back street abortionists", "cunning herbalists" or their equivalents have always performed abortions as there have always been unplanned pregnancies and unwanted children. I do not wish to downplay those bleak facts in any way. However, we also know that in some parts of the world women had access to menstruation huts (or "red tents") and that they lived much closer to their own monthly rhythm, the Moon and the way all these cycles drop into alignment when women live closely and intimately together. The red river that is menstruation is one manifestation of the River of Life. Our blood is also the blood of our ancestors. They are no longer alive, but their blood continues to flow in our veins.

The moment we start calling this life-giving phenomenon The Curse – we literally curse ourselves and all women. We create (or call in) a phenomenon where women perceive themselves as "being cursed" (rather than being blessed with fertility and life-giving powers). Essentially, we are always making up stories to explain the facts of our human existence. The Curse or Life-giving Power? The choice is ours! However, the way we choose to perceive this will shape our experiences and the experiences of our daughters (unless they reclaim a different story, a different lens of perception for themselves). *Choose your Reality Tunnel with great care – because it will affect your life quality immensely!*

Cursing

In everyday language one of the meanings of cursing is using offensive words in anger or annoyance (for instance when you hurt yourself or nothing will go right). We even use acronyms, for instance "WTF" has become a common utterance on Facebook.

In my profession cursing refers to invoking a curse against someone. That means setting an energetic trajectory in motion that is going to bring the person (or people) concerned ill fortune, nasty things. I once worked with a family where all the men died before age forty. When we unravelled this and located the origin of this issue, we discovered that in a dispute between neighbouring families over an "unsuitable marriage" the father of the bride had cursed all men for all generations to come, in the family of the groom, about two centuries earlier.

Creating undesirable outcomes and manifestations in energetic form and then sending them somewhere is the phenomenon at the heart of what we call black magic. The popular image we have of this is sticking needles in dolls, or effigies, but it can be done in many other ways as well. In ancient Scandinavia people used cursing poles:

In the Norse sagas, creating a níðstǫng (scorn pole) is a unique practice used to curse and express hate toward an enemy. Dr.Jackson Crawford has a video on his YouTube channel titled Níðstǫng: The Old Norse "Scorn Pole".

Toxic Thoughts

Old Norse cursing poles are an extreme version of the cursing phenomenon, but we need to be more concerned about negative thoughts others have about us (or direct at us). Many forms of spiritual hygiene and spiritual protection are about deflecting (and even transmuting) such thoughts by erecting an energetic shield. One single toxic thought may not hurt us but when we receive a large volume of such thoughts (say from one angry person or from a group of people who do not agree with us) then negative energy (unless deflected and transmuted) can start accumulating in our energetic field and eventually pool in our bodies where it causes intrusions and physical health issues.

Brene Brown[8] suggests that we always have a choice in arriving at an interpretation of someone else's behaviour: "When we own our stories, we avoid being trapped as characters in stories someone else is telling." For example: my Dad never attended any concert where I played the violin, as a teenager. I can identify the following options for interpretation (but there might be many other possibilities):

- Attending music school concerts was my mother's job (as the church organist)
- He didn't care if the concert went well or not and if I played the violin or not
- He never had the privilege of an education in music, so he might have been afraid of demonstrating ignorance or making a fool of himself
- He needed some time to himself, home alone, more than he needed to attend his children's activities
- He suffered from PTSD and could not manage to sit still on a chair for two hours. Sounds and noises of any kind were difficult for him to handle because it intruded on his fragile state of mind. For that reason, my mother had long

stopped playing her small collection of vinyl records of classical music.

Today I choose the final interpretation. For people with PTSD the world just simply does not look, feel or sound the same as it does for more balanced or healed people. I don't think it was possible for him to sit through a youth concert.

To this I will add that I ran this exercise once with my shamanic group for teens: The Time Travellers. They all agreed: "Nope! When a person intends to hurt me, I can read their energy and know for sure – I do *not need* softer alternative explanations!" – That too is a valid take on this.

Activity #8: What Reality Tunnel do we choose in Life's Playground?!

In this activity we will choose our Reality Tunnel with greater awareness!

Go to a place where you can be undisturbed for a while. Bring paper and pen. Light a candle and play relaxing music. Take a moment to drop all everyday concerns – however pressing they may feel.

Use your imagination to see life as an Amusement Park with many rides to choose from. Especially those rides where you scoot through tunnels, powered by water!

For the duration of this exercise suspend all disbelief, any thought along the lines of "But of course I know what reality is, this is silly!" Seek admission to this park (can you walk straight in or do you need to pay for your ticket? This tells you something about the workings of your own mind!)

Walk around and check out the rides, especially the reality tunnels. They have different colours, twists, turns and destinations. Choose one and take the plunge. Prepare to see the world in a completely different way. You may even want to try a few of them. (You are likely to get wet and dirty!)

Anything could happen…if you are Pagan you may see the world through the eyes of a fundamentalist Christian. A pacifist may see the world as a terrorist perceives it. If you enjoy good mental health, you may see reality distorted by mental illness. If you are elderly – you may see the world through the eyes of a child. *Anything is possible!*

Return. Make notes. Try to hold on the insight that other reality tunnels can be just as convincing as your own…. Does this change your interactions with people in any way?

Chapter 9

Imagination and the Art of Telling Ourselves Stories

Aldous Huxley commented, "I had motive for not wanting the world to have a meaning; consequently assumed that it had none, and was able without any difficulty to find satisfying reasons for this assumption. The philosopher who finds no meaning in the world is not concerned exclusively with a problem in pure metaphysics, he is also concerned to prove that there is no valid reason why he personally should not do as he wants to do ..."
Calvin Smith[1]

In a universe of blind physical forces and genetic replication, some people are going to get hurt, and other people are going to get lucky; and you won't find any rhyme or reason to it, nor any justice. The universe we observe has precisely the properties we should expect if there is at the bottom, no design, no purpose, no evil and no good. Nothing but blind pitiless indifference. DNA neither knows nor cares. DNA just is, and we dance to its music.
Richard Dawkins[2]

Creationism has surprisingly little difficulty accommodating dinosaurs. Indeed, the first thing you bump into at the museum is Boris, a 20ft model of a tyrannosaurus rex. Conventional scientists think T-rex died out at the end of the Cretaceous period, about 65m years ago. Creationists, who argue that the world was created no more than 10,000 years ago, believe dinosaurs and man co-existed in the pre-Flood period (they date the Flood to around 1,600 years after the creation), that there were dinosaurs on the ark, but that they were eventually wiped out by the changes in climate which followed the Flood.
Stephen Moss[3]

> *"Murder is not about lust and it's not about violence. It's about possession. When you feel the last breath of life coming out of the woman, you look into her eyes. At that point, it's being God."*
> *Ted Bundy*[4]

> *John George Haigh "Acid Bath Murderer" Born in Yorkshire in 1909 to John & Emily Haigh, two devout members of the deeply conservative Protestant sect known as the Plymouth Brethren, young John George Haigh grew up with no friends, as his father (an engineer) had erected a 10 foot wall around their garden to lock out the "disgusting" influences of the outside world. As an only child, Haigh retreated into solitude, a crazing for attention and his own imagination, which in his teens manifested as theft, lies, fantasies and animal cruelty.*
> Michael J Buchanan-Dunne[4]

We all tell ourselves stories.

It has been said that all is vibration and that vibration is the ultimate nature of everything.

It has also been said that "all is story and story is the ultimate nature of everything.

Creation Stories

I love and collect creation stories. Why does this interest never wane? Because these stories hold kernels of timeless truths about the human condition and mythic memories of events, that predate the arrival of human beings on our planet.

People all over the world tell creation stories to explain how the world and her creatures and features came into being. Those stories often (but not always) show interesting parallels: they speak of a creator god/goddess or plurality of gods. Common themes are The Flood, The Fall from Paradise and the Birth of Sacred Twins or Hero Twins (often representing duality) and the adventures of Animal Ancestors.

People can feel very strongly about their creation stories. Well into the 21st century some parents choose to keep their children off school when evolution and Darwinian concepts are taught.

Creation stories from around the world often attempt to explain what sociologist and a professor emeritus at Harvard University Daniel Bell once stated: *Culture ... is the effort to provide a coherent set of answers to the existential predicaments that confront all human beings.*

Common sense and Uncommon Sense

... if you believe mankind was created by a warlike being that simply overpowers his opponents, then adherents to that system probably won't have a problem subjugating other people by war. If you believe there is a loving God who created us, then you would probably believe we should treat others fairly. What we believe about origins determines the 'rules' or 'laws' that a culture is willing to live by, as that narrative reflects how we should conduct ourselves as we live our lives.

Calvin Smith[1]

Common sense is often used as shorthand for the assumption that "anyone in their right mind would do this or think that!" However, the religious wars we are seeing in our world today teach us that *common sense is only common when there is a commonality of thought (perception or belief system) between people!*[1]

We live in a time of spiritual fragmentation. The Judeo-Christian stronghold in most Western countries has been eroded and this dominant cosmology has been replaced by a much wider range of beliefs. In addition to that many people are on the move and people from very different ethnic backgrounds living closely together now make up the demography of many communities.

Adam and Eve and Darwin

For nearly two millennia Christianity was the dominant religion in Europe. The book of Genesis is the first book of The Hebrew Bible (or Tanakh) and the Old Testament. It tells the story of creation: how God created the world in seven days (He spent six days creating and rested on the seventh day). In the 19th century Charles Darwin presented a very different creation story.

The theory of evolution by natural selection, first formulated in Darwin's book "On the Origin of Species" in 1859, describes the process by which organisms change over time as a result of changes in heritable physical or behavioural traits. Changes that allow an organism to better adapt to its environment will help it survive and have more offspring.

Evolution by natural selection is one of the best substantiated theories in the history of science, supported by evidence from a wide variety of scientific disciplines, including paleontology, geology, genetics and developmental biology.

> *The theory has two main points, said Brian Richmond, curator of human origins at the American Museum of Natural History in New York City. "All life on Earth is connected and related to each other," and this diversity of life is a product of "modifications of populations by natural selection, where some traits were favoured in and environment over others," he said. (…)*
>
> *The theory is sometimes described as "survival of the fittest" but that can be misleading, Pobiner said. Here, "fitness" refers not to an organism's strength or athletic ability, but rather the ability to survive and reproduce.*
>
> Ker Than[5]

Some people have pointed out that if all evolution is rooted in biochemical processes, then our cherished concept of free will is called into question. If we take this "story" to its extreme, free will is an illusion because human existence is dictated by chance chemical-physical processes. As noted by Lady Barbara Wootton, the British criminologist, *If mental health and ill health cannot be defined in objective scientific terms that are free of subjective moral judgments, it follows that we have no reliable criterion by which to distinguish the sick from the healthy mind. The road is then wide open … to dispense with the concept of responsibility altogether.*[1]

Darwin[6] wrote in his notes that: "This view should teach one profound humility, one deserves no credit for anything. Nor ought one to blame others."

Can Life have meaning if Death has no meaning?!

One very interesting thing we can extract from this is that there is a strong connection between gods, cosmology and (beliefs in) an afterlife and human ethics: why bother being good if there is neither punishment nor reward for this?!

> *A Japanese company has launched what it claims is the world's first funeral drive-thru service. In a country with a shrinking population, where the death rate far outstrips the birth rate … It enables the elderly and immobile to see off their friends and family from the comfort of their cars, streamlining what can be a lengthy service into a simple affair lasting just minutes.*
> John Robson[7]

> *Let me summarize my views on what modern evolutionary biology tells us loud and clear … There are no gods, no purposeful forces of any kind, no life after death. When I die, I am absolutely certain that I am going to be completely dead. That's just all—that's gonna be the end of me. There is no ultimate foundation for ethics, no ultimate meaning in life, and no free will for humans, either.*
> William Provine[1]

Another balancing comment I wish to make in this context is that there are (apparently) serious issues even with Darwin's theories. Below I will list just some taken from Evolution News and Science[8] today:

- Lack of a viable mechanism for producing high levels of complex and specified information
- Fossil records do not support Darwinian evolution.
- The failure of molecular biology to provide evidence for a grand "tree of life."
- Natural selection is an extremely inefficient method of spreading traits in populations unless a trait has an extremely high selection coefficient
- The failure of chemistry to explain the origin of the genetic code
- Humans show many behavioural and cognitive traits and abilities that offer no apparent survival advantage (e.g. music, art, religion, ability to ponder the nature of the universe!)

It is not for me to say who is right or wrong or whether every author quite possibly perceives a part-truth. The aspect we will explore here is that we all tell ourselves stories. Human beings are wired to tell each other (and themselves) stories because it is how we find meaning in events. Human brains are wired to spot patterns. Some would say that we even impose patterns where there were none to start with.

> *The shortest distance between a human being and truth is a story*
> Anthony de Mello[7]

> *Jesuit Retreat Master Edward Kinerk suggests that "the closest description [of spirituality] is life-style," continuing that any definition of spirituality "should contain the idea of personal*

growth . . . What distinguishes the human condition is growth beyond self, self-transcendence.

Edward Sellner, scholar of Celtic spirituality, proposes that "Spirituality in its broadest sense is, quite simply, a way of life that reveals an awareness of the sacred and a relationship with the Holy One in the midst of our human fragility, brokenness and limitations."

Ernest Kurtz and Katherine Ketcham[9]

According to Kurtz and Ketcham, D.H. Lawrence observed observed that *however smart we may be, however rich and clever or loving or charitable or spiritual or impeccable, it doesn't help us at all. The real power comes in to us from the beyond. Life enters us from behind, where we are sightless, and from below, where we do not understand. And unless we yield to the beyond, and take our power and might and honour and glory from the unseen, from the unknown, we shall continue empty.*[9]

We tell ourselves stories. We interpret some things. We misinterpret other things. We fool ourselves. We make things up. We listen to other people's stories. We believe some – not others. We get inspired. We get bored. We get religion. We get angry. We lose our will to live. We laugh. We love. We laugh at ourselves. In the Ginnungagap (the primordial void in Norse mythology) there was said to be great cosmic laughter (according to some authors).

Our culture often perceives stories as "something for young children" but we all tell ourselves stories in many ways. We often think that stories are about us – when they are not. We tell stories about others – but don't realise how these stories say more about us than about others. Other times we talk so much that we fail to listen. We are in a constant dialogue with ourselves.

The wheels on the bus

This morning I attempted to board a bus in London. It took me a moment to realise that the driver wanted me to use the back door instead. As I stepped on board, he hit the gas pedal, accelerated and took a sharp bend before I had gained a proper foothold. I went flying, crashed into some people and fell down on their feet and bags. I scrambled back upright and apologised in all directions. People gave me a stony stare. They obviously thought I was drunk or mentally deranged. I held on tight with two hands and got to the desired destination. No one helped me up. No one said: "Are you OK?!"

I was shocked because I am used to having wonderful encounters on London buses. People often tell me "how unfriendly and rude Londoners are" and I jump right in there to explain how friendly a city London *really is.* Once I got home again, I thought: "Woah… I daily experience London through the eyes of a well-educated middle class white European woman with a home to go to. I do not often get to experience London "through different eyes". This morning I just got the tiniest taste of London as perceived by a homeless person or unstable person (an "undesirable" no one is keen to talk to). And I didn't even break an arm – what a gift and life lesson!

I also felt shame: my stories about London being "almost as friendly and community-spirited as Amsterdam" are told from a place of privilege. They are not a truth every Londoner agrees with (or indeed ever experiences). One year ago, I visited Amsterdam and people were not especially friendly there either. Not the way I remembered from three decades ago. However, in those days I was a tall skinny bohemian girl with long blonde hair. Salesmen at Amsterdam's street markets would slip me free clothing or fruit and vegetables with a wink, saying "come back soon!" At the age of twenty-three years old I moved to Stockholm (definitely not a friendly city!) The thing is that my perceptions of all these cities were heavily coloured by my own youth and appearance. I very much doubt any "Amsterdammer" would slip me free clothing or sheet music for my violin today!

Amsterdam has moved on since I left. I have changed too. The Amsterdam I remember from my student years is now only a collection of stories. It does not exist any longer. The person I was then does not exist any longer either (though I still have the long hair). In those days I disliked men whistling at me as I cycled around the "grachten" (canals). I craved invisibility more than anything. Today I have more invisibility, but other doors have closed along with that one. There are many Londons and many Amsterdams, millions of them, and that is not counting the tourists! These millions of cities are like only loosely connected parallel universes...

The story I am telling myself

Brene Brown[10] suggests that we use the following preface: *"the story I am telling myself"*, when talking to others, because it leaves space for the speaker to be wrong. If we are to have joyful and balanced relationships with other people, it is important not to jump to the worst-case-scenarios the whole time. Other people might be having experiences that we are not aware of. They may also be operating under challenges or restrictions we are not aware of.

Parents of small children do not have "free time" the way couples at the before-children stage do. They are always on call in either their work setting or their own home. They generally need to pay for child-care by the hour – doubling the cost of a meal out with friends. Meeting someone for tea means that something else (invariably urgent) does not get done. You can only spend the time once.

This simple fact changed my life forever. Since our three children arrived and I decided to be a working mum, I think carefully before accepting invitations. Is this something I really want to do? Are these people I really want to be with? Am I going to come away feeling inspired and uplifted (or drained and in need of recovery time?) Add to this my profoundly solitary temperament and, indeed, I say no to more invitations than I accept. People often perceive that as rejection but for me it is a positive choice: I reserve the right to spend my (very limited) amount of free time as I wish.

Some empathy goes a long way in these situations! A mum who finds herself in the supermarket with a screaming toddler (or even worse: on a ten-hour flight with a colicky baby) does not a need parenting advice or criticism. A comment to the effect of: "Mine did this all the time, what a beautiful boy!" will go down much better than "tut-tut" or "the evil eye".

I thank the people on the bus this morning for showing me how London looks to less privileged people. It opened doors of perception. It was a gift.

Belief

Another thorny issue is whether we choose our beliefs or if many of our beliefs are deeply ingrained until we make a conscious choice to shift them, examine them, release them and replace them with beliefs that serve us better. (This is the work I do for myself, with clients and with students).

In our time Richard Dawkins embodies the voice of atheism, though professionally speaking he is an Oxford-educated biologist. I invite you to read the following blog, which gives an account of a public debate between Dawkins and Rowan Williams, the archbishop of Canterbury. The title of this debate was: "The Nature of Human Beings and the Question of Their Ultimate Origin"[11]:

Both great minds agreed on three issues:

- That there is such a thing as truth
- Both believe in logic (as in, two contradictory statements cannot both be true)

- Both believe in the claims of science to describe the observable world

Williams, as a priest, believes that one of the things that makes us human (and sets us apart from animals) is our consciousness. It allows us to join our consciousness with an unconditional creative energy (that he calls God). Essentially, he is saying that his faith is what sustains him and provides his moral compass in a world admittedly rife with suffering and darkness.

My 18-year son (who has just started university) has become very fond of the word "narrative". While he is sorting out what he believes and what others believe, he has concluded that all these different beliefs follow narratives: the Christian narrative, the scientific narrative, a tribal narrative, a London gang culture narrative...

He is really saying, in 21st century teen language, that "all is story" and that without story there is no meaning. One thing our teen philosopher takes for absolute truth is that a life without meaning is not worth living and that even very tough lives are bearable if people find meaning in their existence. However, often when I talk to him, he will often say: "Cut the narrative Mum, yours is only one viewpoint among many!!" We *all* need that reminder!

Three Agreements

This book does not attempt to solve the greatest conundrums of human existence. However, for the record I would like to give my take on the three agreements reached by Dawkins and Williams:

That there is such a thing as truth

In my early days as a shamanic practitioner I used the word truth a lot in one-to-one sessions. Here I was following one of my own teachers who said: "the spirits will not beat around the bush - the spirits always speak the truth!" The issue is, of course, that what is absolute unquestionable truth for you may not hold any truth for me at all. Therefore, we could perhaps say that truths (plural) exist or can co-exist (your truth, my truth) but the moment we speak of one truth, which truth are we talking about except our own?

Practicing shamanism this issue gets even trickier because the spirits have a habit of cutting through layers of illusions, delusions, projections and defence mechanism we wrap ourselves in (enabling us to survive in the world). Many a time have my helping spirits said something to me that made me feel outraged: "What?! How dare you say that? You really have gone too far this time!!" -but then I always sit deeply with their guidance, I sleep and dream on it, I open my heart to it -and I discover that they are right, that there is yet another layer of self-fooling or self-comforting I need to peel right off, OUCH!

On the level of human existence, any truth is relative because there are limits that delineate human existence. Even scientists operate within those limits, but they cannot impose those same limits on the universe. (This is why many indigenous peoples speak of Dreaming).

Both believe in logic (as in, two contradictory statements cannot both be true)

In my own life there was a time where I too believed this and took it to be a corner stone of human reality. This was challenged at art school where one of our teachers (a philosopher called W. van Ringelestein) presented material from his own book about phenomenology called "Beeld en Werkelijkheid" (Image and Reality)[12]

Our word phenomenology comes from Greek (phainómenon: "that which appears" and lógos "study"). It aims to study the structures of human experience and consciousness. It was founded in the early years of the 20th century by Edmund Husserl in Germany and seeks to determine the essential properties and structures of experience through systematic reflection. It is neither a doctrine nor a philosophical school, but rather a way of thinking and questioning that can be almost disorientating.

What I remember best from those lessons in Amsterdam in the 1980's is how he took apart the notion of what a chair is. He asked all of us to name the defining characteristics of "a chair":

- *It usually has four legs*
- *It is often made of wood*
- *Its primary purpose is for people to sit on it*
- *(and so forth)*

Then he proceeded to take it all apart again: obviously some chairs have three legs, or two legs or no legs at all (think of an outdoor wooded seat perched on a concrete block!) Chairs can be made from many conventional and unconventional materials.

You can't sit on a tiny chair for a dollhouse but the doll can sit on it...

Modern art has taken things to surreal (or even absurd) limits and we can now collectively conceive of a chair you cannot sit on.... Imagine a chair so huge that only a giant can sit on it, larger than surrounding buildings. I can also conceive of a chair with a spiky seat that only a fakir would manage to sit on, perhaps a symbolic existential commentary on how uncomfortable the human condition is...

Van Ringelestein took all of us to the conclusion that there are chairs but there is no such thing as "chair-ness" (as in one defining characteristic all chairs have in common), only a large collection of phenomena in which chairs feature and manifest. In this discourse logic triumphed over "chair-ness" and he actively encouraged our class to entertain the notion that two contradictory statements can both be true at the same time as both can offer valid windows of perception on a given phenomenon.

A few decades later I found myself sitting in circles with teachers of shamanism. One of the things I soon discovered was that two contradictory things could be true here too. Not only that, but there are multiple layers on which we can perceive reality. The spirit world is *non-consensual reality.*

There is one layer where a chair can't be a not-chair at the same time (everyday reality, think of the family breakfast table!)

On another level there is such a thing as "the spirit of the chair concept" or "the spirit of all chairs" that would express its essence through whatever shape a chair took. One could (conceivably) create two chairs following completely contradictory descriptions and specifications and both would still be expressions of "the dreaming of the Great Universal Chair Spirit" (I am deliberately using non-Western language to make this point).

Regarding the final claim that Dawkins and Williams make:

Both believe in the claims of science to describe the observable world
Due to my training and practice in shamanism I view this slightly differently: Science is one way of describing the observable world. It is the dominant lens of perception in western 21st century culture. Yet there are many other equally valid ways of describing the observable world. I have come across the statement that "science is just another mythology", because it is a belief system that imposes its own lenses and limits. Assumptions are made – until proven wrong. Further assumptions are built on those foundational assumptions. I have also come across the statement that mathematics could exist independently of human form and existence, because it is abstract and deals with the numerical properties of the universe. (I am not a good enough mathematician to disprove this statement). In a very different way (using story) mythology deals with the larger cosmic "truths" that underpin reality.

The implications of Goedel's Incompleteness Theorem and Heisenberg's Uncertainty Principle are routinely ignored in most of the sciences. Specifically the assumptions (the mental perspectives) of the observer change what is being observed; scientific systems such as mathematics are based on unprovable, often unrefinable assumptions and to understand the limits of a system and refine its underlying assumptions it is necessary to stand outside it, to literally be in a different system.
Stephen Harrod Buhner[13]

In these kinds of discussions (where the parties with opposing views will never reach agreement) one example that is commonly used is that our scientific paradigm makes us think that the indigenous peoples of (let's say) the Amazon region developed their plant medicine through trial and error over centuries. (Meaning that initially there would have been way more mishaps and fatal outcomes than healing outcomes). Our dominant culture teaches that anything else is impossible. However, when we actually interview the elders and medicine people of these tribes they unfailingly give a different answer: "the plants spirits themselves taught us what plant remedy to make for what ailment". They will say that "the plant spirits came and communicated by means of dreams and visions". To us that is "nonsense" or "impossible". For them that is *native science*: it provides the right cures for the right situations. (And often 20th or 21st century investigations in labs prove that tribal people have arrived at exactly the right way of extracting a key ingredient or biochemical compound. However, they were doing that many centuries before microscopes and biochemical analysis existed!) Each culture is a unique experiment in the human encounter with the nature of reality.

In 1962 Thomas Kuhn astonished his academic contemporaries by proposing that scientific theories should be looked upon not only

as dealing with pure objective facts, but rather as systems of belief.
Stephen Harrod Buhner[14]

We are not necessarily doubting that God will do the best for us; we are wondering how painful the best will turn out to be.
C. S. Lewis[15]

Activity #9: Finding the Gold Nugget in Adversity

Go to a place where you can be undisturbed for a while. Bring pen and paper. Light a candle.

I invite you to think of something that happened in your life that you have always perceived as entirely negative. (And I am not denying that some things *just are devastating,* such as death and the loss of a loved one).

Do some time travel: go back to that period (or that moment) and then scroll forward in time (to return to today). Pay careful attention to the course your life took: did this life event shape you? Can you identify any positive things/developments/outcomes that only exist today because this incident/time/transition in your life?

Perhaps you received poor parenting, but this made you determined to be a far more aware (and therefore better) parent for your own children.

Take the broadest possible view: has any other person benefited from what happened to you (in an honourable sense, not an abusive or criminal sense)? Has anyone felt safer, better understood or well supported because of your experience? – And if so, are you willing to reframe the experience for yourself: e.g. "it was very negative at the time, but it also shaped me and harnessed forces for the good within me..."

Given enough time, finding the gold nugget or gift in adversity can become a spiritual practice. In my own life the time this process takes gets shorter all the time. That means that any time I spend feeling "victimised" or "traumatised" or "knocked for six" has reduced significantly. I start looking for the gold nugget much sooner and that has improved my life quality. I wish to "pay this forward". (I also wish to reiterate that truly dreadful things *do* happen, and no amount of positive thinking can change that fact!)

Chapter 10

An Imagination in Evil

None of us stands outside humanity's black collective shadow.
Carl Jung[1]

Good can exist without evil whereas evil cannot exist without good.
Thomas Aquinas[2]

Most definitions of psychological abnormality are devised by white, middle class men. It has been suggested that this may lead to disproportionate numbers of people from certain groups being diagnosed as "abnormal".
Saul McLeod, Abnormal Psychology[3]

Toxic People

Toxicity is the degree to which a substance can damage an organism. Toxicity can refer to the effect on a whole organism, such as an animal, bacterium or plant, as well as the effect on the sub structure of the organism, such as cell (cytotoxicity) or an organ such as the liver (hepatotoxicity). By extension, the world may be metaphorically used to describe toxic effect on larger and more complex groups, such as the family unit or society at large. Sometimes the word is more or less synonymous with poisoning in everyday usage
Wikipedia[4]

Let's start our exploration at the "lightweight" end of this spectrum. The end of the previous chapter brings us to the phenomenon of "toxic people". I once wrote an article exploring that concept by the title: Toxic People -Toxic Concept[5]. Please note that I am challenging the use of the word "toxic" and question the way we throw it around too carelessly. I do not deny that there are people out there who are "very bad news" for others! There is no doubt that we all need to operate cast-iron boundaries in many situations and do what we can to avoid energetic vampires (or even worse) predators. Narcissists are best avoided too.

It has become common usage to apply the word toxic to people. "You won't believe how toxic my mother-in-law is!!" A friend has pointed out to me that there are now many books on the market: TOXIC PEOPLE, TOXIC RELATIONSHIPS, TOXIC PARENTS, TOXIC LOVE.... I just ran a quick search and they are grouped with books about psychopaths!

Now, I truly and completely understand that there are people and situations that are not good for us, therefore we must put distance between us and those things/people, and ideally avoid them altogether.

Unlike snakes, bees or scorpions, human beings do not carry venom. Not physically or literally any way. Human beings can (and frequently do) behave in nasty ways and resort to survival mechanisms that others perceive as pure toxicity. However, leaving aside the field of psychopathology for a moment, this is (at best) a coping mechanism or (at worst) profoundly dysfunctional behaviour displayed by damaged (wounded) individuals.

No expectant mother dreams of putting a Poison Baby on the planet. And most (so called) Toxic Individuals will have areas of competence, generosity and their moments of loving kindness. Your *toxic parents* may be the neighbours who get the weekly shopping for the elderly man next door. Your *toxic colleague or boss* may be a wonderful Dad who runs the Saturday football club for Under Fives.

The first thing we need to release is the fantasy that *other people are toxic and that we are not.* We all weave in and out of behaviours that range from severely dysfunctional to evolved or inspired, all the time. This means that we make delightful and uplifting company some of the time and poor friends at other times.

It is irresponsible to describe other people as toxic. Words have an energy all their own and they can be used as poison arrows. The moment we say that "so and so is toxic", we affect them energetically. People who may have been positively disposed to so-and-so will now actively start looking for trouble and hidden motives; they may project negative interpretations on all so-and-so's actions and statements. *We and only we* chose to set that in motion – not the individual. *We are using language in an irresponsible (and yes!) toxic way.*

> *A word is dead*
> *When it is said,*
> *Some say.*
> *I say it just*
> *Begins to live*
> *That day.*
> Emily Dickinson[6]

The next thing we need to do is reflecting deeply on our own toxicity. When we gossip, we are displaying toxic behaviour. The same thing goes for breaking confidentiality, shouting swear words at other road users in heavy traffic (even if we are alone in our car), flipping someone the bird or using an offensive nickname behind their back, and so forth.

Having thus established (I hope) that we are all more than capable of toxic behaviour and resort to this at least on occasion, we can start to look at what feels so wrong about it and how often it is not even remotely intended as toxic behaviour.

I find visiting my family of origin challenging. Not because my relatives intend this, but because I have lived in other countries for decades and completely changed my boundaries, settings and cultural perceptions.

I feel like a more aware person creating better outcomes and healthier relationships, when I behave my way and follow my chosen principles. However, this does not give me the right to describe my family as "toxic" – even though I do sometimes feel the sting of their judgements and criticisms of me. Their inability to see who I have become (rather than who I was decades ago) hurts. Then again that is my journey; learning about not taking that to heart. *It ultimately teaches me that actually very little of what others say and do reflects on me – it only reflects on them, even when they are talking about me!* That insight was a life-changing insight and was a gift from my beloved family!

Taking this to the next level, what about people who cause problems wherever they go? I have heard a colleague refer to this as *social pain*. Those individuals will keep joining collectives (classes, clubs, groups, circles) desperate for acceptance, on some level knowing that this will inevitably backfire and soon they will find themselves in the role of outcasts or scapegoats again. The human need for belonging, for having a community and rewarding social interactions with others is a core need and deeply wired into us, not a luxury.

Reflect on this for a moment, (we all know several people who fit this description), and we see how incredibly sad this cycle is. Those people are not so much *toxic* as *hurt*. They carry a lifetime of rejections and bad experiences. Unless a group is actively therapeutic (meaning that it exists for the explicit purpose of healing and permanently changing our "wiring") those processes will stay "on repeat". These people's own behaviour creates the defeating outcomes, but they do not realise it and they have no way of breaking free from it. Instead they end up thinking that "the world is against them". This is a tragedy.

En-souled and Inspirited

Human beings are sentient beings, ensouled beings. A Divine

spark animates us. We are not robots! In the moment of our conception a marriage of spirit and matter occurred, allowing us to take physical form and become a human being.

When people (including ourselves in unguarded moments!) display toxic behaviour we can still make an active choice to see their soul, their spirit, their timeless Divine self, their divine spark – if you like. Quantum physics teaches that the presence of the observer changes the outcome of an experiment. This is called the Observer Effect.

We can apply that principle in the spiritual dimension by setting a strong intention and choosing our level of awareness with care. If many people around you commit to seeing the best person you are capable of being (on a personal and professional level) then you will feel encouraged to show your best side. Just as a whole team of colleagues constantly (and secretly) referring to us as toxic will flatten us, push us right down, doing the opposite will lift us.

This spiritual choice is ours to make, in every moment. On occasion we may even choose to deliberately walk into toxic situations to be the breath of fresh air, the catalyst or change agent. Not for too long, not to the point where we risk injury or illness – but long enough to make a slight difference by responding to a situation from a different level of consciousness.

Becoming a Crucible

> *My introduction to the Concept of the Poison Mother and subsequent work with her alongside a group of amazing women changed my life beyond my wildest imaginings!*
> Katharine Lucy Haworth[7]

In 2016 in Sweden a mysterious female figure started appearing in my dreams. She introduced herself as The Poison mother. She did not immediately disclose her full identity. After a year and a day of immersing myself in her teachings and "unwrapping" her message I discovered that I already knew her as one of the Norse goddesses (Sigyn, trickster god Loki's wife).

In the poem Lokasenna in the Poetic Edda[8], the Norse Trickster god Loki has been bound by the gods with the guts of his own son Nari (for an unspeakable act of betrayal that led to the death of the young god Baldr). Loki's son Vali has been turned into a wolf. The goddess Skadi fastens a venomous snake over Loki's face, dripping venom, but Sigyn tends to him and empties the bowl at regular intervals. However, as it fills, she is forced to step away and empty it. During this interval venom drips on Loki and this causes him to writhe so violently that earthquakes make the entire earth tremble.

Sigyn's message is neither easy to comprehend nor comfortable to put into practice. Essentially, she is inviting us to become a human crucible for the transmutation of poisons in our world. The etymology of the word crucible tells us that it is a ceramic or metal container in which metals or other substances may be melted or subjected to very high temperatures.

Her greatest teaching is that every single one of us is a chalice, a crucible.

Her Handmaiden is Death, unfailingly in service to Transformation.

Engaging with this teaching required an exploration of what poison is: all living things produce substances to protect themselves from being eaten, so the term poison is generally only used for substances poisonous to humans. In contrast substances that are mainly poisonous to a common pathogen (disease agent) to an organism and humans are called antibiotics instead. Throughout human history intentional application of poison has been used as a method for murder, pest control, suicide and execution.

The Poison Mother explains how human beings seek pleasure and avoid pain. Keeping ourselves safe is one of our primary tasks as a human being. However, as our spiritual journey unfolds, and we discover hidden powers within ourselves, we may well be called to willingly stay in (or venture into) challenging situations to be the change agent, or kernel of healing, that is planted.

We can only be a crucible for transmutation when we face our ordeals and see them what they are: opportunities to evolve and grow, to move to higher levels of consciousness – by embracing adversity and transmuting it.

Sigyn asked me the following tricky questions:

- What is the poison in your life?
- Who holds the bowl?
- What happens when they are forced to step away to empty it?
- Do you hold the bowl for others?
- What happens when you are forced to step away and empty it?

I keep working this material myself, on different levels. I have also taken groups through this material, inviting people to work with her and build a personal relationship with her. The results have been nothing short of life changing.

For more please watch my art video about The Poison Mother.[9]

School Shooters

You don't have an ordinary kid who wakes up one day and becomes a mass murderer.

Peter Langman[10]

Dangerous people do exist!

Research shows that many school shooters classify as psychopaths, in that they are akin to serial killers – it is an incurable condition -but they kill on a larger scale at a younger age (and often kill themselves too so then we do not know what their adult selves might have become).

I hope to have a conversation with an FBI profiler or criminologist one day. Google profiles of young people who committed school shootings in the US show that all of them had extremely dysfunctional and abusive childhoods. No emotionally balanced teenager wakes up one morning and spontaneously decides to shoot fellow students and teachers that day. Such acts are many months in the planning (and many years in the making as an individual becomes more and more alienated from their community).

The mother instinct in me says: Imagine having a childhood where all you knew was abuse – not love. What kind of individual would you grow into? At the very least, a twisted, damaged and extremely angry person. I often wonder if school shooters are externalising their pain. If by shooting and traumatising others they are forcing the world to look in a mirror and perhaps see the "soul murder" that happened to them. – But even if I am right, is that the whole picture?!

> *Also what comes into play is the fact that even when school-related homicides are going down, when they do occur, it seems like they are occurring en masse. It is not just one kid shooting another kid or stabbing another kid. It is the large-scale rampage attacks that gets the media's attention.*
>
> *In terms of numbers, school shootings are such a rare phenomenon. Most of us will not see a school shooting in our lifetime. Someone once put together statistics on secondary school shootings, and you would have to be at that school for like 6,000 years before you would see a school shooting. That is how rare they are.*
>
> Peter Langman[10]

Peter Langman identifies three types of school shooters:

- *The traumatised shooter*
- *The psychopathic shooter*
- *The psychotic shooter*

He says that: "The traumatized shooters—they come from dysfunctional families, poverty, abuse in the home, a number of them were sexually abused outside the home, parents are poor, kids bounce around between mom to dad to grandma, sometimes they are in and out of foster care, there is no stability. And eventually, the rage and depression build.

The other two types come from essentially stable and intact families. One type is the psychopathic, someone who is narcissistic, doesn't care about other people, no empathy, no remorse, no respect for laws and regulations or authority, they are going to do what they feel like doing. They are often sadistic, so they get a thrill over having the power over life and death. "There is often peer encouragement of some kind. Sometimes the shooters have role models for violence. They look at Eric Harris and Dylan Klebold at Columbine High School as a role model or Charles Manson or Hitler. They get into various ideologies that would support violence as appropriate. There are a lot of things coming together." [10]

Some research shows that many school shooters become obsessed with the film Natural Born Killers. Disturbingly, famous school shooters become heroes or role model for another generation of school shooters. In my first book, Natural Born Shamans[11], I wrote a section titled "The Price of Instant Fame", about the role the media and all of us play in feeding this sinister phenomenon.

Dangerous People

FBI profiler Joe Navarro[12] published a book by the title Dangerous Personalities, based on two decades of studying victims and perpetrators. In this book he lists four types of dangerous personalities and he provides checklists (not to label people but help us in being alert to risk and danger).

The four dangerous personality types are:

- *The Narcissistic Personality*
- *The Emotionally Unstable Personality*
- *The Paranoid Personality*
- *The Predator*

For the details you will need to read the book but in an article in Psychology Today[12] Navarro (interviewed by Marty Nemko) gives some interesting pointers:

> *Their behaviour can be subtle, and it can take a long time before others become rightfully concerned.*
>
> *Pay close attention to actions that violate the boundaries of normal behaviour.*
>
> *Use others as a soundboard if you are not sure about your own perceptions.*

In a nutshell:

- Send a narcissist strong messages letting them know you will not tolerate being disrespected (and keep a log of events)
- Don't buy into the emotional dramas of emotionally unstable people. Set hard boundaries and disengage.
- Try to avoid paranoid people as reasoning with them leads absolutely nowhere.
- Don't ever let your guard down with predators, guard your safety, finances and loved ones

Perhaps his most important teaching is this: *no one has a social obligation to be victimized - ever.*[7]

Suicidal Terrorism

This is the only language which you understand... It is very painful to innocent people and very painful for anyone to lose a close relative or a friend, but it was necessary. This is what it takes to make you feel the pain which you are causing to other people.
Ramzi Yousef[13]

Yousef dreamed of causing half a million deaths and untold casualties.

In Chapter 7 we wondered where killers go in the Afterlife. This question applies especially to suicide bombers and suicidal terrorists: *Where do suicide-bombers go in the Afterlife, if they truly believe that they will be rewarded or immortalized for their acts?!*

The word kamikaze means *divine wind* or *spirit wind*. The Kamikaze were members of the Japanese Special Attack Unit of military aviators who performed suicide attacks against Allied naval vessels during World War II, destroying war ships. About 3,800 kamikaze pilots died during the war and more than 7.000 naval personnel were killed by those attacks.[14]

What motivates a suicide bomber? *Professor Arie W. Kruglanski*[15] *of the University of Maryland, College Park, examines recent analyses of the motivations for suicidal terrorism and suggests that factors identified as personal causes of suicidal terrorism, the various ideological reasons assumed to justify it, and the social pressures brought upon candidates for suicidal terrorism may be provide an integrative framework that explains diverse instances of suicidal terrorism as attempts at significance restoration, significance gain, and prevention of significance loss.*

What makes seemingly unexceptional human beings willing to take the lives of innocent people as well as their own lives? According to Kruglanski there is a compound of powerful motivations at work here:

- Absolutely all human beliefs have a motivational basis (You would not sacrifice your life for something you don't believe!)
- Many Muslim youths feel alienated and disempowered (by the dominant culture)
- Every human being needs meaning and significance in their lives. If that is lacking it makes people vulnerable to being recruited in service to fundamentalist (even terrorist) doctrines
- If you are not at all happy in this life, the promise of meeting Muhammed, being the presence of Allah and being a celebrated figure in the Afterlife becomes more attractive pretty fast
- Not only that but committing large scale acts of terrorism mean that your name makes it into world history and history books in the way that success in almost no other profession does
- Personal trauma and pain may swing the balance (for instance having lost loved ones to the conflict playing out. You may then feel you are "honouring your brother" by committing such acts etc.)
- Depriving people of their sense of belonging increases death ideation

Please note that Freud proposed that all human beings have both a life instinct and death drive and that those twin principles are active within all of us.

> *In many countries during times of war, suicide rates drop. In some countries when homicide rates are low, suicide rates rise, and vice versa. Interpretation of this data lends itself to the belief in an innate drive which compels balance in destructive forces (Comer, 2011).*
>
> William Berry[16]

Where do martyrs dying for a good cause go after death? Who makes the ultimate decision on what is a good cause?

Please note that here we have another example of a phenomenon appearing in a higher octave – lower octave expression:

Higher Octave
Martyr: a person who is killed for their religious or other spiritual beliefs and who heroically chooses death over changing their ways or belief system

Lower Octave
Scapegoat, victim of a witch hunt
Later in this book we will examine what the Buddhist concept of the *near enemy* means and how we can work with it. For now, I will just provide the near enemy for the Martyr/Scapegoat figure, as food for thought:

Near enemy
The Suicide Bomber as "martyr to" e.g. extremist Islamic doctrine: a person who kills many other people because of religious or spiritual or other beliefs is a terrorist believing that they are performing a heroic religious act in service to a good cause.

What I witness in shamanic work is that Suicide Bombers may initially arrive in an otherworld realm that appears to support their beliefs. There could even be spirits present taking the forms of Allah and Muhammed. However, as The Higher Loving Divine Power (I am trying to stay clear of culturally specific names, gender and titles here) would never truly support mass killings (it blatantly violates a key commandment in all and any religions!) things will evolve. I observe how over time, (here I mean: as their souls continue to evolve, because time does not exist in the same way in other realms), Divine and angelic beings will come forward and work with them individually to make them see the error of their ways. They will be shown the consequences of their actions and the suffering of the people affected.

Two things can then happen: they embrace the pathway of karmic consequences and start crafting an existence of making amends (either in the other world or reincarnated on Earth) or they remain entrenched in their chosen doctrine and join the criminal masterminds (mentioned earlier) in shady territories acting as hang-outs, where they will continue to influence the minds of the living in malevolent ways (obviously this does not free them from the wheel of karmic consequences and therefore karma continues to pile up).

While on this subject, please note that forces in service to the greater good can *also* choose to work through the living from other realms. Involvement in this can be part of a soul's pathway or trajectory in clearing karmic debt.

What is normal anyway?

The next question to ask is: What is normal? When I visit my family as an almost-foreigner following an incomprehensible spiritual path, they could be forgiven for thinking that I am "abnormal". This is literally true: as Dutch citizens go I hardly represent the norm for anything Dutch.

Psychology is the study of people. Within psychology there is a division that studies people who are "abnormal" or "atypical" in comparison with other members of the same society. The concept of abnormality is hard to define. The three categories psychologists use to define this[16] are:

- Statistical infrequency (a comparison with others expressed in numbers but being left-handed or having red hair does not make you abnormal!)
- Violations of social norms (please note that most societies

have both laws and many unwritten rules and those can change over time -for example the phenomenon of political correctness, has changed our social climate and norms for public conduct in just one generation)

- Deviation from Ideal Mental Health

What causes Psychopathology?

Research indicates that there are many layers to this process and all those layers have an impact on other layers.

Many mental disorders are caused by a lack of security in the early years. Children who do not receive enough attention will develop challenging behaviours and act out to get this attention. This process often misfires and produces the opposite result: punishment, abuse or abandonment. This dynamic will cause what psychologists call *attachment disorder,* which sets people up for a lifetime of serious issues.

Psychopathy is a spectrum disorder. Brain anatomy, genetics and a person's environment can all be a contributing factor in the development of psychopathic traits.

The terms "psychopath" and "sociopath" are often used interchangeably, but in correct parlance a "sociopath" refers to a person with antisocial tendencies that are ascribed to social or environmental factors, whereas psychopathic traits are more innate, though a chaotic or violent upbringing may tip the scales for those already predisposed to behave psychopathically. Both constructs are most closely represented in the Diagnostic and Statistical Manual of Mental Disorders (DSM) as Antisocial Personality Disorder.[17]

The stark and unsettling truth is that no one really knows if serial killers are born or made. The most likely answer is this: *the majority of the most prolific and dangerous serial killers were genetically disposed to behave anti-socially and furthermore grew up in an environment* that cultivated a disregard for the lives of others.[18]

According to the FBI, for a killer to be a serial killer he or she must commit at least three murders over a time period of at least three years at three different locations with an emotional cooling off period in between.

Many brutal serial killers have antisocial personality disorders, not infrequently in combination with other disorders such as inflated ego or narcissism. Antisocial Personality Disorder is the clinical term for what we call psychopathy or sociopathy in everyday life.

Characteristics of Antisocial personality disorders:

- A disregard for morals, social norms, and the rights and feelings of others.
- Exploitation of others in harmful ways for their own gain or pleasure (sadistic tendencies).
- Manipulation or deceit of others using superficial charm, feigning innocence or disability, or pretending to be working for an admirable cause.
- A lack of empathy for others and a lack of guilt or remorse about harming others.
- Explicit or hidden hostility, irritability, agitation, aggression or violence.
- A lack of fear of dangerous situations and behaviours that often leads to unnecessary risk-taking.
- A failure to learn from the consequences of their good or bad actions.
- A history of unstable relationships (including romantic relationships, friendships and relationship with parents).
- A failure to fulfil work and financial obligations.
- Recurrent fall outs with authority figures, including law enforcement, and sometimes sanctions, arrest and conviction.

Most people with anti-social personality disorder do not become serial killers (or even criminals). Many lead miserable lives as human beings without committing crimes. Others actively thrive in leadership positions and jobs that give them control over other people's lives. (This provides a part-explanation for some of dynamics we observe in contemporary society. Just look at politicians and CEO of large companies!)

Contributing factors that have been investigated are extremely high levels of testosterone and abnormal levels of the brain chemical dopamine (responsible for pleasure and motivation). Essentially a very low level of this means that an excess of stimulation and excitement is needed to feel stimulation or motivation. (Serial killers sometimes describe killing as the ultimate thrill). They also take extreme pleasure in having total control over another human being. In addition they (often) derive great satisfaction from media attention and being a source of public fear. Over time they become desensitized and always need greater thrills and risks to gain the same satisfaction.

Author Maria Kvilhaug[19] describes how it is believed that for Old Norse people there was a blood mystery in killing an animal because it allowed a person to then follow (even ride) this animal into the underworld. A similar thing is said about hangings and human sacrifice: that possibly sitting out under the corpse of a hanged man allowed a person to follow their soul into other worlds. Those were initiation techniques.

I sometimes wonder if the gory killings we witness (as well as the insatiable appetite for horror movies) are not an expression of a lost blood mystery. In Viking times villages stank because of the butchering that went on as a routine act at the heart of community life, for everyone to see. Today our lives have become so sanitized that the need for initiation into blood mysteries goes unmet.

Any primary human need, which is deeply wired into the human psyche, will seek expression in other ways. Horror movies are preferable to gang killings (where gang members are expected to "take out a person" to gain their place in the gang hierarchy).

Are serial killers born or made?

Psychologist and author Glenn Geher suggests that psychopaths have proliferated since human beings stopped living in the small and close-knit communities of their ancestors, where nothing went unobserved and communities cracked down on bad behaviour. Ostracism had grave consequences in such a setting! Today many of us live in mega-cities, with populations numbering millions. That is what he calls an *evolutionary mismatch*. This provides exactly the anonymity and social control that serial killers (and sociopaths) thrive on.[20]

Just for the record: it is estimated that 1% of the general population are psychopaths and 6% have narcissistic personality disorder, meaning we all encounter them and know some!

Psychopaths and Psychopomps

On my YouTube channel[21] you will find a video by this title. It is about young people exploring death and "being recycled" in spiritual, fearless and often funny ways.

What is the spiritual cause of psychopathic disorders? What is the underlying spiritual dynamic? Is there anything we can learn from this?

One of my greatest regrets is that human beings are averse to really looking in the mirrors that history serves up. (This phenomenon could be called a form of *collective psychopathy* in its own right!) World War II showed us that Nazi death camp commanders were devoted to their own families but felt no compunction about killing other people's children. This appears to demonstrate that extreme circumstances and false doctrines can push more of us in the direction of complete empathy failure and the psychopathic spectrum than we like to think.

We live in an era of political correctness. We like to think of ourselves of upstanding citizens who take pride in our rational thinking and compassionate views. Yet the media and politics serve up many reminders that this viewpoint does not stand up to scrutiny. One example is how Muslims have been demonised since the horrific events of 9/11.This is scapegoating: we perceive ourselves as "good" (the group following the right principles etc.) and another group as "bad" (despicable, sub-human). It is undeniable that some terrorists committed dreadful crimes. It is equally undeniable that most Muslims lead non-violent lives of high integrity and community spirit – as people of all faiths and denominations actively set out to do. It is also extremely obvious that some white western people commit heinous crimes while many others lead exemplary lives.

Wetiko

It is always very difficult to live in this life so as not to be a damaged person or one who damages others
Jack D. Forbes[22]

The demon we really need to wrestle with (as Jacob did in the Bible) is not the serial killer or mass murderer (those are best left to law enforcement and the FBI) but the toxic belief that there are "two kinds of people": good people and bad people, superior races and inferior races, people like me and people different from me: "Us and Them". That way of thinking has caused some of the greatest atrocities in human history. Unless we police our own consciousness and activate our Inner FBI (as it were) all of us carry within us the seeds of such things occurring again.

> "We have all heard people describe other people in a derogatory way, as being 'full of imagination.' The fact is that if you are not full of imagination, you are not very sane."
> *Buckminster Fuller*[23]

American Indian thinker Jack D. Forbes wrote a ground-breaking book titled Columbus and Other Cannibals[22]. This book ought to be on university reading lists for many disciplines – it is on my reading list for students of shamanism.

Forbes calls this, the disease, (expressing itself as imperialism, colonialism, torture, rape, slavery, terrorism, brutal violence, greed etc.) *cannibalism* or *Wetiko cannibal psychosis.*

The word Wetiko comes from the (Native American) Algonquian language. Another author, Paul Levy, wrote a related book titled Dispelling Wetiko[24]. In this book he examines the psychic epidemic, collective psychosis or cancer of the human soul called Wetiko and it is highly contagious. This "virus" operates through blind spots in the human psyche, rendering people oblivious to their own madness.[25] Levy says that 'Those afflicted with Wetiko consume, like a cannibal, the life force of others – human and non-human – for private purpose or profit, and do so without giving back something from their own lives. Wetiko acts as both a filter through which and mirror in which we see ourselves.'

One clear example of Wetiko is the destruction of the Amazon rainforest. Another obvious example is provided by the manifold manifestations of consumerism-gone-mad. Levy's message (paraphrased by me) is that Wetiko "makes predators of all of us". Because we use reasoning, self-justifications, products and services sourced following this principle, we are all implicated in this collective dynamic, of making others pay the price for our excess and cultural megalomania.

Carl Jung[26] worded it this way: *We are always, thanks to our human nature, potential criminals. In reality, we merely lacked a suitable opportunity to be drawn into the infernal melee. None of us stands outside humanity's black collective shadow.*

Whether the crime lies many generations back or happens today, it remains the symptom of a disposition that is always and everywhere present – and one would therefore do well to possess some "imagination in evil," for only the fool can permanently neglect the conditions of his own nature. In fact, this negligence is the best means of making him an instrument of evil.

Wetiko has its origin in the image-making psyche. We can use our imagination to create a utopia or we can use it to fool ourselves and hide from ourselves. Because of our ability to tell (and sell) ourselves stories, we can find justifications or supporting evidence for almost anything. One of the problems is that most people get through a whole human life without serious self-reflection, without delving too deeply into their own psyche.

> *Your mind is like an unsafe neighbourhood; don't go there alone.*
> Augusten Burroughs[27]

We need to put alchemy on the school curriculum again. We need to teach our young people how to wrestle with these internal demonic forces in order to obtain the treasures: soul-full-ness and creative lucidity. Might this be the teaching of the Genesis narrative where Jacob wrestles with the angel? On his way back to Canaan he spends one night alone by a river. Here he encounters a man who wrestles with him until daybreak. The story ends well: Jacob is given the name "Israel" while the "man" refuses to give his own name. Jacob then names the place where they wrestled Penuel: "Face of God" or "Facing God"[28]

Was this demon-angel perhaps Jacob himself, a part of him demanding to be acknowledged and embraced? Was it the divinity of Jacob, "God in Jacob"? Does the God in Jacob (the God in us) arrive accompanied by a demon because we have free will in what we choose?!

For alchemists, the imagination is the divine body in every person, a refined, rarefied "subtle body" that is not humanly constructed but divinely implanted in us from a source beyond ourselves. Through the alchemical art of the imagination, the soul is empowered to become an instrument for the divine imagination in such a way that it can literally change the world.

The following question is asked by Levy[24]: "Is Wetiko simply evil, or is it a disguised form of the divine that is literally helping us awaken?" Is it a virus, vampire, parasite, cannibal, disease or is it a teacher? Is it perhaps all of those things and more? – This goes right back to the concept of the god-in-us, the demon-in-us.

For diseases of the imagination – the cure is also found in the imagination

The Ojibwa word Wetiko or Windigo, may be related to the word meaning excess. The human propensity for excess is where wetiko gets to us. In Levy's words: "Evil preys and thrives upon excess". It feeds itself through creating cravings for more-more-more (never enough) and me-me-me, Greed and Narcissism. *The notion that it is somehow OK for others to pay any price for me having those things.* One very everyday example of this is buying our own children clothes from shops known to sell items produced using child labour in India. We see the price tag, not the true cost of the item.

Spiritual paths and "Spirituopaths"

The world of "spirituality" (be it shamanism, Buddhism, Wicca, yoga, Druidry, heathenism etc.) certainly has its fair share of narcissists, sociopaths (and yes *near enemies).* One of the mistakes that "beginners" (people who take their first baby steps exploring a specific path) make is that they often cherish the illusion that "spiritual people are safe people to be with". This is simply, sadly, madly and badly not the case!

On one course in shamanism I myself attended I ended up with two individuals displaying prolonged bouts of stalker-ish behaviour. (One male sending me daily text messages along the lines of "I was just flying past your window and saw you getting undressed") and the other was once spotted sitting in his car, with the engine humming, in front of my house at 2 a.m.

The "beauty" of this is that it serves up a mirror and unflinching reminder: the boundary between spirituality and psychopathy can be razor-thin. This is what makes spiritual practitioners who do not engage in any form of shadow work and supervision so incredibly dangerous.

Wim van den Dungen[29] writes: *In the case of a psychopath who is not spiritually insane (and so lacks religious mania), the possibility exists that he or she uses and abuses spirituality in a psychopathic way, and thus without having experienced anything resembling the Self or higher states of consciousness. Such psychopaths are bogus spiritualists. They may confuse altered states with higher states, or they may feel they have a "special" spiritual mission, but because they actually lack a direct experience of the Divine, their spiritual stance is nothing more than a fraudulent disguise enabling them to better manipulate gullible others. They use the trappings of religion & spirituality to further their narcissistic cause. This comes in functional, dysfunctional, neurotic or psychotic formats.*

Shamanic practitioners actively work with the souls of other people and even their families (performing for instance soul retrieval and ancestral healing work). Any shamanic practitioner who does this work without brutal self-appraisal essentially becomes a "spirituopath", a word I coined impulsively to refer to "dangerous practitioners of spiritual techniques". Yet I would say that failure to do shadow work is extremely common. On the practitioner training in shamanism I myself attended this practice was not even taught. *This means that people are expected to do something most feel serious resistance to without ever being taught how to do it properly*! (If ever there was a recipe for disaster!) This is just one "psychopathic dimension" of western shamanic practice today (there are others).

It is a well-known fact that absolutely all schools of spiritual thought produce their own version of "inverted practitioners": false gurus, priests who sexually molest children, charismatic figures founding cults, narcissistic shamanic teachers, fake bodhisattvas, fundamentalists –turned-terrorists and so forth. One only needs to follow the news to see many manifestations of narcissism masquerading as compassion and enlightenment.

What makes this situation even more complex is that no practitioner is an enlightened being. All practitioners occupy many places on various spectrums (in terms of compassion, in terms of talent, in terms of self-involvement, in terms of being financially motivated or being dangerously otherworldly and impractical, in terms of level of experience etc.) That is what makes human interactions such a minefield. Even when we pay for someone's professional time, we may receive a service that greatly varies in quality from one practitioner to the next (or even from one day to the next!)

Gas lighting refers to manipulating someone by psychological means into doubting their own sanity (and often making them appear crazy in the eyes of others). It is a surprisingly common technique used by abusers, cult leaders, dictators and indeed high school students! The phrase comes from the 1944 movie Gaslight, where a man uses manipulation to make his wife think that she is losing her mind.[30]

Pardon My Sanity in A World Insane
Emily Dickinson[31]

It was while volunteering at a suicide hotline in Seattle that Bundy took his duties intensely seriously. As co-volunteer Ann Rule later wrote in her book The Stranger Beside Me: *"Ted Bundy took lives, he also saved lives."*[32]

People who commit serial crimes, especially serial rape and murder, often do it because they're trying to feel something. A 1997 study that looked at the behaviour patterns of twins raised in separate households found that both sensation-seeking behaviour and impulsivity were not matters of nurture, but of nature. In other words, it's a quality that many serial killers are born with. Author Becki Robins[33] says that people who are engaged in selfish pursuits are almost always trying to fill an emotional void. Psychologist Marcia Sirota says such people may not have received much love and affection as children, or that they observed others engaged in selfish pursuits and are trying to emulate that behaviour as adults. Serial killers in particular are often described as emotionally vacant and incapable of forming meaningful personal relationships.Serial killers have this quality in common with drug addicts — people who abuse drugs are looking for some sort of emotional experience that can replace the emotional experiences they don't have access to, usually relationships with other human beings. Having healthy relationships with others is a crucial component of psychological health — it's what makes us human.

Even billionaires have something in common with drug addicts seeking their next fix and vacant serial killers seeking their next thrill: their relentless pursuit for money is ultimately an expression of filling an emotional void, the place where love, human affection and friendship ought to live within us. Wetiko leaves tracks we can follow.

> *Big deal. Death always comes with the territory. See you in Disneyland.*
> Richard Ramirez[34]

When healers do harm: Implanting False Memories

We will now look at some other areas where something dark took over and healers or therapists did actual harm to vulnerable minds. One such therapeutic technique was called "retrieving repressed memories" but it has been discredited and today we call this *implanting false memories.*[35]

Therapists and clinicians used techniques such as hypnotic regression or forms of guided visualisation where vulnerable people were actively encouraged to imagine events (that never happened) or to look for different personalities living within their own psyche (that did not exist before the suggestion was made). This was commonly done, for instance with teenage girls with eating disorders, or people receiving psychiatric care after a mental breakdown.[36]

Over time, especially in people with a lively imagination (remember "the fantasy prone person"?) the memory of an imagined event is misinterpreted or stored as the memory of a real event (which happened, and other people could certify that). Hypnotic regression is a particularly powerful technique for such (unintentional perhaps but powerful) "programming".

A word that comes to mind is *brainwashing:* to pressurize (someone) into adopting radically different beliefs by using systematic and often forcible means.

Implanting false memories in someone (especially memories of abuse that never took place) is an abhorrent crime. It has devastating consequences, not only for the victims but also their families, who often become the targets of such allegations. It is hard to see any positive aspect to such scandalous techniques, other than the fact that such tragic cases have brought the issue to collective awareness. We need to acknowledge here that family breakdowns and miscarriages of justice have occurred because of this. The *Wetiko* of that still entangles (and emotionally strangles) many people today. This cannibal devours families and causes mental illness in high functioning individuals (such as loving parents who never did any of things they stand accused of and this fact was corroborated by many other adults close to the situation).

Psychiatrists and psychotherapists have since demonstrated by now that victims of childhood (sexual) abuse *have difficulties forgetting – not remembering!*

Alien Abduction

While discussing extreme phenomena: psychologists now say that accounts of alien abductions also come under the heading of false memories. The same thing goes for large numbers of people claiming that they were Cleopatra or Napoleon in a previous incarnation.

As a shamanic practitioner I sit on the fence when it comes to alien abductions. I know people personally who believe in aliens and are actively trying to connect with them using mind techniques. I feel no temptation to join them, but I would not rule out that Earth has been/is being/will be visited by aliens. Going on my own limited experiences of this I believe that they will not bring their bodies if they do so, they may well arrive in astral (energetic) form instead.

Reincarnations of famous people

Every once in a while I meet people who tell me that they are Napoleon or Cleopatra reincarnated in the twenty-first century! For obvious reasons I operate a healthy dose of scepticism around such statements.

I will add that I have personally performed healing sessions with people where the key to a life-long block was found in another time and another life. Some would then say that issue was of an ancestral nature in origin: meaning someone who lived earlier left the issue in the family field and another person picked up "the ball". This is possible. Other people would say that powerful memories (both good and bad) live on as vibrations and frequencies and that sensitive people have a talent for receiving those signals. Here we can think of Rupert Sheldrake's morphogenetic field.

From a healer's point of view, it is less important to figure out "what is empirically true and what is not". *It comes to attention*

- therefore it seeks acknowledgement, healing or balancing.

For many people, it is all too easy to believe, even in the absence of convincing evidence, that memories of childhood sexual abuse may be repressed and then recovered during psychotherapy. This is partly because sadly it is true that such abuse is a lot more common than was once accepted.

The psychoanalytic notion of repression is that when something extremely traumatic happens, an automatic involuntary defence mechanism kicks in that pushes the memory for the trauma into an inaccessible part of the mind. But this is simply *not supported* by the empirical evidence we have today.

Satanic Ritual Abuse (SRA)

Satanic ritual abuse was the subject of a moral panic that originated in the United States in the 1980s and then spread throughout many other locations.

David Finkelhor[36] divides SRA into three categories:

- Cult-based ritualism in which the abuse had a spiritual or social goal for the perpetrators
- Pseudo-ritualism in which the goal was sexual gratification and the rituals were used to frighten or intimidate victims, and
- Psychopathological ritualism in which the rituals were due to mental disorders
- Subsequent investigators have expanded on these definitions and also pointed to a fourth alleged type of Satanic ritual abuse, in which petty crimes with ambiguous meaning (such as graffiti or vandalism) generally committed by teenagers, were attributed to the actions of Satanic cults.

Ed Cara[37] writes: *Many law enforcements agencies and teams conducted investigations (sometimes even excavations!) looking for evidence of satanic cults engage in unspeakable acts (murder, torture, cannibalism, the killing and eating of babies etc.) FBI special agent Ken Lanning, then a member of the bureau's behavioural science unit, examined hundreds of satanic ritual abuse claims and found no compelling evidence that such cults existed. He wrote in a 1992 report: "Now it is up to the mental health professionals ... to explain why victims are alleging things that don't seem to have happened."*

The way out of the labyrinth

The human psyche is sometimes compared to a labyrinth. A Minotaur appears to lurk at the heart of that labyrinth. Ed Cara[37] says that the only definitive way to tell false memories from real ones is by reference to independent external evidence. Subjectively, false memories can be every bit as detailed and compelling as real memories. The best that can be hoped for is that, by appealing to external evidence, one can convince the victim that their memories do not reflect reality thus converting them into what psychologists refer to as "non-believed memories".

Allegations of childhood abuse should always be listened to and examined carefully. But we must treat stories based on "recovered memories" with the level of scepticism they deserve.

Psychology expert and memory expert Elizabeth Loftus[38] researches how memory is malleable to suggestion and social influence. In 1994 she published a book, The Myth of Repressed Memories: False Memories and Allegations of Sexual Abuse, challenging the fundamental tenets of recovered memory therapy: 'People don't recall the past but reconstruct it, moulding it to the demands and beliefs of the present moment. Therapists' assumptions that their clients held hidden memories of abuse, she asserted, could be a key factor in creating those very "memories.'

Other researchers found that people who have survived atrocities such the Holocaust, genocide or natural disasters do not have the ability to seal away their traumatic memories and experiences (By this I mean: keeping the memories locked away completely and then recalling them with clarity, at some later time). People do not have that choice. Human beings do have other choices, in any situation, as described by concentration camp inmate turned ground-breaking psychotherapist Viktor Frankl, in his 1946 book Man's Search for Meaning[27].

Speaking as a shamanic practitioner, people can suffer serious soul loss in harrowing situations and that can make them feel disconnected from their own selves, as if "they are not all here". However, they will have flashbacks and often even talk about their terrible experiences in a flat tone of voice, as if it happened to another person or in a film. A therapist will still notice that the emotional tone of those memories continues to colour their whole lives. You observe this in the moment these survivors walk through the door: they shuffle, they hunch over as if they carry the suffering of the world on their shoulders, often then whisper (for fear of being heard and abused again) and so forth.

One quote used in Twelve Step recovery programs is: *"It is better to know and remember than to know and not to remember".* People *know.* Human bodies store memories in their own unique way.

Multiple Personality Disorder (MPD)

Christopher Barry-Dee[39] writes books about his interviews with serial killers. His book titled "Talking With Serial Killers"[40] describes how the search for multiple personalities has now become part of interview techniques for serial killers. We have already established that some serial killers are extremely clever and calculating. If they think that evidence of MPD is going to get them off Death Row, they will work hard on manifesting evidence of this. They will have fun with the challenge too.

Dee is an independent investigative criminologist and he conducts interviews with notorious serial killers. This book is poorly edited and typeset but Dee does a good job mapping (and infiltrating) the mind set of sociopaths and psychopaths.

In his descriptions of events and interviews in high security prisons we see serial killers actively cooking up sub personalities in the attempt to then blame them for the ghastly deeds. ("It was not me; it was Robbie!")

Ed Cara[37]: *In 1992, Harold Merskey, a professor of psychiatry from the University of Western Ontario, published a paper in the British Journal of Psychiatry in which he examined all cases of multiple personality disorder-like symptoms in the historical record—and couldn't find one that wasn't contaminated by suggestions from clinicians or other forms of social encouragement. "It is likely that MPD never occurs as a spontaneous persistent natural event in adults," he concluded. "Suggestion, social encouragement, preparation by expectation, and the reward of attention can produce and sustain a second personality. Enthusiasm for the phenomenon is a means of increasing it.*

Research shows that serial killers sometimes (not always!) are better-than-average looking people who exude a certain charisma or charm. Superficial charm can lull just about anyone into a false sense of security, so it's important to be on the lookout for it. Monsters do not look like (our mental picture or children's book representation of) monsters!

One of the FBI's favourite techniques for interviewing serial killers is flattery. Psychopathic killers tend to have a grandiose sense of their own self-worth, so investigators can use praise to get them talking. In an FBI document about serial murder, behavioural analysts said psychopathic serial killers don't respond to "altruistic interview themes," in other words, trying to make them experience feelings of guilt or sympathy for their victims is a waste of time. Instead, interviewers might praise them for their intelligence or for their skill at outwitting investigators.

> *Forensic psychologist Stephen A. Diamond calls this quality psychopathic narcissism, and likens it to an "immature, selfish, self-centred, resentful, and raging child inside a powerful adult body." Children are inherently narcissistic and must be taught the rules of social behavior, but when children grow up physically but remain in a state of immaturity, they can become extremely dangerous people.*
>
> Becki Robins[33]

Activity #10: Meet the Inner Minotaur!

Go to a place where you can be undisturbed for a while. Bring a notepad and pen. Light a candle.

Take a moment to meditate on the biblical story of Jacob wrestling with the demon. Does this resonate in any way at all? Do you have any sense of "wrestling your own demons" at times?

Perhaps every human mind is like a labyrinth?! At the heart of that labyrinth we find our own personal Minotaur. A hybrid: half human and half-other. On him or her we project our shadow: all the aspects of ourselves we don't like (and/or that we have discovered that other people do not like!)

To be loved, accepted and occupy a secure place in our families and communities we often disown (push away, deny) a big piece of ourselves. The Inner Minotaur represents that piece, the missing piece of the puzzle.

Close your eyes and express the wish to meet this Minotaur. Release all self-judgment and expectations as you start walking this labyrinth (your own mind!) Who is waiting for you at the centre? Meet this special being with an open heart. When you lock eyes with him or her– approach slowly… Some people may be able to embrace him/her on the first visit. Others may need to make repeat visits and get a little closer every time.

Now ask: what does he/she want to communicate? The answer may not come in words, but feelings/ images/a smell/ an intuition... Express gratitude for whatever you receive. You may wish to speak other words from the heart: I accept you; I love you just the way you are.... (or whatever comes).

I am willing to meet you here in this sacred space! I hear you! I see you! I accept you! There is no need for you to appear in external form or in the form of nightmares any longer. Let's have a direct dialogue from now on....

Return by walking out of the labyrinth that is your own mind. Make notes or a sketch. Commit to repeating the exercise if there is more to be learned or unlocked.

Chapter 11

Shadow Seeks Expression

One does not become enlightened by imagining figures of light, but by making the darkness conscious.
C. G. Jung[1]

Black light

I am writing this chapter the week that The Golden State Killer (who terrorized California but eluded law enforcement for decades) was finally identified and arrested (April 2018).

Like many people (I guess) I committed to a spiritual path thinking that it was going to be the Path of Love and Light, as in "the ultimate nature of everything is light" and "love heals all". As my journey unfolded, I soon discovered that true treasure is found in darkness and that there are many different types of darkness. I am a "Darkness Worker" at heart: I find my greatest inspiration and allies in the deepest Darkness of the Scandinavian Winter, in the Land of the Dead, in the Great Below where Sumerian goddess Inanna makes her descent, in the less well-trodden realms of the human psyche where luminous treasure awaits. In my second book, Sacred Art: A Hollow Bone for Spirit[2], I make a distinction between darkness (lower case, as in low vibration energies and actions) and Darkness (capitalised) as in sacred darkness, the womb of Mother God, the fertile earth that incubates a seed.

Please remember that Darkness cradles the seed of light and Divine Child, and that light has a twin in black light:

... we enter into the light of angels; we enter into another kind of Darkness called by the mystics the "Night of light," the "luminous Blackness" or the "black light." This other-worldly light is the light

> *of the soul, the light of consciousness rising over the Darkness of the subconscious in which the divine Cloud of Unknowing gives birth to an interior burst of initiatic light – the light of the "Midnight Sun."*
>
> Henry Corbin[3]

Over the years I made the transition from being a student to becoming a teacher and I learned very soon (and this rattles my soul!) that taking groups of people through spiritual material and teachings flushes out the personal and collective shadows in a way almost nothing else (politics and religion excepted) does. This is a painful truth. As the teacher one becomes the focal point for all projections and many unresolved issues that students carry – so while teaching about higher perspectives and the continuation of consciousness after death, in reality one finds oneself in the underworld (and the doghouse) a lot of the time.

As I gained spiritual maturity (and confidence) I deliberately started taking groups of people to the underworld (in the most literal way I knew how) because that is the realm where profound mystery teachings are found.

Trading healing skills for writing crime stories

If I have one confession to make it is that at one time, I developed an appetite for quality crime and forensic procedure novels. I devoured books by Patricia Cornwell about the fictional character Kay Scarpetta[4]. On the shamanic practitioner training I attended there was one man who soon dropped out of the program and decided to focus on writing crime stories and novels instead. In our circle this created quite a stir: how could anyone trade learning healing skills for writing crime stories?! Isn't that the proverbial upside down world?! -Not just that, a close friend on the same program once visited my house, eyeballed the collection of Cornwell books on my shelf and said: "Imelda, those books need to leave the house! ASAP! Give them to a charity shop or something... These books are way too low in vibration for a shamanic practitioner and healer to have on her shelf!" I followed her advice!

The fact is that the aspiring-practitioner-turned-crime-writer had been a policeman. Through his profession he had explored the underbelly of human existence (and he knew what he was writing about). Today I understand his urge to write about crime – as opposed to focussing on healing others. I no longer agree with my friend's take. I have learned that the very opposite is true: Shadow will out!! Shadow will always seek expression!! This is a fact outside human control. However, *human beings have a lot of choice in how/when and where shadow is given expression.*

For me two of the most mind-boggling but also life-changing principles my own first teacher of shamanism (Simon Buxton[5]) imparted were:

1. As teachers of shamanism we have the sacred duty to create safely held experiences of initiation for our students
2. The spirits make no distinction between what is "real" and what is "not real", meaning that a symbolic enactment of something means that "it happened", from their point of view.

These key teachings have changed my life and shaped my own approach to shamanic teaching.

Different kinds of darkness

Before we wade deeper into the luminosity and enlightenment found in deepest darkness, we need to make one important distinction. For the purposes of this book I will, once again, refer to darkness (not capitalized, as referring to intentional harmful acts) and Darkness (the power of hidden teachings, shadow work, ancient mystery and underworld journeys of initiation).

As a teacher of Seidr, working within the Northern European

Tradition and teaching the indigenous ancestral pathways of Northern Europe, I know that the heathen tribes of Old Northern Europe did not make a distinction between good and evil the way we do. The concept "evil" did not exist until Christianity became the dominant religion of Europe. This is not to say that people did not make any distinction between good and bad outcomes or good and bad choices and actions (we have every reason to believe that they did) but they did not believe in a personification of evil (as in Satan or The Devil) as we know this from a later period. Instead they operated a code of honour: warriors were expected to make honourable decisions and fierce women (going on the sagas) prioritized their tribe and kin over personal gain or fulfilment. They aligned themselves with ancestors, gods and powerful spirits in order to do this.

It was only in the thirteenth century that Christians made attempts to identify trickster god Loki with Satan. "Hell" (as an otherworld realm of punishment and eternal suffering) was named directly for Hel – the realm of the Norse death goddess Hel. Yet her great hall for the dead was nothing like Christian "Hell". When teaching classes in Norse shamanism this always requires exhaustive explanation.

The notion of "finding ourselves" is a very contemporary concept indeed! In the medieval period people were concerned with finding their place in a larger Divine Plan instead. The climate of Scandinavia and Northern Europe was harsh. A bad harvest could (and would) bring starvation and kill people. Bad decisions could kill in this unforgiving climate and or not offering hospitality could kill strangers, as homesteads were few and far between, in remote areas.

The dualistic concept of Good and Evil as opposing forces with personifications ("an omnipotent good male god and an evil male devil") only arrived on the scene with the Christianization of Europe. Until then people were polytheistic (possibly pantheistic) and their gods and goddesses provided a more holistic role model for human beings in that they were perceived as having both a bright and dark manifestation. (Freyja is said to be a "love goddess" but she is also the leader of the Valkyries and the Chooser of the Slain, as well as a powerful vǫlva or Norse witch, and that is where her true power and greatest teachings lie).

When a new religion takes over, the old religion and old gods are (often) demonized and various things commonly happen:

- The old gods become the "new demons"
- New interpretations or characterizations are forced on older phenomena (In Old Europe churches were built on the sites of pagan temples, older mother goddesses became identified by Mother Mary, plants with indigenous names acquired Christian names, pagan festivals were rebranded as feast days in the year of the church calendar and so forth)
- Cultures that truly celebrate polytheism sometimes add the "new god" to the "old pantheon" without much ado

One of the most disastrous effects of the advent of Christianity is that the male church fathers (never Jesus Christ himself - important distinction!) demonized wise women and men. Their herbalism and healing skills were branded as witchcraft and black magic and this resulted in the witch trials of the 16th-18th centuries. Until today we Europeans collectively hold a deep ancestral fear in our collective consciousness (and possibly even DNA – this is called genetic memory[6]) of all things esoteric/magical/supernatural and we carry a deep fear of "burning at the stake for our beliefs". In healing work this issue comes to attention in the ancestral field of incredibly many people of European descent.

The phenomenon of witch hunts existed long before the notorious European era of the witch trials and it has flared up in world history in different locations. I highly recommend the book The Witches' Ointment by Thomas Hatsis, researching and mapping this.[7]

Women have traditionally been wise in the "ways of Darkness": they assisted at both birth and death, they had a medicine chest of herbs and folklore remedies in the days where the medical profession (as we know it today) did not exist or most people could not afford (or even reach) the services of earlier practitioners of medical care.

Personal Darkness

Our word esoteric comes from the Ancient Greek word esōterikós ("belonging to an inner circle") and this referred to the secret or hidden teachings of Greek philosophers as opposed to their public or exoteric material. The word *apocalypse* literally means *uncovering*.

In western society the Christian paradigm still goes strong (meaning that it is wired deeply into our perceptions and cultural assumptions even when we do not consider ourselves practicing Christians).This means that the word "darkness" tends to cause alarm and anxiety because people will assume that it refers to black magic or other forms of intentional harm.

We all come from darkness: we gestate in the darkness of our mother's watery womb for nine months. Seeds need to be planted in the darkness of the fertile earth in order to sprout and see daylight. We often need to keep something to ourselves and reflect on it deeply before we can share it with others. There are many forms of profound life-giving and wisdom-inspiring Darkness.

The human shadow

We live in a culture that encourages us to hide our personal shadow from view. By shadow I mean those aspects of us that others do not like and do not wish to engage with. From a very young age we receive powerful messages from our parents and carers about what is OK and what is not OK. (Have you ever parented a two-year-old? Or even looked after one, for just a few hours?!) We learn to shut parts of ourselves away. We do this so successfully that our conscious mind no longer remembers that these parts exist. What then happens is that these parts start making noises, acting out and generally causing havoc in our lives -because they will not be denied and disowned. They continue to exist.

I already mentioned my collection of crime novels. Another aspect of me that many people around me do not comprehend (and often take personally) is my great need for solitude. My social skills are fine (I had to really work on that as a teenage misfit!) so people habitually mis-read me as a sociable person. I receive many kind invitations to meet up and hang out. This can stir a dark resentment in me because I need a lot of space. I can and do spend time with close friends and colleagues and I will always have time for my family. However, I have no appetite for small talk, gossip or mindless conversation. When my time alone get compromised for long periods, (as it inevitably does in the modern life of a working mother), this yearning and need for time alone turns into a loud growl. This is the bear in me -the part of me that needs to withdraw and hibernate![8]

When that need goes ignored for too long, I become positively antisocial. I will go to any lengths to create time alone. To me this is a positive choice in terms of my own needs and lifestyle. Most of my books, paintings and art videos would not exist if I did not retreat from the world. It is not a reflection on other people or my love for people. It is not intended as a "rejection" either. It has taken me decades to see that I do not owe it to other people to pretend to be something I am not (a party animal, dinner-party-hostess or lover of loud live music).

The Not So Strange Case of Dr Jekyll and Mr Hyde

Linking back to the "Inner Minotaur" meditation in Chapter 10, please take a moment to reflect on the following questions:

- *What is your shadow?*
- *Which "characters" lurk deep inside you, thus seeking expression against the desires of those around you, or against the norms of mainstream culture?!*

The Strange Case of Dr Jekyll and Mr Hide was a book published by the Scottish author Robert Louis Stevenson in 1886. Today "Jekyll and Hyde" has become short hand for people showing very different faces on different occasions. Apparently, Stevenson was friends with a man who poisoned his own wife with opium.

Here one could embark on long literary debates. Does this story mostly tell us about the fundamental dichotomy of the Victorian era (with its focus on outward respectability and repression of inward last and darker urges)? Was this story perhaps an allegory or an examination of the duality innate in human nature (do we all have an inner struggle between good and evil? If this is so, did this inner struggle exist before Christian times and the advent of the word evil?!) The Native American tale about two wolves indicates that all people and all cultures grapple with this: An old Cherokee is teaching his grandson about life. "A fight is going on inside me," he said to the boy. "It is a terrible fight and it is between two wolves. One is evil – he is anger, envy, sorrow, regret, greed, arrogance, self-pity, guilt, resentment, inferiority, lies, false pride, superiority, and ego."He continued, "The other is good – he is joy, peace, love, hope, serenity, humility, kindness, benevolence, empathy, generosity, truth, compassion, and faith. The same fight is going on inside you – and inside every other person, too." The grandson thought about it for a minute and then asked his grandfather, "Which wolf will win?"The old Cherokee simply replied, "The one you feed."[9]

We are all both Dr Jekyll and Mr Hyde! It seems telling that the unsavoury character is called Hyde (a thinly veiled variant of the English word "hide").

Years of working as a practitioner and teacher with both my own shadow and the shadow material of others have taught me the following things:

1. We all have a personal shadow
2. That shadow seeks expression (it will "out!") and it is preferable to be aware of his and exert some control over how and where this happens
3. We cannot engage with other people without encountering their shadow *(make sure you marry someone whose shadow you can live with!)*
4. We project shadow material we are not able to own onto others -meaning that they end up carrying this for us (really meaning that all of us do this for others all the time)
5. We also collectively disown and project shadow material onto other groups of people and this is the cause of much suffering in our world (religious wars, racism, apartheid, discrimination, homophobia and so forth)

Shadow cannot be denied or suppressed -it will just seep out, in ever less acceptable ways, the more it is pushed down. The Golden State Serial Killer was actually a policeman and US Navy veteran, meaning that he used his professional skills in heinous crimes and rapes. The bitter irony is that his day job was law enforcement and protecting the public (might he have been involved in man hunts for himself?)

Finding safe expressions for Shadow

There is an industry out there that satisfies our need for shadow material: crime novels, horror movies, police–procedure-inspired TV series and so forth. It has been claimed that those films ought to be banned because they provide inspiration for unstable characters. I certainly believe that there is some truth in this (I myself have written articles about school shootings[10] and a youth culture where on-line killing games loom large just now).

The Never Again Concept

However, I believe that there is also truth in the opposing argument: that most people who watch horror movies would not dream of acting out material from those sources. The very opposite thing is true: watching horror movies or reading crime novels satisfies the part of us that needs to walk on the dark side and explore the underbelly of the human mind. Once the yearning is satisfied, it no longer seeks expression through acting out "in real life".[11]

Do many young people today play on-line games where killing is a central feature because they are not exposed to death and the killing (of e.g. chickens or farm animals) any longer? Many European countries no longer enforce military service either. (Some call this the only ramaining rite of passage open to young adult men in our culture!)

Can we use our imagination to find additional creative ways of expressing our shadow so our society ends up seeing fewer actual manifestations of disowned shadow material?

In contemporary youth culture we find gangs devising their own rites of passage where one such initiation is killing a human being. This is a completely upside-down and horribly twisted version of a core truth in human nature: any classical/tribal/shamanic initiation always refers to a symbolic death followed by rebirth where the person concerned graduates to a new status in the community (and often a new identity and even name as well. The human soul knows that the processes of death and rebirth are found at the very heart of human existence and evolving human consciousness. This is the reason why elders of communities traditionally initiate teenage boys and tribal shamans do initiate their apprentices by means of a ceremonial and symbolic death.

Young people, left to fend for themselves, (with little access to quality opportunities and no involvement from wise elders acting as mentors and role models) will inevitably arrive at a twisted version of this mystery, in order to "belong" and progress up the ranks of the collective (gang). It is wired into their soul. All of us collectively bear part responsibility in this -because we are not meeting a core spiritual and developmental need in our children!

Huge variation exists: many young people from decent families go on to do well even without formal rites of passage. (Often Life initiates them, or their peers do). A surprising number of young people from dysfunctional and disadvantaged backgrounds still goes on to do well despite almost insurmountable obstacles and adverse early experiences. Informal mentors often play a key role (a caring teacher, neighbour, youth leader or parent of a close friend...) Many young people express this core need through sporting or academic achievements, political activism or volunteering. Those are positive expressions of the need to be initiated and show what we are capable of.

Here I am speaking on the level of soul and archetypes (blueprints active in the human soul). It is time to speak those uncomfortable truths. It is time for all of us to realise that we do not only have responsibilities for our own children but also for the children of our tribe and communities.

We may need to look at actively offering containers for human shadow to young people: perhaps through theatre and drama, film making, volunteer work in prisons, soup kitchens and so forth. We may need to organise this as part of their educational curriculum or families may need to wake up to the importance of this.

Another example of this principle is festivals such as the Roman Saturnalia, where role reversals occurred between masters and slaves, parents and children. I know that similar festivals existed in Old Europe and indigenous societies where a short period of license and lawlessness acted as a "circuit breaker" that allowed communities to keep the lid on the kettle for the rest of the year. Another example is the Bacchanalia where *"celebrations and initiations featured wine-fueled violence and violent sexual promiscuity, in which the screams of the abused were drowned out by the din of drums and cymbals."* [12]

Life after Death is not a straight-forward matter

All cultures impose a set of moral values. Our moral values are defined by religious beliefs and spiritual laws. Those same beliefs also shape our cosmology, our beliefs about where we go after death.

Shadow is a (largely) unconscious expression of personal darkness. However, the Abrahamic religions have a word for conscious expressions of personal darkness: sin. Sin is defined as an immoral act and considered to be a transgression against divine law. Sin is moral evil, perceived from a religious standpoint. In Judaism and Christianity sin is viewed as the deliberate and purposeful violation of the will of God.

In my Roman Catholic upbringing the Seven Deadly Sins still loomed large. They pose fatal obstacles on the path to spiritual progress.[13] Not only that, they are also said to affect our destiny in the Afterlife.

Christians might believe that they burn in Hell for all eternity unless they ask for forgiveness and return to the embrace of Jesus (who died for the salvation of all our sins). However, as some authors have pointed out, this (possibly simplified) belief opens the door for mass murderers, serial killers and other committers-of-atrocities to ask for forgiveness in the moment of death and "go to Heaven".

Buddhism teaches that there are three types of death: the end of life, exhaustion of merit and premature death. On the brink of death, good and evil karma will flash before a person's eyes. The Chinese say: "At the time of death, the ghosts that feel injustice will come and ask for one's life." For that reason, serial killers might see a procession of dead souls seeking justice, by means of karmic action.[14]

In Islam murder is seen as a grave sin and death is viewed as the termination of earthly life and the beginning of the afterlife. The Angel of Death appears to extract a person's soul. After the burial, two angels come to test the dead on their faith. Wicked souls are thrown in hell or the underworld where they are punished until the Day of Judgment.

Judaism believes in an afterlife and regards the preservation of human life as one of its supreme moral values and forbids doing anything that might shorten life. Euthanasia is murder, full stop. Injustice is addressed by divine agents in the afterlife.

> *The value of human life is infinite and beyond measure, so that any part of life – even if only an hour or a second – is of precisely the same worth as seventy years of it, just as any fraction of infinity, being indivisible, remains infinite.*
> Lord Jakobovits[15]

Serial killers and the Afterlife

The notion of divine justice being meted out to serial killers, school shooters and terrorists in the afterlife is profoundly comforting. Unfortunately, it may also be simplistic, even naïve.

One thing is a person dying knowing that they committed bad deeds, feeling guilt and remorse. A person who is incapable of feeling such things, in other words: a person without conscience, is a different thing. Their humanity is in question and they dehumanise others through the crimes they commit.

We discussed earlier how some religions or faiths teach that the state of mind in the moment of death decides the trajectory of the human soul after death. Remorse and a desire to make amends is clearly an example of this.

One of my own shamanic teachers was very fond of using the phrase "high magnitude beings" in the context of what we call compassionate de-possession work (more commonly and horribly called exorcism in everyday language). That work is a steep learning curve, in the context of the questions addressed in this chapter.

Based on years of doing (too) much of that type of work I will share some observations from the "scene of action", that differ from the overt teachings of major religions (here it is worth mentioning that many religions also have secret teachings and ways of transmitting specialist skills behind closed doors, only for initiates. This certainly is true for exorcisms performed by Christian priests).

My observation is that people who do not die "a good death", (boarding a direct flight to the right destination in the Afterlife as it were), often end up in the energetic parallel version of our reality.

Spirit assistance is available but free will is honoured here too. This makes it possible for severely corrupted minds (who still have an eternal luminous soul but are completely disconnected from that) to seek out dark, low-frequency places to hang out and continue their nefarious activities.

In its "milder" form we are talking about dead alcoholics clustering around pubs (and so adding to the energetic field that surrounds public "watering holes"). At its worst we are speaking of the vibration of fear, violence and torment. These earth-bound spirits often hang around earth-based terrorist cells, mafia leaders, prisons, mental hospitals and dangerous criminals. (This is an additional reason why such places make for unhealthy places of work where employees really need to master forms of spiritual protection and clearing themselves before going home – you don't want to bring those energies home to family life and your children!)

Evil

One question begs asking: is it possible for extreme soul loss to occur to a person (read some biographies of the most notorious killers in world history) allowing groups of nefarious spirits to take over and commit deeds through their directing their minds and bodies? – In shamanism that is viewed as perfectly possible (if frightening!) It is also one of the reasons that I would not agree to work the most dangerous cases of possession as a solitary practitioner.

This is partly what creates the larger aura of inhumane terror, of the quality we call "evil" in civilized society. We know that we are in the presence of something huge and extremely chilling: an energy or presence that does not observe any moral rules or the commandments of any religion or god. We are talking about something that feels larger than ourselves – yet that something is not without its match or medicine. We always have the option of calling in beings of a higher frequency and magnitude, but this requires skill and a committed relationship to spirit. Our society does not value or encourage this so only very few individuals develop this skill.

We often wonder how a single person (think of any serial killer here) can commit such deeds and turn into a complete monster. I believe that such killers may be loners in earthly terms, but they do not (necessarily) act alone in otherworld terms. That is a creepy though, yes... but to effectively deal with something we need to comprehend what we are up against.

This obviously raises moral questions about responsibility and accountability. If a person is "not all here" can we hold them 100% responsible for their actions? In everyday life we know of an "insanity plea" but I think that the real issue is infinitely more complex than declaring someone "sane or insane". There is a spiritual continuum in operation with many "grey zones". Undoubtedly that makes forensic work and profiling diabolically difficult.

> *He who fights with monsters should be careful lest he thereby become a monster. And if thou gaze long into an abyss, the abyss will also gaze into thee.*
>
> *[Anything which] is a living and not a dying body... will have to be an incarnate will to power, it will strive to grow, spread, seize, become predominant -not from any morality or immorality but because it is living and because life simply is will to power... 'Exploitation'... belongs to the essence of what lives, as a basic organic function; it is a consequence of the will to power, which is after all the will to life.*
>
> *In music the passions enjoy themselves.*
> Friedrich Wilhelm Nietzsche[16]

This awareness also raises questions about Death Row and the death sentence. We may eliminate a person from the streets and from a high security prison population, but a death sentence may send them to a place where their minds can satisfy their infernal appetites again by influencing or "possessing" the minds of others. One thing agreed on by everyone who has interviewed serial killers, is how shockingly clever they are at playing mind games and messing with people's heads.

It is easy to speak as a backseat driver. What do I suggest instead? Dealing with e.g. a serial killer needs a multi-disciplinarian approach that includes highly skilled spiritual specialists (and here I am not referring to a Christian priest hearing confession or talking about the Bible before an execution). Just as law enforcement uses teams of police officers, forensic specialists and profilers I believe that a team of shamanic detectives needs to work the case as well and unravel the energetic structure that exists around such a person (and the forces that feed on him or her). This would range from care for (and communication with) victim's families (the victims and their families also need shamanic help after gruesome deaths) in tandem with actions performed in the other world to de-activate or lift disharmonious otherworld influences.

Western society has chosen not to believe in "woo woo". This means that spiritual specialists are not granted the same standing and respect as experts in other professions (scientists, big screen actors. medical doctors, lawyers...) What we are inadvertently doing is stockpiling a lot of energetic problems and spiritual entanglements (that only some individuals feel called to work with quietly). Until we give spiritual work its proper place again, our society and daily life will be blighted (even haunted) by these issues.

Not believing in things does not make them go away. The opposite is true: often it creates the very places where such things can feed and fester.

Last but not least, we can all take (some) pressure off "living high magnitude beings" (terrorists, serial killers, criminal master minds etc.) by doing our shadow work and owning our personal shadow. I have explained before how we all project onto others what we do not wish to own in ourselves. As well as embodying evil these people carry some serious garbage for us – allowing us to think well of ourselves. We need to actively take back those part-responsibilities. In me too, somewhere in all of us, lives a cold-blooded killer. Thankfully most people alive never get close to acting from that place.

If, collectively and individually speaking, we commit to doing spiritual work on this (all possible forms) I think this will take our understanding of "evil" to complete new level. It will also take our spiritual toolkit to a whole new level and empower us.

Core shamanism sanitized the material it adopted and

stripped it of its underbelly. In living breathing tribal shamanic traditions the shadow is and was not edited out. It is freely acknowledged that there is a very fine line between shamanism and sorcery. What I am learning through my return to the Northern European Tradition is that teaching people on that level of perception keeps them disempowered. In my classes I compare this to parents and children: when children are young, good parents keep them safe and supervised 24/7 and they do not want them to know about paedophiles or rapists. However, when those same children become teenagers about town, good parents do inform them of dangers and predators – or else young people will not stand a chance of being alert and staying safe. The same thing holds true for spiritual teachings: any New Age (or core shamanic) teaching stating that all we need is love and light, ultimately lets people down, because it leaves them defenceless in the face of the very dark things that exist within us and around us. Raising awareness of this is one of my reasons for writing this book.

Fictional characters and spirits

The spirits come out to play in any creative work!

The Kay Scarpetta character was apparently inspired by former Virginia Chief Medical Examiner Marcella Farinelli Fierro. However, when a talented author starts writing, I observe that spirits come forward to assist in the process of creation. They might just be the spirits of long deceased forensic pathologists wishing to engage once more in work they loved passionately. Writing about murders may just call in the restless souls of (real life) crime victims that have not crossed over and their voices may blend with the author's in imperceptible ways.

I will go as far as saying that any endeavour in our world is met by a cast of characters in other worlds. Our creative efforts provide outlets for those spirits to taste human life or bring an issue to attention. From the shamanic point of view such authors would do well to set strong intentions *and* boundaries around their work.

I have heard stories about people with mediumistic gifts who found reams of writing in their rooms, recognising their own handwriting but not recognising the narrator's voice and not remembering that they ever wrote any of it. This is extreme but it illustrates the phenomenon I am trying to address.

On a lighter note: in Chapter 2 we introduced the concept of the fantasy-prone person. I observe that spirits come forward through play and toys as well. When one such character starts leading a life of its own – it is inspirited. My youngest son has a "toy" jaguar with a larger-than-life personality. I don't think my son is a fantasy-prone person – he has got a very good grasp on current affairs and politics. I do think that this jaguar has a spirit of her own and that she likes living with us. And why not?! (And yes, as a large predator animal she has a rather narcissistic personality…) The same thing happens with much-loved teddy bears, they actually become en-souled or in-spirited beings.

Activity #11: Describe your own Cosmology

Different cultures have different cosmologies. Spiritually aware people actively work on their cosmology: they make tweaks through releasing limiting beliefs and actively visiting other world realms through meditation and astral travel. This can also be viewed as a form of death-preparation work.

What you believe (about divinity and the true nature of the cosmos and everyday reality) shapes both your life and your death. Please write down your key beliefs, addressing (but not limited to!) these questions:

- Do you believe in other worlds and a continuation of consciousness after Death?
- Do you believe in deities and divinity, in powers greater than yourself?

- Have you (through dreams and moments of profound reflection) glimpses other worlds, parallel realms? (Not everyone "sees" in the visual sense, but have you received information through other senses such as hearing, touch, deep inner knowing, smell etc.?)
- Have you ever sensed the presence of a loved one who is deceased? How did you sense them? Was there a message, smell or strong emotion?
- Do you believe in angels, power animals or other guides and helpers?
- Do you ever try to navigate realms other than everyday reality?
- Have you ever used music/drumming/singing bowls or other forms of sonic driving to achieve this?
- When other people talk about their cosmology and belief system, is there anything that resonates with you and sounds true?

Write down what you believe about the afterlife and what you believe will happen to you after your physical death. To help you get started you may use the following sentences (but feel free to fly free!):

- *I was brought up with XYZ belief system (or none) and I still follow this but my thinking has evolved in the following ways…*
- */over time I adopted different beliefs/ I now believe…*
- *If I had to sum up the key principles of my belief system, they are…*
- *I believe in a power (or powers) greater than myself and this/ these takes the form of…*
- *I have sensed other world beings (describe) and I perceive them as… (angels/ ancestors/nature spirits/power animals) etc., describe…*
- *My spiritual practices are… (and failing that: the spiritual*

practices I would like to follow are…)

Did this exercise open a dialogue with yourself?! Make notes and keep them at hand for you to return to!

Chapter 12

Moral Law and drawing Moral Lines

(Moral Law is) a general rule of right living; especially such a rule or group of rules conceived as universal and unchanging and as having the sanction of God's will, of conscience, of man's moral nature, or of natural justice as revealed to human reason.
Merriam-Webster online dictionary[1]

To one who has faith, no explanation is necessary. To one without faith, no explanation is possible.

To bear with patience wrongs done to oneself is a mark of perfection, but to bear with patience wrongs done to someone else is a mark of imperfection and even of actual sin.
Thomas Aquinas[2]

It is a hotly debated issue whether such a thing as (an ultimate and absolute) Moral Law exists. However, all human beings with full use of their mental faculties will sooner or later need to draw their own moral lines. We have already established that there is a close relationship between our personal (and cultural) ethics and our understanding of death and a possible afterlife.

Moral Law and Natural Moral Law

Moral law is (in some systems of ethics) an absolute principle defining the criteria of right action (whether conceived as a divine ordinance or a truth of reason).

Cicero[4] wrote that *Natural Moral Law includes those ethical theories which state that there is a natural order to our world that should be followed. This natural order is determined by some supernatural power. Natural law originated in the philosophy of the ancient Greek, especially that of Aristotle, and was developed by Thomas Aquinas.*

It is an absolute theory of ethics, but it is not rooted in duty, or in an externally imposed law, but in our human nature and our search for genuine happiness and fulfilment.[3] *True law is right reason in agreement with nature; it is of universal application, unchanging and everlasting; it summons to duty by its commands and averts from wrongdoing by its prohibitions.*

According to Cicero, this natural and unchangeable law will be valid for all nations and all times, and there will be one master and rule -that is God.

Aquinas considered that by using our reason to reflect on our human nature we could discover our specific purpose and, having discovered this, we could then work out how to achieve it. This understanding of God's plan for us, built into the nature of creation, he called Natural Law.

The human imagination and ethics

Arguably one of the most important uses of the human imagination occurs regarding moral law and ethics.

Philosopher and theologian St. Thomas Aquinas was born around 1225 in Roccasecca, Italy. He combined the theological principles of faith with the philosophical principles of reason and he ranked among the most influential thinkers of medieval Scholasticism. He was an authority of the Roman Catholic Church and a prolific writer. Before St. Thomas Aquinas was born, a holy hermit shared a prediction with his mother, foretelling that her son would enter the Order of Friars Preachers, become a great scholar and achieve unequalled sanctity.

Judy Blume[5] explains: *At the forefront of medieval thought was a struggle to reconcile the relationship between theology (faith) and philosophy (reason). People were at odds as to how to unite the knowledge they obtained through revelation with the information they observed naturally using their mind and their senses. Based on*

Averroes's "theory of the double truth," the two types of knowledge were in direct opposition to each other. St. Thomas Aquinas's revolutionary views rejected Averroes's theory, asserting that "both kinds of knowledge ultimately come from God" and were therefore compatible. Not only were they compatible, according to Thomas's ideology, they could work in collaboration: He believed that revelation could guide reason and prevent it from making mistakes, while reason could clarify and demystify faith. St. Thomas Aquinas's work goes on to discuss faith and reason's roles in both perceiving and proving the existence of God.

Thomas Aquinas was a thirteenth century Italian priest, theologian, philosopher and jurist in the tradition of scholasticism. In his Summa Theologica Aquinas called the rational understanding and following of God's divine purpose for human beings Natural Moral Law.

He believed that this law is universal and unchanging, relevant to all circumstances and that it can be found in the natural order of things.

All human beings (that is to say: those who possess the faculty of reason) can perceive this moral law but only people who believe in God and an Afterlife will accept that it has implications for them beyond the grave.[5]

If we accept that Moral Law exists (which for many people is debatable) we immediately reach the following question: is this law wired into the cosmos, (as it were), or does it depend on the existence of an Ultimate Divine Being or Prime Mover? In Western culture the male God of Christianity is a development or later version of what is called The Prime Mover in earlier and pre-Christian sources.

Morality and Ethics

Is morality the same thing as ethics? Generally, those terms are used interchangeably but different communities do make distinctions.

Both morality and ethics are ultimately about telling the difference between "good" and "bad" or "right" and "wrong". Many people think of morality as more of a personal setting (such as *"it is important to teach our children moral values"*) whereas ethics relates to standards applying to a specific community (group of people) and/or social setting.

For instance, I live in a community (western society) where abortion is freely available but not all people living in my community will agree that it should be. Some people (with extreme views) believe that abortion is always wrong ("the murder of a baby, the termination of a human life") while others believe that women "have the right to rule over their own bodies" and therefore abortion is always right (and by extension *a human right*). This is also known as the Pro-Life and Pro-Choice Debate). Many people may come down somewhere on the spectrum between those two extremes. At the time of editing this book (January 2019) there are reports about certain states in the US extending the legal limit for abortion right up to birth.[7] It is my understanding that these exemptions apply *only* to anomalies (extremely serious birth defects and disabilities in a foetus) and the physical or mental health of the mother (once again only grave and extreme situations).

I have never been able to imagine opting for an abortion, but I have never experienced rape and I have certainly not experienced pregnancy caused by rape. I am using this as the most extreme scenario I can personally imagine. My three children were born to a father who wanted them and has stayed around to look after them. I have not faced medical issues that made a pregnancy risky for my health either. I have spent most of my life in (Northern European) countries with a high standard of living.

I am the first to admit that I have not personally lived through many scenarios that I know other women all over the world face every single day. Neither have I ever been in the situation where I have not been able to feed my children or provide a roof over their heads. Tragically this is not true for many mothers on our planet. Therefore, my personal experience says little about abortion being "wrong", and the global situation says much about the challenges that women face in the 21st century. We can fly to the Moon -but we can (apparently) not prevent wars or famine. We can produce genetically modified crops but we cannot adequately feed all members of the Human Family and so eliminate the problem of people literally starving to death.

Here are a few more questions for you to sit with:

- Is stealing always wrong?
- Is adultery always wrong?
- Is euthanasia always wrong?
- Is murder always wrong?
- Is killing a person under any circumstances wrong?
- Is the common trend to opt for a termination when medical tests show that a foetus has Down's Syndrome, right or wrong?

For many western people the word morality has Christian overtones (for me personally it has the association of being judged by a power or being larger than myself). In the world of business, education, medicine or law we use the word *ethics* instead. It refers to a personal code of conduct. This is often informed by our moral compass. Also, even within one single profession there can be heated debates about ethics.

Any code of conduct we arrive at in our personal lives will be informed by our moral compass (and therefore our religion, faith or spiritual orientation or even lack thereof). Our code of conduct in our professional lives will also need to take into account any boundaries which others and appropriate bodies have drawn up for good optimal practice.

One command from the Bible (attributed to Jesus in his Sermon on the Mount) is:

Do unto others as you would have them do unto you!

This is the heart of the matter: if we do not have empathy or compassion (literally "fellow feeling") for others, if we cannot even briefly put ourselves in their situations, why would we operate a personal code of conduct (perhaps beyond knowing where law enforcement draws the line for human behaviour in our community because we don't fancy spending time in jail). Law enforcement certainly has its own shadows and it has plenty of corruptions too but not having access to law enforcement is far worse because it marks a return to the "justice of the jungle".

Moral Crimes

I think that most of us can think of scenarios we might call moral crimes. My husband used this word yesterday. We heard that an elderly neighbour of ours in Sweden had had a heart attack and been rushed to hospital. The issue dominating his every waking thought is that his family has lived for three generations on land that belongs to a nearby manor house. As the tenancy agreement now runs out, the landowners ("the people at the big house") decided to push for more income, without taking into account the lifetimes of back-breaking work, ancestral memories, deep love for the land and so forth this farmer feels. It is the only home he has ever known. To reduce three generations of loving care for land, farm buildings and animals to an attitude that translates as: "Pay more money or move out!" feels like a moral crime to us.

Other examples of moral crimes we can observe around us might be children who never visit their elderly and ailing parents -thought we do not know what really played out there. A seemingly adorable elderly grandma or grandpa might have been a very abusive parent in a younger incarnation. The Golden State Killer was described as a harmless grandpa type by his neighbours who clearly did not live in fear of him.

I have had clients who told me that they clocked up two or three abortions in one calendar year. I can't help but think: didn't you learn your lesson after the first one?! That is three small potential human lives...[8]

Here we also see that there is a very fine line between "drawing a moral line" and "being judgemental"! We live in an era where having a strong opinion on anything means people call us "judgemental". The higher octave manifestation of "judgemental" is discernment.

Moral absolutism

This refers to the ethical view that specific actions are intrinsically right or wrong.

Returning to the questions I posed earlier:

- *Is stealing always wrong?* Even when "we steal from the rich to give to the poor ", Robin Hood style"? -However, if we make an exception for that, then we open the door on large scale burglaries and plundering in areas where affluent people live....
- *Is adultery always wrong?* We live in an era where adultery is perceived as a "private offense". Most people would still say it is definitely wrong but in today's world committing adultery will not bring the village priest to your door nor will it cost you your job or stop you from getting a job you are the best candidate for (And perhaps that is part of the problem, thinking back to the concept of *an evolutionary mismatch*?!)
- *Is euthanasia always wrong?* This is another debate that rages and rages without resolution. "Going to Switzerland"[9] has become a synonym for "elected assisted

death" and my country of birth (The Netherlands) now also makes euthanasia available to people who experience insurmountable suffering and no hope of a cure or improvement (subject to assessments by several medical doctors).

Is murder always wrong?

Earlier I mentioned one incident that occurred on a flight where a passenger became a danger to other people and he had to be restrained by crew members and other passengers – but actually died. Is this homicide (technically it is) or an act of bravery and civil service? Was a far more dangerous situation (he tried to break into the cockpit and what exactly was he planning to do to the pilots or the controls?!) narrowly avoided?! We don't know. We *do know* that the people involved were not prosecuted.

If a parent takes justice into their own hands and kills the paedophile which tortured and killed their son or daughter. Is this intentional killing? Yes, it is, no doubt! Is it morally wrong? Yes – this is what we have a justice system for! Would many parents feel a degree of compassion -if not reluctant admiration or gratitude-for this parent?! I suspect that might be a second yes, especially parents living in the neighbourhood concerned.

There have been cases in the news recently where mothers of a dead child became a global inspiration by not walking the path of revenge and instead speaking up for forgiveness, compassion and the value of a human life.[10]

Is killing a person under any circumstances wrong?
If this is so -why are wars so common?
Does the concept of a mercy killing have validity?

We already mentioned the concept of one death occurring to prevent many other deaths.

If law enforcement kills a would-be terrorist or suicide bomber while doing their job – is that wrong or right?!
Is the common trend to opt for a termination when medical tests show that a foetus has Down's Syndrome, wrong?

Parents of such children often say that they arrive as teachers of unconditional love. I know people who parent a child with Downs with immense love, satisfaction and a magical touch. I also know people who were devastated by the test results and opted for a termination for "medical reasons".

Parenting any child is a mammoth task. Even people who are parents by choice suffer from moments of complete overwhelm and self-doubt. When we add mental disability into the mix and add the fact that a person with Down's needs supervision and care for life (meaning beyond the parents' own lifespan), can people-who-do-not-face-this-challenge sit in judgement on an agonizing decision such parents face and eventually make?

Some people are so desperate to adopt a child and experience parenting, that social workers find good homes for children with Down's syndrome with relative ease. There are so many people whose lives are blighted by not having children. Yet today almost no one considers a carrying a child full term allowing the new life to thrive and another person to live their dream (I have been told that this is more common in the U.S.!) I appreciate that doing so is a huge practical, physical and emotional undertaking. Are we encouraged to engage our imagination and compassion fully when we make these life-or-death decisions? What is our soul-contract with the unborn life and "The Other"? What is the dream of the unborn child?

Did we check on any of those things before we made our decision?!

We can tentatively conclude that moral absolutism is elusive and ephemeral, that context and intention give meaning to human actions. Perhaps the value of struggling with these ethical dilemmas lies in that very act: by tossing and turning and giving ourselves a headache pondering all possible dimensions -we grow as human beings; we take our place on the larger spectrum of human values that connects all of these things -and ultimately all of us. We could not do this without the miraculous faculty that is the human imagination.

Moral Law may or may not exist, but the human imagination allows us to draw moral lines.

Bless a thing and it will bless you. Curse it and it will curse you... If you bless a situation, it has no power to hurt you, and even if it is troublesome for a time, it will gradually fade out, if you sincerely bless it.
Emmet Fox[11]

Adversity introduces a man to himself.
Attributed to Einstein[12]

Moral Panic

A moral panic is a widespread fear, most often an irrational one, that someone or something is a threat to the values, safety, and interests of a community or society at large. Typically, a moral panic is perpetuated by news media, fueled by politicians, and often results in the passage of new laws or policies that target the source of the panic. In this way, moral panic can foster increased social control.

Moral panics are often centered on people who are marginalized in society due to their race or ethnicity, class, sexuality, nationality, or religion. As such, a moral panic often draws on known stereotypes and reinforces them. It can also exacerbate the real and perceived differences and divisions between groups of people.
Ashley Crossman[13]

The phrase "moral panic" and the development of the sociological concept is credited to late South African sociologist Stanley Cohen (1942-2013), who introduced the social theory of moral panic in his 1972 book titled Folk Devils and Moral Panics.[14]

It could be argued that the witch hunts were examples of moral panic. There is always a dimension of this phenomenon that reinforces the authority of leaders, really meaning it leads to increased control of the population due to the sense of "law and order" appearing to return.

This is a phenomenon where an encounter with The Other in any form (people who are different in any away in terms of religion, race, sexual orientation etc.) sparks off fear, and the desire to control the situation and re-establish previous values that the threatened group felt more comfortable with.

On a human level this understandable. Most people do not like an interruption of the status quo or a reduction their level of privacy and entitlement. On another level people shut themselves off from genuine soul searching, personal growth and cultural fertilisation when this occurs.

Shadow dimension: this easily turns into empty rhetoric and spin-doctoring, where the situation does not really change long-term but a spin is put on things and politicians further their own career by taking on the cause.

Celebrity

The average person has little idea of the shadows carried by celebrities (because we all freely project onto them). However, once people acquire celebrity status (wanted or not) they become public figures and role models. That carries the responsibility of reflecting on what example is set, what message is sent, how any actions may speak louder than words.

If you have access to this mysterious power – use it well! Promote causes that deserve attention, model right action made from a moral compass (not vanity and self-interest), raise funds for charities that truly relieve suffering.

Activity #12: Audience with the Siberian goddess Umai

There is an old belief in Siberia that after death shamans go to a special place in the other world, organized around the World Tree. Here the great Siberian goddess Umai lives. She sends the souls of children-wishing-to-be-born out in the world in the form of small birds. Women hoping for pregnancy can visit and petition her.

The River of Life runs by this World Tree, where it passes the Veil between worlds it becomes the River of Death. In the Other World, houses of shamans line the shores of this great river. While still in our world they visit and prepare for death.

Our middle son kept telling us, as a toddler, about his house in the spirit world (in a place he called Yellow Land, a place made of golden Light). He visits this in his dreams and checks that all is well. This takes the sting out of death because he knows he will "go home" after death.

Ask Umai to take you on a journey on this river. She may lend you her birch bark boat! Ask if you have shaman ancestors living there. They belong to The Deep Past (meaning you cannot trace them in your family tree -but they exist and contributed to the making of you!) You may be invited in for a visit!

Return to your starting point. Thank Umai! Thank your shaman ancestors! Feel free to return other times and prepare for your own death.

Chapter 13

Imagination and Compassion

Don't judge a man until you have walked a mile in his shoes.
Cherokee proverb[1]

Pain is unavoidable but suffering is optional.
Haruki Murakami[2]

Empathic people feel the pain of others acutely. Is it possible to be too empathic? Could feeling too deeply for someone else's pain or sorrow actually hurt you?
Tara Well[2]

Are human beings capable of feeling compassion without flexing the muscle of their imagination? In the previous chapter we danced around some thorny issues, issues that scratch and snag on the gossamer fabric of our souls.

Compassion, Empathy, Pity

The word compassion literally means "suffering along with another". The contemporary English word comes from the Old French word compassion, meaning "sympathy, pity" (12th century) and that word comes from Late Latin. The room stems are "pati" (to suffer) and com (with). An Old English loan-translation of compassion was efenðrowung.[3]

In everyday life we often use the words compassion and empathy interchangeably and the word pity is not far off.

The word pity has less than positive connotations: you are looking at person suffering from a place of not opening yourself to their suffering. In everyday language we often speak of "Poor so-and-so..." No matter what is happening in my life, I hope no one will ever speak of "Poor Imelda" because it feels destructive, like the person is not even using their imagination to believe that I will make the best of the cards I was dealt, that I can and will survive (physically or spiritually) whatever is happening to me. Pity feels dark, sticky and patronizing.

The word empathy refers to the ability to feel the pain of others acutely. You feel what others are feeling on a physical level. In my younger days (when I had much to learn about developing healthy personal boundaries) I often felt the pain of others to the point of losing my appetite and ability to sleep. It was debilitating! As I gained more life experience, I began to see other aspects of this:

- Suffering so intensely on someone else's behalf does not actually take one ounce of their pain away (having been brought up on stories about saints and martyrs I had got hold of the wrong end of the stick here!)
- If I join a person in the space of acute suffering my ability to help them is reduced. I can only help a person when my own strength is up so I can make full use of my skills and energy.
- People often ask for help but don't truly want to make changes. They want sympathy and supportive listening without committing to *acting on any help and guidance they receive.*

An article in Psychology Today explains how neuroscientists Tania Singer and Olga Klimecki[3] conducted studies actively training people to use empathy and compassion, using two separate experiment groups for this. This research revealed fascinating differences in the brain.

First, the empathy training activated motion in the insula (linked to emotion and self-awareness, in the human brain) and motion in the anterior cingulate cortex (linked to emotion and consciousness), as well as pain registering. The compassion group, however, stimulated activity in the medial orbitofrontal cortex (connected to learning and reward in decision making as well as activity in the ventral striatum (also connected to the reward system).

Second, the two types of training led to very different emotions and attitudes toward action. The empathy-trained group found empathy uncomfortable and troublesome. The compassion group, on the other hand, created positivity in the minds of the group members. The compassion group ended up feeling kinder and more eager to help others than those in the empathy group.[3]

Human beings have a perceptual bias to pay more attention to negative and potentially threatening information, (surely a survival-mechanism!) To stay safe, we need to be aware of possible threats and problems. This can cross a line into overwhelm and lead people to believe that the negative outweighs the positive. For that reason, we are advised to *limit our exposure to negativity.*

The philosophical problems of empathy

My friend Rick Lewis, publisher of Philosophy Now magazine, wrote an online article[5]. It questions whether empathy is even possible, speaking from a philosopher's point of view. People are extremely complicated beings and we have "no direct access to their minds".

There are (apparently) two "philosophical problems" connected with empathy: the first one is the question how much we can truly share other people's mental states and emotions (can we do so at all?!) The second one relates to ethics and society. Does it matter whether we understand other people's feelings? Lewis says yes, definitely, it is preferable to be surrounded by sympathetic people and empathy oils the communication between individuals. Empathy helps us assess the behaviour of other people. Lewis also suggests we approach the issue by coming at it from the opposite direction: what happens when empathy fails?! He gives the example of the 9/11 attacks on the twin towers in New York. One example that comes to my own mind is of the Manchester bombing at the Arianna Grande concert in Manchester in 2017, where the intention was to harm (kill and mutilate) children. On 22 May 2017 a shrapnel-laden homemade bomb was detonated as people were leaving the Manchester Arena. The perpetrator was a 22-year old Muslim man of Libyan ancestry.

Here we have left the realm of "empathy failure" and we have well and truly entered the realm of intentional harm or "evil". Lewis believes that a reasonable degree of empathy can save the world from barbarity. I do not agree!

The people who master-mind terror attacks, same as Nazi death camp commanders, are (generally but not always) capable of feeling empathy for their personal loved ones but they compartmentalize: empathy for some but not for others. It appears that for people prone to a fundamentalist persuasion the very human-ness of others comes into question as a larger issue takes priority: world dominion of their chosen belief system. (I refuse to call this a religion because people who commit acts of terror are not acting in service to *any* religion).

Suicide attacks

A suicide attack is any violent attack in which the attacker expects their own death as a direct result of the method used to harm, damage or destroy the target. Suicide attacks have occurred throughout history, often as part of a military campaign such as the Japanese kamikaze pilots of World War I, and more recently as part of terrorist campaigns, such as the September 11 attacks.

Suicide attacks tend to be more deadly and destructive than other terror attacks because they give their perpetrators the ability to conceal weapons and make last-minute adjustments.

They also cancel out the need for remote or delayed detonation, escape plans and/or rescue teams. Suicide attacks constituted 4% of all terrorist attacks around the world over one period (between 1981 and 2006), but caused 32% of all terrorism-related deaths.[5]

Suicide attacks have been described as a weapon of psychological warfare to instil fear in the target population, as a strategy to eliminate or at least drastically diminish areas where the public feels safe, and the "fabric of trust that holds societies together".[6]

The word kamikaze means divine wind or spirit wind. The Kamikaze were members of the Japanese Special Attack Unit of military aviators who performed suicide attacks against Allied naval vessels during World War II, destroying war ships. About 3,800 kamikaze pilots died during the war and more than 7.000 naval personnel were killed by those attacks.[7]

Far and Near Enemies

Up to now we have identified "lower octave" and "higher octave" manifestations. The third classification is *the near enemy.*[8]

Buddhism teaches a set of virtues called The Four Immeasurables[9]. When a Buddhist takes the Bodhisattva vow, he or she dedicates their life to cultivating the following virtues:

- Loving-kindness: wishing well towards all beings.
- Compassion: recognizing the suffering of others and wishing for them to be free of suffering.
- Empathetic Joy: rejoicing in the joy of others, even if it is not your own.
- Equanimity: even-mindedness and serenity, treating everyone impartially.

Those Buddhists use special meditations and daily life practices to actively cultivate these qualities. People practising this are also taught about the *far enemies* and *near enemies* of these qualities. Identifying the far enemy tends to be quite straightforward: ill will (or active intention to do harm) is the far enemy of loving kindness. Cruelty is the far enemy of compassion and jealousy is the far enemy of empathic joy.

However, *near enemies* are much harder to spot and deal with! This concept refers to a phenomenon that, at first sight, resembles (or even masquerades as!) the virtues mentioned, but it is fundamentally different and dangerous.

The near enemy of proper love is conditional love or clinging attachment. The near enemy of friendship is people acting friendly *because you are useful to them.*

Pamela Fox says: *On a personal level, I've found it incredibly helpful to remember the near enemies. For example, I'm always working on reducing my anxiety and being less emotionally reactive (being more equanimous, a word I can rarely pronounce). However, I'll admit I often fall into the near enemy of disassociation and indifference. Thankfully, since I am aware of that near enemy, I can realize when that's happening and apply the antidotes*.[8]

The *near enemy* is the aspiring suicide bomber (/terrorist/ mass murderer etc.), who takes the shape of the pleasant and unfailingly polite boy (or girl) next door and who is actually building nail bombs in their bedroom or bedsit.

Higher Octave

Martyr: a person who is killed because of their steadfast commitment to religious or other beliefs

Lower Octave

Suicide Bomber as "martyr to" e.g. extremist Islamic doctrine:

A person who kills other people because of deep-held beliefs

Near Enemy
Aspiring suicide bomber as the handsome boy next door (whom your teenage daughter fancies) constructing nail bombs in his bedroom, one wall away from your own bedroom. (Any permutation of gender is possible in this example!)

Reducing suffering for all sentient beings

One key principle in Buddhism is actively trying to reduce the suffering of all sentient beings[9]. Commendable as this is, operating from a different belief system, I put my questions about this to author friend Todd Wiggins[10], a professor of English based in Paris. He explains that Buddhism is not "one unified belief system", there are different schools, lineages and traditions operating under the umbrella of Buddhism. The differences are both geographic (Tibetan/Tantric and Zen disciplines) but also there are different pathways with a different focus or emphasis.

Recovery programs and shamanic healing work teach that people need to hit "rock bottom" so they themselves realise that "the only way out is up". If that point is not reached, they will gravitate back to that exact place. Sometimes the larger intelligence of the universe is trying to teach someone a lesson. It is not in their best interest if someone, however well-meaningly, steps in and tries to prevent a tough outcome. The person needs to master the lesson and climb out of a hole by themselves. (We can give them a hand -but we cannot stand between them and the hole).

This raises the spectre of *collusion*: research into addiction demonstrates that the behaviour of many addicts goes relatively unchecked for long periods because family members cover up for them, make excuses or clean up messes so that in the eyes of the world things look better than they are. In similar ways the Church has covered up cases of priests abusing young boys, schools cover up complaints about abusive teachers and so forth.

This type of collusion also occurs in many personal

relationships. Privacy is one thing (no one wants the world to know everything about them!) but collusion is more sinister: it enables a person to continue their severely dysfunctional (harmful to self and others) functioning.

Enabler: a person who encourages or enables negative or self-destructive behaviour in another person

What makes this issue so tough is that enablers generally don't realise that they are enabling – they truly believe that they are lovingly supporting the dysfunctional person (and that belief in itself is deluded and dysfunctional!)

I was taught to (professionally speaking) "never help a person who is not asking for help", speaking on the level of healing sessions/interventions/major spiritual work. Obviously, most people practicing shamanism will commit many random acts of kindness. Catching a toddler who is on the run from a harassed parent with another baby in a pram is not "enabling", it is known as "the kindness of strangers"! It is also known as "being the person who happened to be in the right place".

Returning to Buddhism Wiggins says: "This is, as you can imagine, quite a vast subject that, at its ultimate level, is not interpreted in the same way by all schools. The bodhisattva vows are a hallmark of the Mahayana branch (as opposed to the older Theravadan school), and are therefore central both to the Tibetan/Tantric and Zen disciplines but the emphasis isn't quite the same, in that Zen says: Beings are numberless, I vow to liberate them all; whereas the Tibetans refer specifically to "sentient" beings. The simplest way of understanding loving kindness and compassion - the first two of the four "Immeasurables" - is to say that *people in general will find themselves to be much happier if they are able to put others first.* For Buddhists this means intervening on the appropriate level according to the particulars of the situation and one's own capacities: helping someone cross a street, lending them money, feeding them... if these are within our capacities, and if the situation calls for such actions, we should not hesitate in performing them. In this Buddhist appears no different from other religions.

The perspective changes (or deepens) the more one practices. There is, as in shamanism, a distinction to be made between helping people in a formal student context and helping them in general. Teachers do not instruct others in the dharma --considered the highest form of liberation -who have not asked for this. These aspects form part of the original imperative to respond to every situation in its particulars, never out of some general rule or dogma. A master may well respond very differently to two people who appear to be in the same circumstances. This is the first point: *every context is unique, and the capacity of response varies according to person.*

The second point he makes is that compassion is often misunderstood as empathy which it is not. (Here empathy is understood as feeling another person's suffering as intensely as they do. This would, by definition, render any helper as impotent as the sufferer!) Compassion is about the interconnectedness of all beings, when truly understood there is no "individual" helping "another." A high bodhisattva no longer thinks, "What can I do for this person?" The more "realized" they are, the more impersonally they act, until they have no sense of "actively" helping anyone. It just happens. This is an important point, because all of us, at the beginning, may sincerely think, "I'd really like to help other people and do good things." This is fine as far as it goes, and a good motivator, but is something that will fall away as one's comprehension increases and the sense of one's own separation diminishes.

One's compassionate action is simply the universe expressing itself through an apparent individual who longer perceives themselves as such. This is the level of Buddha, understood not as a separate historic individual, but pure egoless manifestation. So again, to summarize: *the higher the realization, the more one is effective without being "active" as such. Compassion is the seamless web of all apparent phenomena in their great display.* Put another way, what really distinguishes Buddhism from almost every other discipline (aside from Advaita Vedanta and Taoism) is *nonduality,* the transcendence of subject/object, good/bad, me/you, one/two, this/that, etc.

The great virtue of Buddhism is that, properly understood, it is *absolutely pitiless*! The deepest sanity depends on that very fact. The annals of Zen and Tibetan masters tend to recount stories that would strike most Westerners as sadistic! Again, it depends on the situation and the student (or non-student), but the whole notion of "progress" on the Buddhist path does not involve avoiding obstacles but running straight at them! The student must realize that the only path to Buddhahood lies *within themselves*. The master illuminates that path -but he/she cannot carry the student on it. Buddhism is about stripping away every layer of pretence, protection, self-regard... in brief, every story one has ever entertained about oneself, no holds barred, to see the stark-naked truth; and as one teacher of mine said, this state of exposure is something few beings can withstand...

Social Imagination

Our imagination plays a key part in the way we relate to other human beings. Empathy involves using our own imagination (as well as feelings and physical sensations) to attempt to walk in another person's shoes for at least a few meters (we may not complete the mile).

It is often claimed that individuals on the autistic spectrum lack in imagination because they are so literal-minded. All human beings move through a developmental phase where metaphors are taken literally. I remember saying once, years ago when my three sons were toddlers: "So and so hit me with an unexpected deadline" (for a piece of creative work). My two eldest sons looked at me in horror: "Who did you say hit you

Mum?!!" They believed that a crime had been committed and we had better report this "assault" to the police!

Children "on the spectrum" crave routines, "sameness" and predictability. Any changes can cause immense distress (a level of distress that is hard for neurotypical people to imagine). In truth all of us (probably) have this to some extent: to feel secure all human beings need a degree of sameness and being able to predict what will happen next, how a person will respond or what constitutes an appropriate range of responses to others at our end. When that social knowledge drops away, the world suddenly becomes a far more menacing place. I can only imagine how the same must be true for people with Alzheimer's and dementia: a (previously) familiar world turns unpredictable and frightening.

> *People with autism have trouble seeing things from the perspective of another person. This affects their ability to recognise, understand the feelings of other people and predict their possible reactions. One obvious consequence of this way of being wired is that they cannot predict the consequences of their own behaviour either.*
> Autism Toolbox[11]

Children with autism typically have limited skills when it comes to creative and imaginative play. I have heard parents of children with severe autism say that their child treats them like a piece of furniture: climbing them or pushing them out of the way (as if they were an object). Therefore, many authorities on this subject claim that that such children (who become adults on the spectrum) have issues with social imagination. This affects their ability to:

- accept others' points of view
- accept changes in routine
- cope with 'mistakes'

- be aware of unwritten rules ('hidden curriculum')
- deal with rules being broken
- organise their time as well as equipment and appearance

This gives us a thought-provoking list of things that we would *all* struggle with, if our imagination did not function flawlessly![11]

Autism and the Neurotypical Imagination

Autistic people are wired differently from (so called) neurotypical individuals. For vivid (even poetic) descriptions of life with autistic children, check out the following books: George and Sam by Charlotte Moore[12], as well as two books by Rupert Isaacson, father of autistic son Rowan: The Horse Boy: A Father's Miraculous Journey to Heal His Son[13] and The Long Ride Home: The Extraordinary Journey of Healing That Changed a Child's Life.[14]

In shamanism we speak of *the healing journey* -because is a long journey with many encounters and adventures along the way. Isaacson used his imagination to craft the most perfect healing journey our planet could offer his son. By doing so he gifted his son the opportunity to be fully alive and engaged with this planet, within his own talents and limitations. His family inspires other autistic families to reach for non-conventional ways of healing and acceptance.

To do this, we need to step away from our individualist me-me-me thinking (or as we say in English: thinking of "Number One"). Just as taxes are supposed to be about funding collective resources (roads, education, health care) a collective pooling of resources means that those with a large dose of "healing imagination" need to reach out to those who can only make limited use of their imagination.

Not just that: we owe it to all members of our community that they be given opportunities to make their unique contributions. In some cases that will require extra support and thinking-outside-the-box. We all get so busy just supporting ourselves and our own families that we fail to use our imagination in service to others.

Diverse Thinking

The most interesting people you'll find are ones that don't fit into your average cardboard box.
Temple Grandin[15]

You say you love your children above all else and yet you are stealing their future in front of their very eyes.
Greta Thunberg[16]

I feel strongly that most research done involving autistic people does not do their abilities and gifts justice. Here are some balancing viewpoints:

Autistic people lack a special type of imagination called social imagination. This is nothing to do with the ability to be creative! Many (but not all) people with autism are gifted musicians or artists. Their work opens portals for other people. However, most autistic people are not *savants*, which is a rare phenomenon.

Research on autistic people recognises areas of ability in mathematics, data processing and IT where a logical, systematic method is required. Autistic people tend to be superior to non-autistic people in many tasks that require processing large amounts of information, picking out details of objects or scenes, or detecting changes in the environment.

Regarding "Aspies" (people with Asperger's), Jonathan Alderson[17] writes: *As I discuss in my book Challenging the Myths of Autism , I believe that the myth that autistic children don't have an imagination likely began in 1979 when a well-respected and important autism researcher Lorna Wing and her colleague Judith Gould popularized the idea that lack of imagination should be one of three main criteria for diagnosing the disorder. Their ideas were quickly adopted by the medical community and most professionals. People added their own spin on what exactly they believed lacking imagination meant. Soon enough it was used to explain a whole range of behaviours*

His advice:

- Keep your eyes open for autistic children's own unique expressions of creativity.
- Make sure to praise (and encourage) new forms, innovations, and unusual designs as much as you would for any child.

Temple Grandin is the world's most famous autist, autism activist and livestock handling designer. As an expert on animal behaviour she has designed humane handling systems for half the cattle-processing facilities in the US. She consults with the meat industry to develop animal welfare guidelines. She did a TED talk in 2010 titled "The World Needs All Kinds of Minds".[15]

She says that autism helps her understand animals because she thinks in pictures. Animals do not have a language, their memories are sensory-based, not word-based. Many nonverbal children with autism really understand animals. Parents tell her that their nonverbal child has an almost telepathic ability to communicate with their dog. This is not telepathy the child is observing subtle body posture changes that many people do not notice. The child is observing detailed changes in the dog's behaviour.

I have a sensory-based empathy with animals and can really relate to animal welfare issues when it comes to housing. One form of restrictive animal housing that must be changed is sow gestation stalls. It would be like living in an airline seat and never being allowed to walk in the aisle. I can feel the muscle cramps I would

get if I could not move around.
Temple Grandin[18]

For the sake of sows (and all animals subject to cruel cage farming techniques) this is an important observation. It is equally important for neurotypical people to understand that autistic people can feel empathy, but this connection is wired and sensed in a different way.

Why is it OK to do things to animals that we know we should not do to a human being? Our imagination fails us in our dealings with other sentient beings…

What we focus on grows

So how do we best support others on the road to becoming the best person they have the potential of becoming? And what role does our imagination play in this?! We have learned that it is preferable to support the innate strength and talents in others. Rather than saying: "Oh you poor thing!" say:

- "I stand in awe of you, you inspire me!"
- "Next time I face a serious challenge I will take inspiration from you!
- I know you can do this – and I will support you all the way!

People will then smile through their tears -because you see their divinity, their innate strength, beauty and courage. This is one of Sandra Ingerman's key teachings.[19]

The Alchemy of the Imagination

Our imagination is not unlike a cauldron. In a recent art video, titled The Poison Mother[20] I used the line: *"I am witch and cauldron both"*.

We can actively use our imagination to perform alchemy

on situations that come to our attention. One way of making a difference is using Hawaiian H'oponopono, apology and forgiveness work.[21]

Human beings can only take so much pain. Too much pain messes people up for life. Psychiatric hospitals all over the world are full of people who have felt more (or more severe) pain than they were able to process and handle (often at a very young age). The human psyche responds with fragmentation and defence mechanisms. Those defence mechanisms serve us for a time but long-term they turn on us and become counter-productive because they distance (even alienate) others.

In a similar way we can only take so much suffering in others. We tire of people who are always complaining. We avoid the friend who tells us the same pain-stories for years and years but never makes any changes and fails to move forward. We look away when we see pictures of wounded children in Syria or people hurting animals. Something in us yells: *"If I am forced to absorb even more pain I will go to pieces, I will lose my ability to function and meet my commitments."*

The shift we need to make is to engage with these issues imaginatively. If you see a picture of someone hurting an animal or person -use your imagination to call in spirit forces (assuming you believe in them). Use your imagination to send a soul-to-soul message of love and strength to the person or sentient being concerned. Use your imagination to visualize better outcomes: a good home for the animal, a safe sanctuary for the person, a criminal caught and safer streets. Every time we see the "good" in people, that part of them receives a boost. When many people do this, things may just start tilting (or up-shifting) on the level of soul.

Oxford research psychologist Kevin Dutton argues that psychopaths are poised to perform well under pressure because they keep a cool clinical head. Psychopathic personality traits—charm, confidence, ruthlessness, coolness under pressure—can, in the right doses, be a good thing. Not all psychopaths are violent, he says, and some of them are just the sort of people society can count on in a crisis![22] Do we all need a small dose of Psychopath Power or Psychopath Medicine on occasion?!

Activity #13: A Dose of Psychopathic Medicine

Please go to a place where you can be undisturbed for a while. Bring paper and pen.

Human beings are emotional creatures. We like to think that we are extremely rational but often our emotions run the show. In contrast psychopaths are known for keeping cool under pressure.

Try to think of situation in your life that would benefit from an extremely unemotional, sharp-eyed clinical approach. Sweep aside all emotions (both your own and those of others involved in this situation) and look at things from a completely cool-headed and strategic frame of mind.

Your emotions are no longer stopping you – what will you do?

- Ask your employer for a salary rise or promotion that has failed to materialise?
- Disentangle yourself from a situation that unfailingly drains you of energy and makes you lose your will to live?
- Make a bold move and reach for something that attracts and frightens you in equal measure? (Rock climbing? Paragliding? Leaving your job and starting your own business…)
- Dare greatly and ask the person you fancy out on a date?

Imagine that your emotions are not acting as a brake – what would you do?

Would you do anything a sane person would regret?

An exercise like this one will not turn you into a psychopath if you were not born one but it may help you dial up your bold/clinical/self-asserted side enough to accomplish something you yearn for. Did you enjoy meeting your Inner Psychopath? Was he/she more or less frightening than you expected? Will you set another date with him or her?

Chapter 14

The Human-centred Paradigm: Anthropomorphism

> *The sceptics continue to argue however, that God did not make man but man made God. The fact is that God and man make and remake each other, but both are real and yet utterly interdependent.*
>
> *If we cannot move beyond the ego and return to God through the cultural doorway of mythos (mythology), there is only the pathway through pathos (suffering). With culture committed to the ego, rather than spirit, nature gets its revenge.*
>
> David Tacey[1]

> *These were not ordinary animals, of course. They could talk, a common talent at the time of Creation, when everyone is an ancestral spirit and a participant in the inauguration of the way things are going to be.*
>
> E.C. Krupp[2]

Anthropomorphism means attributing human characteristics, behaviour or appearance to non-human phenomena (animals, gods, elements, nature). Our modern word is derived from the Greek word *anthropos* (human) and *morphe* (form). The term was first used to refer the process of assigning human characteristics to deities. By the nineteenth century it had acquired a broader meaning of projecting human characteristics onto anything, (a forbidding mountain, a smiling cloud and so forth!)

We live on a hill in London. I vividly remember walking down this hill one day when our eldest son was a three-year-old "hyper-active monkey". He burst into tears and started kicking a tree. I had been busy with one of his brothers and missed something. What happened: "That tree came walking up the hill and smashed right into me!!" -Oh dear... really?

People in all cultures have attributed human characteristics to deities. The Bible says that "God created us in his image" but it would seem that "we create the gods and goddesses in our own image" in equal measure. We cannot escape this phenomenon:

> *Language, widely considered a human characteristic, must also be present in deities if humans are to pray to them.*[3]

In cultures all over the world we find personifications of human qualities such as love, liberty, revenge, death, envy.

Aidos

The Greek goddess Aidos was the goddess (or personification) of modesty, shame, reverence and respect. She was a companion of the goddess Nemesis, the goddess of divine retribution. Aidos represents the feeling of shame and tenderness which restrains human beings from doing wrong, while Nemesis represented righteous indignation aroused by the sight of wicked men receiving undeserved good fortune. Aidos was worshipped in both Greece and Rome. There were altars and sanctuaries dedicated to her.[4]

The Statue of Liberty in NYC is another example of a personification of important values. Sculptor Frederic Auguste Bartholdi was commissioned to design a sculpture to commemorate the centennial of the American Declaration of Independence. The Statue was named "Liberty Enlightening the World" and was a joint effort between America and France, completed in 1886.

Anthropomorphism even occurs in science. The discoverers of the first pulsar initially mistook its regular radio signals for messages from outer space. Then there is the issue of "the canals on Mars"...

One of the greatest astronomers of the nineteenth and early twentieth centuries, Percival Lowell, published some widely read books titled "Mars and Its Canals" (1906) and "Mars as the Abode of Life" (1908). He became obsessed by the straight lines he observed on Mars through his telescope and he concluded that the Red Planet had once been covered by lush greenery but was now desiccated. Therefore, the desperate yet highly intelligent Martians were digging these "canals" to save their home planet. Lowell was proven wrong. However, photographs that NASA has taken in recent years lead us to believe that these "canals" may be evidence of melted salty water running down slopes during the Martian summer period. As is often the case, with rather wild and way-out theories, a small grain of truth (as in *correct perception*) is discovered in them at some later time, when technology advances.

Dragonish Clouds and the Faces of Mountains

Scottish philosopher David Hume (1711 – 1776) said that there is a universal tendency among mankind to conceive all beings like themselves, and to transfer to every object, those qualities, with which they are familiarly acquainted, and of which they are intimately conscious. We find human faces in the moon, armies in the clouds; and by a natural propensity, if not corrected by experience and reflection, ascribe malice or good- will to every thing, that hurts or pleases us.[5] This phenomenon is called Pareidolia.[5] It refers to a type of illusion or misperception involving a vague or obscure stimulus being perceived as something clear and distinct. The historian Ernst Gombrich said that perception is a bet.[6] Pattern recognition was key to the survival of our Neanderthal ancestors, allowing them to identify poisonous plants, distinguish predator from prey, and interpret celestial events.[7]

Total sensory bombardment was essential when, in absence of

libraries, the brain itself had to serve as a library
John E. Pfeiffer[8]

Europeans commonly see a Man in the Moon while Asian people speak of a Moon Rabbit.[9] Even more bizarrely, a significant number of people refuse to believe in events perceived as a proven or historical fact by the rest of the world population. Some people choose to believe that the Holocaust never happened or that well-documented school shootings were "made-up events by the media" (this despite grief-stricken parents appearing on national TV to talk about their loss).

Conspiracy theories

Conspiracy theories are as old as mankind itself. Some people believe that Jesus and Mary Magdalene were married. Others believe that the Nazis did not kill six million Jews during World War Two or that the Holocaust never happened. Despite moon landings and an abundance of space photography some people still choose to believe that the earth is flat. Others believe that Elvis Presley is still alive. Some people believe that the US government has covered up evidence of aliens landing on Earth, and that they are in possession of the dead bodies of said aliens.

Why do such beliefs persist, often despite much evidence to the contrary? For reasons for personal safety and protecting loved ones, a degree of suspicion may be a good thing. We all know gullible people (and how they end up being exploited, misled or hoaxed) and we warn our children of "stranger danger" (though by far the largest amount of child abuse is committed by people the child lives with or knows well, not "strangers").

Expert Sander van der Linden coined the phrase "conspiracy effect".[10] He demonstrated how watching a brief video can colour people's perception of some phenomenon. The example he used was global warming. The fact is that 97% of leading climate scientists have independently concluded that human-caused global warming is real. Yet people will ditch that awareness, within minutes after watching a conspiracy video.[6]

Denial of scientific facts can have serious societal consequences. It may reduce the belief in other scientific facts, such as the link between smoking and lung cancer, or between HIV and AIDS. There currently is a huge debate whether there is such a thing as a vaccination conspiracy theory (or a cover-up of devastating evidence) or if we have a major public health risk if many people do not vaccinate their children. The jury is still out on this one. The jury is still out on hidden evidence of alien visits as well. What we can say is that if vaccines can cause autism, then medical doctors, as authority figures obeyed by many parents are more dangerous to children than most strangers!

Van der Linden demonstrates that people and governments have definitely conspired against each other over the centuries.[10] History proves that beyond any doubt. Belief in one conspiracy can soon become a worldview instead, a lens of perception. Yet the premise of most (not all!) conspiracy theories is inherently unscientific.

Perhaps the most interesting point Van der Linden makes is that conspiracy theories start out with the need to confirm a particular premise (i.e. some evil actor or agent must be responsible). This is what psychologists refer to as a *fundamental attribution error*: the tendency to overestimate the actions of others as being intentional rather than simply the product of (random) situational circumstances.[10] People find randomness uncomfortable because there is no meaning in it. It breeds uncertainty and feelings of powerlessness. For that reason, it is always more comforting to blame someone. Perceived in that light, conspiracy theories turn out to restore a false sense of certainty and "control": someone is responsible for this!

The psychological phenomenon of "scapegoating" serves a similar purpose. Blame someone and then sacrifice them so the rest of us feel better because "the sins have left the community and we all feel safe again". This phrase originates from the goat that was sent into the wilderness on the Day of Atonement by Jewish people.

Psychologists call this "the ego defence of displacement".[12] The phenomenon can also involve non-human entities (objects, animals, demons). Scapegoating played a huge role in the witch trials in both Europe and Salem.

By now we are aware that projection or displacement of our own shadow aspects never works for long, but we can learn a lot about the human imagination by studying phenomena such as scapegoating and conspiracy theories.[13] Professor of Psychology Joseph Paul forgas[13] says that April Fool's tricks often work because they exploit our baseline inclination to accept direct communications from others as reliable and trustworthy. In most face-to-face situations, the threshold of acceptance is fairly low, he says, as humans operate with a "positivity bias" and assume most people act in an honest and genuine way.

So why do people believe in conspiracy theories? Here are some suggestions:

- An intrinsic and narcissistic need for uniqueness: people like feeling that they have access to scarce or secret information
- People can find it difficult to accept that we live in a world where random acts of violence occur therefore it can be more "comforting" to think that a well-organised group of powerful people is behind such events
- People are literally "addicted to answers" (that this is true I know from my own students!)
- Our personal level of trust is set in childhood and it reflects our level of attachment to our parents (meaning how secure, loved and well-supported we felt growing up)
- Those people actively promoting their beliefs (and

> conspiracy theories) creates a "blizzard of misinformation" (Lewandowsky)[14]

Meteorologist David Grimes[15] says that we all share a single world, and the consequences of what we decide from a policy or ethics perspective, affect all of us. If we cannot even agree on basic science, things that shouldn't even be controversial, we [will] have serious problems making decisions.

We need to realise that we are "drawn to patterns," even when there are none. The reality is, we live in a stochastic Universe. It's tempting to draw a narrative, but there's no narrative, there are no waves, we are joining dots in the sand.[14]

The word stochastic means: having a random probability distribution or pattern that may be analysed statistically but may not be predicted precisely.[16]

> A stochastic radiation-filled world model is constructed in which the equation of state is perturbed with a "white noise". The corresponding Fokker-Planck equation is solved. It turns out that the maximum probability path of the world's evolution is that of the Friedman model. However, singularities are no obstacles for the stochastic evolution, and $\sigma 2 \rightarrow \infty$ as $t \rightarrow \infty$.[16]

Yes, right, this too is a well-documented belief underpinned by mathematical equations. It is a consensual reality for scientists. Science certainly has its place, in my "cosmology" but it is not my dominant lens of perception. Shamanism does not follow the rules of science – though I am enough of a scholar to always compare what the spirits tell me with scientific theories and discoveries. I hope and believe that one day they will be less far apart than they are today.

> *Homo sapiens is probably an intrinsically gullible species. We owe our evolutionary success to culture, our unique ability to receive, trust and act on stories we get from others, and so accumulate a shared view about the world. In a way, trusting others is second nature.*
>
> *But not everything we hear from others is useful or even true. There are countless ways people have been misled, fooled and hoaxed, sometimes for fun, but more often, for profit or for political gain.*
>
> Joseph Paul Forgas[13]

We live in an era of information overload. So much information is just one click, or a brief google search, away that it is hard to work out what the most reliable source is – and what to reject or discount. We also live in an age of spin doctoring, meaning that conscious efforts are made by politicians, manufacturers, media personalities, Youtubers and so forth to present things in a very specific light (that inevitably serves their own agenda in some way). To succeed in this world, we now all need to have a "brand" and market ourselves accordingly. I have huge resistance to all those things. I don't want to *have or be* a brand! I prefer to always vision and to forever learn, rethink, make a fresh start... This is the great cycle of creation and indeed Life itself: vision or seed, creation/gestation, a creation/art object/project and then yielding to destruction. Life renews itself through the eternal cycle of birth-death-rebirth.

Gullibility and credulity also need a mention: gullibility is a tendency to be easily manipulated into believing something is true when it isn't. Credulity is a close cousin. It refers to the willingness to believe unlikely propositions with no evidence behind them.

Inevitably the positivity bias has a shadow manifestation: the Pollyanna Principle[17] this refers to the human tendency to focus on the positive and positive words and terms with higher frequency during a conversation.

Generally, people who are mentally healthy and not suffering from depression tend to focus more on the positives than the negatives, and they are prone to recalling more positive than negative phenomena from their memories. It has also been demonstrated that people prefer communicating good news and avoid looking at upsetting pictures or footage. We like thinking of ourselves as optimists rather than pessimists and apparently many people overestimate (slightly) how attractive they are to others!

> *Doctor Clay Jones puts it this way: "Anyone who isn't clinically depressed is on some level more like Pollyanna than Eeyore".*
> Courtney Ackerman[17]

There is a lot to be said for actively learning to navigate the shadowlands so we are not caught out by shadow and negative events or people. Our powers of perception are sharpened: we operate choices in how we set our filters of perception!

Social media exert a relentless pressure on us to "appear to have the perfect life". We (young people especially) are fooled by these social pressures: we post selfies and profile pictures that make us look (almost) like models (or twenty years younger than our true age!), pictures of (seemingly) perfect families, cute pets, amazing holidays. It does not take much for people, who are struggling to find their identity (or struggling *full stop*), to feel "inferior" because these things feel out of reach.

Animism

Animism refers to the spiritual belief that All That Is (all objects, places, creatures and phenomena) possess a distinct in-dwelling spiritual essence. In plain English this means that all those things - even the ones our culture teaches us to perceive as inanimate - are inspirited entities. Mountains and rivers have indwelling spirits and winds have spirit too (and different winds, from different directions, have very different personalities!) According to anthropologists this perception may well date back to the Palaeolithic Age when hunter-gatherers existing in a close relationship with animals and nature spirits.

"Gods and Other Humans"

My perception of reality is that human beings are always dreaming and co-creating with other life forms. As I go about my business, I actively open myself to the dreaming and whispers of plants, the memories held in land and mountains, to the voice and colour of the wind and so forth.

Walking between the worlds it is my observation that all of Creation is engaged in a constant dance between form and formlessness. We come to Earth to experience a life deeply rooted in matter. This allows us to have experiences we cannot access without having a physical body: food and drink, sexuality and fertility, money and property. Earth allows us to arrive at very physical material (three-dimensional) expressions of our dreams and visions.

In the other world, however, everything is non-material and energetic in nature, meaning that it is evershifting and fluid. When shamans engage in shapeshifting they access that very special otherworldly power: the dance between form and formlessness, the skill of taking on another appearance at will. Spirits and deities take delight in taking different forms (after all they are not "married to one definite physical form" the way that human beings are). They will often take a specific shape just to make a point, teach us a lesson or be of assistance.

I once did a shamanic healing session with a young boy. He was experiencing issues in school with bullying and friends turning against him. His family had a strong connection to (and belief in) angels and angelic helpers. We asked for one angelic helper to commit to being with him 24/7 for him to feel guided and protected. I clearly perceived this being or presence as a "luminous field" around him and shielding him. To my eyes it had no shape or human features at all, but it embraced and enveloped him completely, thus creating a safe zone between him and the world. The boy himself said (the moment his helper arrived): "Wow! It is an angel in a Batman costume -that is so cool!!" His mother could see the superhero as well.

To my mind there is no conflict here. A luminous being, in possession of powers greater than we humans have access to, has arrived and all three people present sense this. I am seeing luminosity, unconditional love and a protective "field". The boy and his mother see an angel (twice as tall as a human being!) wearing a superhero costume. We are all seeing what we need to see for the greatest healing to occur. I can check that the boy's energetic field is secure and guarded. The mother knows that her son is in safe hands. The boy himself says: "Wow, when this helper is with me, no one is going to mess with me!"

To me the debate whether "gods and angels look like human beings or not" is a non-issue. They will take human form (and delight in the details they select for this purpose) when this serves a situation but manifest in a very different way at another time. I have been in situations where I urgently requested guidance and a strong gust of wind came on a windless day -or a cloud of a very significant shape suddenly crossed overhead in a cloudless sky. To me these interactions with other worlds and the spirits are incredibly playful. However, to me an angel-shaped cloud appearing on a cloudless day is not just "my human mind imposing humanoid patterns" - to me this is a message and gift.

You will not catch me joining passionate debates about whether the Norse goddess Frigg always carries a bunch of keys or not, or whether every god that appears carrying a big hammer is a manifestation of Thor. From my point of view those details are ultimately specific to the viewer. An encounter occurs. A human being is fortunate enough to have an audience with a divine being. I won't limit that with pigeon-holes designed by human minds.

Divine in origin but not God

Years of shamanic practice have taught me that the boundary between humans and gods/spirits is less well-defined than Christianity would have us believe. Not all gods are omnipotent, and humans have a divine aspect or divine spark that animates and ensouls them. Divinity is a spectrum with many surprises and permutations.

However, one of the shadows of the human imagination (paired with a heavy dose of narcissism or ego inflation), is human beings believing that they *are God.* Every human has a divine spark that ensouls them and an innate divinity because of that but that is not the same as believing that you are God! Yet, this does occur. It is not an uncommon delusion in acute psychiatry (people might hear voices telling them that they are God and end up in a psychiatric hospital). This is called the God Complex.

My father used to joke that "If I walk the streets claiming that I am God, some people will believe me and follow me". He might have been right about that, but I think he could equally well have ended up being followed by the local police!

The profession of spiritual teaching carries its own unique shadow:

Higher octave: trustworthy spiritual teacher or mentor who imparts genuine teachings and accelerates/supports the learning journey of their students

Lower octave: person who needs to focus on their own healing but is running from pain by chasing the illusion that they are able to heal others. People who are entirely unconscious of their own shadow engaging others in "shadow theatre" (enactment of key life wounds) and charging them money for the dubious privilege.

Near Enemy: guru, charlatan, dangerous deluded leader – are person who is actively out to hoodwink you, have sex with you as "an impersonal godly act" or run off with your money.

It seems obvious that people with narcissistic personality disorder should not become spiritual leaders but surprisingly often they manage to do this! They also become leaders in many other fields: business, science and the medical profession.

Today's business leaders have higher profiles than ever before due to 24/7 media coverage. We are more business-focussed: we actively compare companies (before we hire or purchase), we consult customer review sites, we brand ourselves and actively create on-line profiles. The business world is in transition and collectively we face immense challenges, this calls for charismatic and visionary leadership. However, our need for strong cool-headed strategy-focussed leaders sometimes attracts narcissistic leaders instead. Much has been written about the proliferation of narcissism in CEO's and other top jobs. The word narcissism comes from ancient Greece, but Freud was the first person who used this word in our contemporary sense. He once wrote a key paper about narcissism.[18]

Because narcissists don't "get stuck in empathy" (the way many of us do), they can cut through structures that serve no more and present new ideas with charm and conviction. Because of their charm they can unleash waves of new initiatives and (oddly) social change. In shamanism we speak of tricksters: change agents that upset the apple cart and thus establish a new cosmic order. Narcissistic leaders can be embodiments of the trickster archetype, *but* they can also wipe out many good things that others have laboured to create before them.

The dangers of amateurs and spirituality

When the going gets tough, the amateurs get going.... Spirituality has become a growth industry meaning that many people now wish to claim their "slice of the pie". We see people attending one weekend workshop in shamanism and offering their services as "shamans". I receive many emails along the following lines: "I was born a great healer. Unlike you I did not need to train with any teachers. I naturally know what to do. I do the same work you do!" – Yeah, right.... Red flags flapping and alarm bells ringing... Having a talent is not the same thing as honing it with discipline, a commitment to shadow work, and arriving a professional code of ethics. I would not choose to see an amateur dentist and I take even greater care with my soul!

One very interesting article about this subject is the following one by Spender Orey about the dangers of spiritual amateurism in America[19]. It is a detailed book review for the book "A Death on Diamond Mountain" by Scott Carney.[20]

Carney describes how in February 2012, Christie McNally and her husband, Ian Thorson, retreated to a cave in the high desert of Arizona for a session of intense meditation. They drank only rainwater, and they ate sparingly. They refused to filter their water—preferring to purify it with their minds. They became violently ill. McNally recovered and kept meditating, but Thorson fell unconscious. McNally waited two days to summon help, but by then Thorson was beyond rescue. The official cause of death was dehydration, but what really killed Ian Thorson was a vision quest gone terribly wrong. Their faith in their own spiritual powers and reincarnation was unshakeable and the outcome was death for one of them.

McNally and Thorson were high-stakes meditators. They took vows to act as guides and teachers for others, even after they themselves had achieved enlightenment. Their commitment would end only after every other being became enlightened, too—even if this took many lifetimes. Thorson was attracted by promises of happiness, ancient and timeless wisdom, and a spiritual humanitarian mission. So, when McNally saw her husband dying of dysentery, she had to decide whether to call for help or to trust him to heal his bad karma spiritually. If he failed to do so in this life, she believed, he'd have another chance in the next, or the one after that.[19]

The author of this article goes on to explain that much of the forbidden, obscure, hidden or secret esoteric knowledge that once made Buddhism (or indeed shamanism) and other belief systems difficult to study have now been made accessible through modern media (books, DVD's, interviews with experts, on-line workshops). This puts the material in the hands of amateurs or only-partially schooled people. They often fail to see the nuances a more advanced student will eventually grasp, take things out of context and "run with it". This can literally be lethal as the Diamond Mountain death illustrates.[19]

Writing my first book (Natural Born Shamans[13]) I faced a dilemma: I wanted to write about the luminous power of shamanic healing work in the context of children – but I was terrified of writing a book people would use as a handbook. I described the benefits and key issues, but I deliberately omitted descriptions how certain specialist procedures are performed. For very little money (and even less effort) amateurs can now study a lot of esoteric material.

Author of the Diamond Mountain Death article Spencer Orey correctly points out that the decontextualization involved in learning a religion through DVDs or YouTube videos makes it easy to ignore, for example, the complicated nature of the spread of Buddhism to Tibet—a bloody tale that is more Game of Thrones than A People's History. Western "converts" to Buddhism are often accused of meditating too intensely, as if it were a job or sport. The benefits of meditation are reported constantly in popular media, but few beginners know about the maladies that afflict overzealous meditators. Carney lists a few: restlessness, sleeplessness, and Kundalini syndrome, an uncontrollable oscillation between ecstasy and rage.[19]

Some people like to think that spirituality is "all love and light". Other people know that this can never be so, but they still prefer to believe that they themselves can stay in the love-and-light zone and avoid walking on the dark side. These people soon become a danger to themselves and others. They peddle a spirituality that ultimately fails to deliver and (even worse) they lead others into danger by presenting extreme simplifications.

If any of this sounds like pure fantasy, please log into Facebook and scroll down the pages of some people who pride themselves on being light workers or human angels. Some dialogues are offensive (and yes, dangerous) because they distort genuine spiritual teachings beyond recognition! ("If your son was murdered, he himself must have killed someone in a previous lifetime!" "If this happened to you then you must have created or attracted this on some level and hold only yourself responsible!")

If you wish to understand what might just happen to spiritually naïve people:

Carney ends with his own evolving fears of Roach. As public condemnation of Roach grew, lamas in Tibet offered Carney a protection spell. Carney declined it, and swiftly he was beset by misfortune. Wasps buzzed around him, he grew sick, and his marriage began to fall apart. Carney doesn't say whether he thinks his experiences were coincidence elevated by paranoia or the product of real karmic magic. But his experience shows how potent spirituality can be, even for wised-up outsiders attempting to study it impartially. Hokum or not, this stuff is anything but harmless.[19]

What we speak becomes the house we live in
Hafiz[22]

Activity #14: Dispelling Pollyanna

This activity gives you the opportunity to dispel your Inner Pollyanna assuming that you do not need her services any longer. By now you have more sophisticated spiritual tools for navigating difficult days!

Pollyanna was a best-selling 1913 novel by the author Eleanor H. Porter and a classic in terms of children's literature. The name of the main character has become a byword for a person with a highly optimistic outlook.[17] Pollyanna Whittier is a young organ living with her stern spinster aunt Polly. (Note the opposites: shadow Polly and angelic Pollyanna – it is the same name!) Pollyanna's philosophy evolves around what she calls "The Glad Game" and that involves finding something to be glad about in every situation, no matter how bleak (or far-fetched).

Do a fearless inventory, asking yourself the following question: can I admit to situations where I have used positivity to avoid or stamp out a darker reality or truth?

- Have you ever said to people: "You will be fine!" or "It will be fine!" knowing fully well that this is not the case (but you were in a rush or could not bear to be fully present to their pain or situation?)
- Do you select the most flattering picture of yourself for your website or social media profile – and then allow yourself to think that this is what you always look like?
- Do you drink too much (eat too much, check your phone too often etc.) and tell yourself "I am fine, I could drop that habit any time?!"
- Where else do you use relentless positivity as a shield, a cover, a form of escapism, a social lie?
- Do you use false positivity to be liked or gain popularity?
- Where and how do you lie to yourself?
- Are you willing to stop lying to yourself and, by extension, to others?!

Now take a moment to call in Pollyanna (or your inner equivalent of her and remember that "she" may well appear as a "he" too!) Thank her for the lesson that she has taught you. Tell her that positivity certainly has a place in your life – but that you do not want to overdose on this, that from now on you wish to be honest with yourself and others; fully present to whatever the day or moment brings.

Ask her to move on and move in with someone who needs her special medicine... wave her off, watch her (him) walk away... How does that feel?

Chapter 15

We Are the Ancestors

This week (December 2018) I spoke to a homeless woman on a train. She said that she really looked forward to Christmas because the hostels have more resources during the festive season. This was her wish list for Christmas 2018:

- A bed
- Warmth
- Food

Birth on Earth

Just as the moon cycles through each month every 28-30 days, its energy waxes and wanes through a person's life every 28-30 years in the same pattern, from new to full and back again. We experience the beginning of the cycle as a new start -perhaps a graduation, a marriage or divorce, a new home or job. The energy of this cycle waxes and builds for 15 years, peaking at the Full Moon, then begins to release over the next 15 years, finally reaching the Dark Moon phase. The seeds of the new cycle are planted here, and the next phase of life begins.

Susan Rossi[1]

A human baby is not born a blank slate. Based on years of ancestral healing work with individuals and delving deeply into their karmic history I have come to believe that most human beings have had previous incarnations on earth. On the level of soul, we choose the family and circumstances we are born into because it provides an optimal match for our learning and issues to be activated in this life. *(Our everyday selves do not remember this!)* We are born into an ancestral web where the weave consists of major life events, decisions, choices and unresolved issues left by our ancestors (whose who came before us and so gave us this gift of life). Through our bloodline and DNA, they also pass on their talents and personal/physical characteristics. Then our own life starts rolling with all the positives and negatives inherent in that. In addition to all this we are shaped by external forces such as: the time we live in, the period in history, the cultural and political climate, natural disasters and so forth. Given the right attitude even the negative often turn out to be positives or blessings.

Forces that shape human lives

We all incarnate on earth with DNA, soul karma and collective karma inheritances:

- Unresolved issues from previous lifetimes seek balancing and healing in this life (most commonly referred to as individual soul karma)
- We are all held in an Ancestral web where everyone has their place but unresolved issues and trauma belonging to ancestors' manifests in subsequent generations (as health problems, accidents, nightmares etc.), this is also known as collective karma inheritances
- Physical DNA passes on traits, talents, physical attributes, predispositions to certain illnesses, disabilities or genetic conditions etc.[2]
- Any family of origin will have greatly varying levels of healthy functioning or dysfunctional patterns -depending on individual. *(This presents a double whammy for people who are adopted: they belong to two sets of families and are affected by both!)*
- There is collective karma: families, communities, societies and sub- groups in all those categories consist of people that create (and work out) collective karma together.

(In shamanic healing work, especially working with different members of friendship groups, I observe how groups of people incarnate at, roughly, the same time. As peers they make amends for things they did before, they arrive as change agents at a specific time, they arrive to prepare the Earth for future generations)

- "Life happens" no human being escapes the cards that life on earth deal us: some good and some not so great. The "perfect life" does not exist – human beings learn from mistakes. A human life free of suffering and grief does not exist either. Happiness is a choice, a state of mind – not the absence of negative emotions or painful experiences.
- External forces such as time in history, location, our place on the poverty-privilege spectrum, political events, wars, natural disasters -and so forth play an important part in shaping lives.
- Human beings can have karma (unresolved issues or unfinished business) with land and non-human beings as well: animals, forests, mountains and oceans. Some people come to earth to work specifically on their relationship to those forces. (The spirits told me once that I am an apprentice of the wind, in this lifetime!)

One gift that we typically receive from our family (of origin) is that they are a constellation of people that we did not (consciously at least!) select and we cannot walk away from them so easily either (some people do break all ties, but this is a traumatic and final-resort option for when all else fails). We *choose* our friends, but we ultimately have the option of falling out with friends or losing touch with them (in other words: there is an escape clause!) Our family (by either birth or adoption) tends to stay in our life and shape our lives. They pass on genetic material (as well as ancestral entanglements), provide lasting influences (or conditioning) and they also impose obligations and commitments.

Our family of origin is often a microcosm for the larger world. It holds up a mirror for the much larger entity that is The Human Family. Any family has members who make it their business to push themselves to the very edges of human perception and consciousness – while other members focus on mastering different skills or situations.

The Ancestral Web and honouring ancestors

In all tribal or indigenous societies, the honouring of ancestors plays a central role. Active efforts are made to remember their names and tell their stories. Especially on feast days and at special times of the year the whole community honours them. (The western festival of Halloween is a distorted manifestation of this older custom). The ancestors are consulted about important matters pertaining to community life (by means of divination and oracular work performed by the shaman or religious leader). Offerings are made to the ancestors: special food and drink are prepared and offered. They also receive small amounts of the food and drink prepared for living members of the tribe. If they are ancestors from living memory, their favourite food and drink may be offered on feast days.

Any indigenous elder would tell you that not honouring the ancestors is nothing short of a crime on the level of keeping the ancestral web healthy and vibrant. Not just that but stagnant energies will affect our everyday lives (no matter if we believe in this or not).

Believing that something doesn't exist does not free our lives from its existence and influence on us!

We are not going to have a healthy culture, free of all the old trauma, pain and ancient imprints currently tearing at the very fabric of our lives and therefore society, as long as we do not learn to honour our ancestors again and embrace other ancient tribal values. We need to reinstate the following things:

- Giving the ancestors their proper place and role, honouring and consulting them
- Giving old people their rightful place as highly respected Elders
- Rites of Passage for our young people (in which those same Elders play a key role)
- Rites of Passage for many other transitions in life
- Releasing fears of Old Age and Death, releasing our obsession with youth and a very limited (or narrow) concept of beauty and success

Anything that is hurting, "shouting" or comes to attention in any other way does so because it seeks healing or balancing!

The ancestral continuum

All of us stand on the shoulders of those who came before us. None of us exist in a vacuum. All of us have our place on a larger ancestral continuum. The moment we realise just how profoundly the choices and experiences of our ancestors shape us -we also realise just how many ancestors we have and how huge our ancestral field is!

Transpersonal spirituality

Nations and cultural groups of people have ancestral fields of their own. The social, political and environmental decisions of the past continue to shape us. Not only on the most obvious level (in the sense that we inherited the tangible results of these outcomes) but also on the energetic level: if my ancestors committed atrocities a few centuries ago (and Dutch people did commit atrocities against native peoples in Pennsylvania, by means of just one example I am actively working on right now) I am not free of that. On the ancestral level I carry an obligation to make amends and do what I can to balance this even if these acts were committed long before I was born, by people who were not my immediate biological ancestors or blood relatives.

Contemporary culture is individualistic in the extreme. We like to believe that everything begins and ends with me-me-me; that our lives belong to us, for us to use as we like. Again, tribal peoples will tell us that this excessive focus on self-interest acts as an acid eroding our fragile social web.

Acting in service to another person's soul

I often take my students through a list of the pay offs of illness and drama. When I first put this to the group there generally is a blank look, but people soon get it.

- *Attention!* ("People feel sorry for me meaning that they are now forced to pay me more attention than they normally would")
- *Sick leave* ("We are excused from performing our duties and if we are lucky, we may still be paid while not meeting our professional obligations" -but no such luck for self-employed people)
- *A lessening of expectations* (other people expect less of us, meaning more space for ourselves)
  (Feel free to add your own observations to this list)

In families the threads of web connecting us to others are often yanked on. When we explain that we see a very different picture, we come across as cold and uncaring. (I am not really a cold and uncaring person, but I am actively working to unhook myself from karmic drama and entanglements).

One tough but liberating lesson I have learned over the years is that *it is often preferable to act in service to the soul of the person* -as opposed to jumping every time they push our buttons or pull on our heart strings. This judgement call can never be made from a place of ego. Only our spirit allies and a person's higher self (sacred or divine self that exists outside time) can provide guidance on this.

I impose this same principle on myself. When something hugely challenging happens, I will allow myself some down time, grieving and processing time, cave time, licking my wounds. However, soon I will ask myself the question: what lesson is being served up here *on the level of soul*? Once I gain clarity on what the best (most honourable) way forward is, I will act on that. Often that is not the way other people expect me to behave, but as long I am acting in alignment with divine guidance - I am at peace within myself.

Inner work is activism too

Life is a Hall of Mirrors and we need to work imaginatively and creatively with these mirrors. We will not achieve world peace until we find inner piece! As long as we are at war with ourselves, with our shadow and hidden (undesirable) aspects of ourselves, with the old parental or authority voices ringing loudly in our ears, with the critical self-talk we immerse ourselves in, with the people we have not forgiven, with the things we have not forgiven ourselves for, with the dreams we failed to live, with the brave things we failed to do, there will no world peace.

To go on a world peace march without addressing the conflicts within ourselves and in our own lives, does not bring peace. As one very dear friend of mine said recently: "Inner work is activism too". She is right!

Activity #15: Honouring Our Ancestors

Go to a place where you can be undisturbed. Bring paper and pen. Light a candle. Take one moment to contemplate the fact that you only exist because of all the people who were your ancestors.

Now gaze into the flame and ask your ancestors to step forward. Express a wish to meet them and seek their guidance. You may not "see" them (even with your eyes closed) but you will sense them, smell them, hear them or feel them arriving in your heart.

Thank them for their gifts. Tell them the family news. Seek guidance on some issue that burdens you. The answer may come in many ways (and often not immediately). A friend may send you a link, you may be gifted a book. An acquaintance or colleague might say something and you just know that your ancestors are speaking through them, sending you a message.

Get in the habit of lighting a candle for your ancestors at regular intervals. Consult them. Bring them some small offerings: flowers, food or drink, a thimble of alcohol, scent, incense. Share a little of your own food with them. Mark their birthdays (if you know them). I recommend that you agree on a regular day with yourself for honouring your Unknown or Forgotten Ancestors. What matters is not exactly *how* you do it, *but doing it from a place of genuine honouring and opening yourself to connection*. The blessings will be beyond measure.

PS

When I speak to people about the need to honour ancestors, people will unfailingly mention toxic ancestors, abusive or unworthy ancestors and so forth. If this is an issue for you: add the word *compassionate*. Meet and honour your *compassionate ancestors* (meaning loving ancestors whom you feel at peace with). Dealing with troublesome ancestors who are not at peace falls outside the scope of this book – but means of doing so exist!

Chapter 16

Reigniting the human imagination

What is hedonic adaptation?
A most striking example of this was a 1978 psychological study that evaluated the happiness levels of recent lottery winners, and recently injured paraplegics relative to the general population. As you'd expect, the lottery winners were pretty upbeat immediately after their win, and the paraplegics were pretty pissed off. But within just two months, both groups had returned back to the average level of happiness.
Mr. Money Mustache[1]

The Tomb as Womb

We fail ourselves and others when we do not fully flex the multi-dimensional muscle that is our imagination:

- We often use clichés rather than original speech.
- We don't think enough about the way we think.
- We don't question core assumptions in our cultural heritage and we don't spot the gaps or black holes (that people from another culture see immediately!) either.
- We are blind to the miracles that surround us daily. A healthy human body is a miracle (one we pray for once we lose it). A safe birth is a miracle. Every plane that takes off and lands safely at destination is miracle of modern engineering. Washing machines and computers are miracles and the result of the talent and creativity of some people in service to the rest of us. The internet is a miracle (with its own shadows and Minotaur lurking!)
- Only a relatively small group of people is actively engaged with retrieving old wisdom and returning the teachings of

our ancestors.

- We have lost most of the wisdom of our ancient ancestors and we don't even remember what we have lost or how much.
- We often don't ask the right questions (such as: why do teenage boys not cause trouble in tribal societies living the traditional way?)
- Because we are so blind, things are often hidden in plain view. *(I keep my witches' broomstick right by the front door. Almost no one ever notices it!)*
- After centuries of an uneasy partnership between science and Christianity dominating mainstream western perception, we often do not question what passes for common sense in our culture. We do not make the distinction between common sense and uncommon sense.

> *First, we must accept that every culture has a science, that is, a way of defining, controlling, and predicting events in the natural world. Then we must accept that every science is legitimate in terms of the culture from which it grew. The transformation of the word science as a distinct rationality valued above magic is uniquely European. It is not common to most non-Western societies, where magic and science and religion can easily co-exist. The empirical, scientific realm of understanding and inquiry is not readily separable from a more abstract, religious realm.*
> E.C. Krupp[2]

We collectively choose to believe that God is male (a patriarchal form of anthropomorphism) and that "good" people go to Heaven after death. We do not question the fact that our concept of Heaven resembles something out of a picture book for three-year-olds, who cannot yet read or write. We do not admit either that we all carry the capacity for evil within us. Not just that, we are all implicated in evil because it is not possible to live a "100%

spiritually clean" life. This is an ontological dilemma – but it is also an invitation for tremendous growth on the level of soul.

All it takes to actively do harm is *to be unaware*. We do not need to take to the streets carrying a knife or gun to do immense harm. There is only a hairline crack between blessing and harm. Through lack of awareness we tumble down that crack.

I have spent many hours pondering the difference between personal shadow and Wetiko. An incident that played out between two colleagues on social media was the ultimate teaching for me: personal shadow is where we do not own our negative side and take responsibility for the expressions this seeks (inevitably affecting others unless we are a Desert Saint living in total isolation). However, my conclusion was that *personal shadow crosses over into Wetiko when the actions of one or just a few people infect a whole community and this infection starts leading a life of its own.*

Children, fools, magicians and mentally unbalanced people often show a lot of *uncommon sense*, they will observe that the emperor is not wearing any clothes -but we do not listen. We prefer to keep our blinkers on and not rock the boat.

The conundrum of tamed teenagers

The reason that teenage boys do not run riot in those indigenous societies which still follow their ancestral traditions is that those boys are initiated by Elders. They are taken away from their families and undergo rites of passage (some of which are pretty severe and gruesome by contemporary Western standards). They leave their communities as boys or children but return as young men ready to take their place on society and shoulder the responsibilities inherent in that role.

As a mother of three sons I appreciate that we cannot blindly copy what is happening in those tribes. It would constitute cultural appropriation for a start! It would also be inappropriate for our lifestyle and culture. What we need to do instead is making the effort to understand the underlying reasons and principles. Next we need to use our imagination to arrive at rites of passage that honour our own culture. We need to research any traditions our ancestors had that amounted to rites of passage (and they might have been called something else).

Cultural illiteracy

I am using the example of teenage boys as my starting point because I believe this might be the easiest example to understand. There is plenty of evidence in the media of what teenage boys get up to in order to self-initiate or start shadow communities such as street gangs.

A human being needs many rites of passage during an average human life span. In my first book I included suggestions for simple DIY ceremonies marking such occasions. In our culture we celebrate birth and birthdays, but we offer little in the way of marking a miscarriage or stillborn child. That fact makes us behave awkwardly around people who suffer this loss and that can add to the pain and not feeling understood. Our imagination fails us here.

In our culture we are collectively obsessed with youth (and a very narrow concept of beauty at that: young, toned, symmetrical features, skinny and fit) and we fail to make old people the valuable resource they really are: Elders of the community, wisdom keepers, initiators -and also those who often have time to really listen to young people and be fully present to them. (Instead we have young people running riot and older people who are made to feel "past their sell-by-date").

Wise blood

We view menstruation as a Curse and the menopause as an affront. We speak of "women of a certain age" and this is neither kind nor imaginative. When I started the menopause early (at age 37!) the words that gave me comfort were *wise blood.* This refers to the spiritual teaching that when women do not bleed any more, knowledge and wisdom accumulates in their blood helping them become wise women and true elders.

Collectively we are in denial about death and we hide it from view. Death is our greatest teacher: we can only live life to the full when we face death and conquer our fear of death. Most human beings die many small symbolic deaths before making their final transition.

In traditional/tribal societies girls are initiated into the mysteries of birth and death by the women. In interviews I have been challenged on this by feminists, transgender people and women's rights campaigners. They told me that it is no longer politically correct to say out loud (or on camera) that girls are treated differently from boys in tribal societies (and that there might be anything remotely desirable about this!) With all respect for contemporary western views and the acceptance of gender fluidity – the fact remains that tribal and ancient societies live(d) by different principles than we aspire to and I am not going rewrite history to please a contemporary audience. The same principle applies when I teach material from the Northern European Tradition and talk about eighth (or eleventh) century Scandinavia. Contemporary standards of political correctness are not appropriate for that period.

It has been stated that "We live life backwards and therefore we never appreciate what we have: we should experience old age before we get to youth, we ought to raise our children and then enjoy our child-free years.... the natural order of things is upside down!"

The hedonic adaptation principle

This brings us to the hedonic adaptation principle: there is no absolute standard for anything: everything depends on our frame of reference. Over time we take even our most tremendous strokes of good luck for granted and we learn to live with the most appalling setbacks.

I have tried extremely hard (as many parents do!) to provide for my children certain things I lacked and craved as a child: stability, commitment to one location, continuation of schools and education, freedom of expression etc.

My children have never known any other "parenting climate" so they will never thank me for it. For them this is "the norm". Not only that, they still feel they have plenty to complain about – and this normal in our culture! As someone who has worked with slum children in developing countries, I admit that this gets to me at times! My rational mind knows that I cannot compare them to street children in South America. They do not have that frame of reference.

Happiness averaging

Hedonic adaptation means that "you will pretty soon get used to whatever you achieve or lose in life", also called *happiness averaging.*

Harvard researchers have delved into the most challenging issues of aging, in the hope that their work would reveal clues to leading healthy and happy lives. They started their longitudinal study during the Great Depression. After nearly 80 years (!) only a few of their subjects are still alive (all in their mid-90s now). Unfortunately, women were not in the original study but over time the scientists expanded their work to include the offspring of these men (now in their 50s and 60s). Their biggest "revelation" was that how happy we are in our relationships has a powerful influence on our health. Taking care of your body is important but taking care of your relationships is a form of self-care too!

Here is a list of their findings, (taken from Science Says Happier People Have These 9 Things in Common by Kevin Loria, Independent)[3]:

1. Key relationships: we all need strong relationships with other people we can trust to support us
2. Time beats money: happier people prefer more time over more money
3. Having enough money to support yourself and pay your bills (people's well-being rises only up to a certain point, as income increases)
4. Slowing down to reflect on the good things in life (appreciation and gratitude practices, "counting your blessings", smelling the roses...)
5. Performing random acts of kindness for others
6. Increased levels of physical activity are connected to higher levels of happiness. (Exercise can apparently help mitigate the symptoms of some mental illnesses)
7. Fun over material items -spending money on valuable experiences increases happiness
8. Staying in the moment, being fully present to What Is (people who practice mindfulness experience greater well-being)
9. Time with friends, especially time spent in the company of happy people

Harnessing the Imagination

I try to actively harness my imagination. Recent example: I work from home meaning that I "get the last shower" in our family of five and I am also tasked with running the family breakfast "show" and clearing up again as everyone dashes out of the house. This daily marathon takes ninety minutes. As my three sons are growing older, I get increasingly annoyed with everyone leaving their dirty dishes in the sink and the milk dripping all over the table, yelling: "Help! I am late!" or "Mum, did you steal my chemistry book?! Where IS it?!"-"Best not to leave things lying around the house darling, as we all know about Dad's obsession with tidying (hiding!), don't we?!"

I hasten to say that our three sons all have domestic responsibilities - they all cook one day a week, mow the lawn and peg out laundry. Sadly, this doesn't stop them from turning their rooms into bombsites and leaving their shoes on the stairs for my students to trip over. So anyway... after some grumpy mornings and a bad start to my own working day I decided I needed to reframe this:

- It is a privilege to be able provide a stable family home for our three children. A home I love and take pride in!
- I may be swimming (occasionally drowning) in testosterone but I adore my three handsome sons!
- Let's put on some music and sing along while tidying this kitchen....
- Most people I know do not work from home. They make their way to work on the London public transport system. I hear constant stories about overcrowded trains, delays and stress.
- I will stand in my kitchen every morning and I say to myself: lucky me! I am not hanging in someone else's sweaty armpit just now on a lurching London Tube train, desperately trying to get to work on time. I will just clear the kitchen and then go to work *here.* I am a most fortunate person: I do what I love and get paid for it without leaving my own home!

This kind of pep talk to oneself sounds silly, but the core principle works. I apply it to other situations as well. When I catch myself thinking: "The way my 80-year old mother repeats things over-and-over drives me a little mad" I reframe this and think: "I am fortunate to still have my mother as many people around me have lost their mother. I shall choose to use this time well. Can I shift her focus to telling me things I actually want to know (rather than telling me things I have heard a million times before)?!" What I have started doing is making a wish list of questions about her own childhood, my grandparents, her childhood experiences during world war II and so forth. I fire those at her during lulls in the conversation. I have also filmed my youngest son interviewing her about her own childhood (he is an eager amateur historian).

By being a bit more organised and bringing some focus to this I have started hearing about things that will be lost to me the day she makes her final transition. She loves being put in the role of Family Elder who has memories to share. *(And yes, of course I sometimes steal a chemistry book from a 16-year old on those days I make love potions or run witchy experiments in alchemy!)*

Harnessing the collective imagination

Collectively speaking we need to get our imagination in gear too. Rather than making certain people feel different, we need to see how they are differently able and meet them on that level with an open mind and supportive attitude. (If you are able-bodied there is a lot you can learn from a person in a wheelchair or a person with missing limbs!) We need to first imagine and then create roles and opportunities for older people to become the compassionate Elders and Wisdom Keepers they are at heart

One morning in November 2016 I was on a red London double-decker bus. Two elderly men, one black and one white (obviously close friends), board the 436 bus in Peckham. I offer them my seat -they say no thanks, love, not necessary! They both walk precariously with a stick. As the bus swings its way through Peckham, they are knocked around and their movements turn into a dance. Says the one man to the other: "I have had not had such fun since I was on a roller coaster as a child!" The other man replies: "Indeed! And as we are both still standing, we are both winners I think!" They leave the bus together, moving *very* slowly and laughing *very* loudly. Oh yes, they are winners, and great teachers for all of us!! We need to:

- Cooperate with minority cultures and colonized peoples in a quest to harness the human imagination to heal rifts, old wounds and unravel old imprints. This can only be a collective responsibility where we hold ourselves accountable for the things our long-dead ancestors did.
- Use our imagination to rise above continuously re-enacting wounded expressions of both masculine and feminine (engaging in a dysfunctional dance). To accomplish this, we need to dance joyfully in the Void place (the Divine Womb) where pristine imprints are birthed and retrieved.
- Use our imagination to release "conflict and war consciousness", celebrating difference, sharing the Earth and all human resources generously and respectfully.
- Release poverty consciousness
- Adopt the principle of supportive cooperation rather than competition
- Find ways of releasing redundant fear. Fear has its place as a red flag or warning bell, but it can never be the base line for every decision we make in life
- Use our imagination to become pioneers and move creatively into areas that need innovation. *(I will never be able to list them all as I do not know them all. You stand in a unique place in this world from which you can see things that I cannot!)*

Lost and exactly where we should be

Many years ago, when I first moved to London (and I felt a bit lost in this humongous city so different from more village-like Amsterdam) I made a painting titled *"Lost and exactly where I should be"*. It came from missing a stop on the Tube and ending up in a completely unfamiliar location. I often think back to this phrase and quote it. It is by unhooking ourselves from routines and expectations that the gods can truly lead us where they need us.

Busyness can become an addiction but being too inactive is just as much of a problem. In my social circle I have observed some people age ten years in just the one calendar year after they retire. To me that indicates that human beings need engagement and meaning in their lives. Just getting through your days is not enough for the human soul. These goals need not be external – they can be internal as well. Write the first chapter of that book you have intended to write for years.... Think large, do something truly worthwhile, do something that changes the life of other beings for the better. Too much free time? Go pick litter on a beach... Volunteer for shifts with the Samaritans (a helpline for suicidal people).

Activity #16: Harness Your Imagination!

Go to a place where you can be undisturbed for some time. Bring paper and pen. Light a candle. Embark on a fearless examination of your own life – without blaming yourself. The point of this exercise is *not about beating yourself up, but about identifying areas where you can do better!*

If you have experience of meditation or shamanic journeying, use those techniques to seek frank spirit guidance. If that is not your cup of tea, take a different route: on a piece of paper write down the names of five key people in your life (ten if you are brave, or if you have many children!)

For every name write a self-appraisal answering the following questions:

- Where do failures in the imagination occur?
- Has this person repeatedly tried to get something through to me – but I have blanked it or ridiculed it (to escape the discomfort of engaging with it)?
- Use your imagination to cook up a positive surprise for these people! (On reflection I will come with you and see that French art film after all/I am aware that you have been

trying to tell me something -now I will sit down and give you my undivided attention!/I know how tired you are on Fridays so let me cook dinner while you enjoy a glass of wine!)

Many decades ago, my mother (newly married and not yet my mother!) once struggled to choose between two pretty dresses in a shop. My father (who was present) went back to this shop the next day and bought her the other dress as well as a surprise! She still talks about this, fifty years later!)

Chapter 17

Imagine Health -A Healthy Imagination

This was the beginning of many dialogues with the pain god. It was the beginning of a different perception of the pain. I felt the pain now to be a presence, an intelligence, an entity, an extremely powerful demon who was intimately involved with me. The pain was still painful, but it was also a companion, a companion who, though he chastened me, also loved me deeply...
Albert Kreinheder[1]

The power of belief

A close friend of mine was diagnosed with cancer about ten years ago. Her husband made a wise comment that remains imprinted on my memory: "Now you know that you have cancer you will need to choose a treatment path. I think what matters most is not what path you choose. What matters is that you choose a path that you believe in 100%. This could be chemotherapy and mainstream medical treatment - I will support you every inch of the way. If you choose alternative treatments - that is fine with me too - those will be equally effective if you believe in their power 100%. It does not really matter what you choose -the only thing that does matter is that you engage from a place of total faith in your path. Your belief will make the treatment work - or *not*.

The power of money

There are many things that pass for "normal" in mainstream health care that I find extremely disturbing. For instance, the fact that every consultation with a primary care doctor in the UK supposedly lasts 12 minutes (but my GP gets this down to less than five!) and the purpose usually is to match the patient up with medicine in the form of drugs. (In comparison: shamanic healing sessions generally last about two hours. The practitioner actively works on seeing deeply into things, re-weaving and mending).

Companies manufacturing those drugs are not charitable foundations: the cancer "industry" is a multi-million-dollar concern. This means, quite simply and brutally, *that it is in the interest of those companies for us to stay ill and for a cure for cancer not to be found (unless even more money can be charged for that!)*

The exact same thing holds true for many other medications but for editorial reasons (i.e. this chapter not turning into a book in its own right), I will stick with the cancer-example.

Courses of chemotherapy are routinely administered to people who have terminal cancer -without any concern for how those toxins are affecting the earth and our environment when death inevitably *does* arrive and the body needs to be buried or cremated. -For far less money this person could have been offered spiritual death preparation work that would serve them on the level of soul in ways that feeding death-denial does not.

Things get worse: one U.S.-based doctor published a book explaining that chemotherapy does not work in 97% of cases: Dr Glidden: The MD Emperor Has No Clothes.[2] He explains that in the US (but please note that this is not true in Europe) the prescribing doctor gets a direct cut of the profits. It is in the interest of the pharmaceutical industry that we continue to fall ill and stay ill. Cancer, he says, is a holistic phenomenon and it can only ever be treated in a holistic way.

Mainstream medical professionals do not work holistically, meaning that they make little effort to see the larger picture or detect the underlying causes of illness. If the triple doses of antibiotics my own doctor prescribed had been successful, I would never have learned the lessons that Gargoyle and Troll Child brought me. I would never have unravelled and addressed some of the darkest dynamics active in my own life, body and psyche.

I used to get terrible chest infections two or three times a year. My shamanic training kicked off with a life burial - I had to dig my own grave and was buried alive for a night. The point of this initiation was facing our demons and I faced a life-long issue: claustrophobia. Many memories returned of having been "confined" in previous incarnations. Especially vivid memories surfaced of a previous lifetime in which I died, as a young Jewish girl, in a concentration camp. In facing the root cause of this fear, a rewiring of my body occurred. After my life burial I no longer get chest infections. Medication to suppress anxiety would never have revealed or healed the root cause of my health problem. Yet that is the route a medical doctor takes: anxiety? We prescribe pills.... Valium, Xanax, Diazepam.... Their names sound like demented Greek warrior gods.

Having said my piece, medication *can* save lives and restore life quality in many cases. I am just making a case for deep introspection and a dialogue with the disease. What is the gift (if any)? What is the symbolism or teaching?

Some research about the role of the imagination in mental health

In the field of psychology there is something called the diametric module of mental illness. Essentially this model shows that autistic spectrum disorders feature deficits in *mentalism* (read: interpersonal skills, mind-reading, theory of mind) while psychotic spectrum disorders feature the very opposite thing: something called *hypermentalism* (meaning an overdrive or caricature of such mental functions).

Between these two "polarities" a new continuum of perceiving these disorders opens. We have already discussed social imagination and now we take a closer look at the "book ends" of this phenomenon: social imagination can swing between two extremes -from non-existent to beyond-all-reasonable limits.

The discovery of these researchers opens the door on a very old question: is there a connection between creativity and mental illness or mental disturbance. The cliché of the "tormented genius" comes to mind.

Autistic spectrum disorders have an early onset because (so called) "mentalistic" development stalls in childhood. Psychotic spectrum disorders typically have a late teen or young adult onset because normal development needs to be completed before "mentalism" can be taken to pathological extremes.

A shamanic perspective on the same phenomena

This continuum of perception once again places human imagination at the heart of things. Of the two, psychosis is the easier one for me to address because prominent people in the field of contemporary shamanism have spoken out about this issue. Especially African-born author Malidoma Some has described spoken at length about how an indigenous, African shaman views the phenomena encountered in a Western-style psychiatric hospital. I highly recommend that you read the article "The Shamanic View of Mental Illness" written by Jason Gaddis[3] in full.

During a psychotic breakdown a rupturing or fragmentation of the usual psychic boundaries occurs. Shamanic peoples often speak of a veil between the worlds. We tend to perceive this outside ourselves as in "stepping into other worlds" or walking into another dimension. However, my own experiences as a shamanic painter suggest that this veil is as much an inner or psychic veil, as one that exists outside of us.

People who experience a psychotic episode or state of mind tumble through that portal unintentionally. Their mind then starts roaming other worlds (where other rules and boundaries apply) and meeting the inhabitants of those worlds, (which neurotypical individuals do not perceive/see). We then say that they are "hearing voices", "hallucinating" or that they have "lost their minds" when I would say it is more a case of not being able to find their way home to their own bodies, minds and brains; to the safe container of a Healthy Self.

The hairline crack between visionary and crazy

It is a common phenomenon for people with paranoid schizophrenia to think that other parties are "out to get them" and that they are being bombarded with messages. Who "they" are usually remains a mystery. Neurotypical care providers and health providers with a western education will write this off as delusions or complete nonsense (and not engage in an investigation who "they" might be).

I often go on omen walks, when some issue requires guidance or clarification. I have also taken my shamanic group for children on omen walks and those are fun sessions indeed because the children soon discover that a larger cosmic intelligence is engaging with us in playful ways. The Universe has a great sense of humour!

The difference is that I do this purposefully and I can weed out the meaningful information from the "other stuff". Absolutely everything can be a mirror -but we draw the line somewhere to preserve our sanity! Do we really have time to see the mirror held up by every piece of rubbish in the street? – It would make an interesting spiritual practice for sure! The line between visionary and insane, between spirit-led and mentally unstable is only a hairline crack. This is the reason why I believe that everyone needs to be educated in navigating those worlds safely, not unlike taking driving lessons.

RD Laing and the anti-asylum movement

A man who challenged medical orthodoxy as much as he did was always going to make enemies within the Establishment. Laing argued that the old Bedlam-based system of incarcerating people with mental illnesses and treating them with anti-psychotic drugs and inhumane electric-shock treatment had contributed to people's psychological and emotional distress and was therefore part of the problem. With his beliefs in the power of self-healing, he became an important part of the anti-asylum movement, which worked towards the community-care model that is the norm today – a process first advocated in 1962 by the then Tory health minister Enoch Powell (for mainly economic reasons).

His boldest experiment was the idealistic concept of the "safe haven" for mental-health patients, without locks or any anti-psychotic drugs, that he and fellow founders of the UK mental-health charity, The Philadelphia Association, set up at Kingsley Hall 50 years ago in Bromley-by-Bow in London's East End. The association, which continues today, was set up to challenge accepted ways of understanding and treating mental and emotional suffering; key to that was, and still is, a commitment to conversation as a way of articulating what disturbs people.

RD Laing: Was the Counterculture's Favourite Psychiatrist a Renegade or a True Visionary?[4]

Autism spectrum -a personal perspective

When it comes to the autistic spectrum, I can only give a personal perspective. There is not (yet) one commonly supported unified view among practitioners of shamanism.

I have been contacted by parents of autistic children in the hope that a shamanic healing session would cure them of their autism. What is really called for there, *is the parents being cured of the yearning for their child to be something he or she is not.* Having said that, shamanism can offer powerful tools to families dealing with members "on the spectrum".

I have written about this at some length in my first book: Natural Born Shamans (Chapter 9).[5] Here are the key points:

- Your child remains the same child that he or she always was, when a devastating diagnosis is made. What *will* change are the expectations we have for that child. Often, we do not admit to ourselves just how many expectations we have of and for our children. Much of that remains unconscious and unspoken until our world tilts on its axis.

- Your child has arrived with a unique gift for your family, community and our whole planet. It may take longer (and far greater effort) to unpick what that gift is -but it is there, yearning to be unwrapped and received.
- No matter how challenged an individual is (child or adult, autistic spectrum or mental health histories, high functioning or needing 24/7 care and supervision) please remember that Outside Time they too have a sacred or higher self, which can be contacted and consulted by a skilled shamanic practitioner. That gives families a way of communicating and honouring the wishes and needs of this person - even non-verbal people.

One dimension of this issue surely is that we have made a right mess of the holy office of being caretakers of this planet. Our ultimate mother, Mother Earth, is being abused in so many ways that she is not in optimal health. We cannot be surprised if that affects her children as well. It seems possible to me that individuals born with autism or ADHD are holding up mirrors *for all of us.*

We are living from a place of shocking disconnection to the Earth and all sentient beings. Is our collective "autism" being mirrored back to us? In our society the pace of life and modern communications are accelerating to the point where being on call 24/7 has become the norm. I have heard stories about young people who keep their iPhone on during the night and wake up several times to ping off responses and messages in a semi-drowsy state. I cannot imagine how such young people will do well in class or at work the next day.

Mapping the territories

My primary concern is that problems, disorders and deviations from the norm are often extremely helpful in mapping a larger territory. I cannot write a book about the human imagination without tracking and recording the darker expressions, malfunctioning, meanderings and out-of-control manifestations of this mysterious "muscle".

Are we collectively ready to imagine and create health and healthy outcomes?! Without balance there is no health. In which areas of our lives do we need to restore balance? Are we willing to really commit to the work that requires of us? Are we willing to work less (in some cases) and commit to creating work-life balance?

Ultimately Wetiko is the collective disease or disorder of excess, of *never enough.* Unless we curb excess in all areas of our lives, we are part of the problem – not the solution. Unravelling this takes right use of imagination and integrity.

It takes a healthy imagination to imagine health

Being healthy also requires us to engage in imaginative ways with what is hurting, what is out of balance, what comes to attention, not just once but on an on-going basis. That is the paradox. The road to the light unfailingly takes us through our own personal darkness. *Not just once but time after time after time.* For people who are new to all this (and who have not mastered the art of either meditation or shamanic journeying) guided visualization is a good starting point. There are many books (as well as tapes and audio recordings) on the market.

One problem is that the word visualization contains the word "visual" meaning that people often feel pressure to "see things". Many people are not wired to "see" mental pictures, but they can experience the other world through hearing, deep inner knowing, touch and other senses. In shamanism we do not privilege one way of knowing or sensing over another!

Spirit medicine and the spirit of medication

Cancer has, sadly, become one illness that affects all of us (either directly or indirectly). There are not many people alive today, who have not lost a loved one to cancer. I am also aware that many people cannot afford, or do not have access to (for various reasons), every type of treatment or medication in existence. Some cancer patients now use crowdfunding to be able to afford highly experimental treatments in a clinic in Germany.

Homeopathy is considered almost a mainstream form of treatment today, where a disease is treated by minute doses of diluted natural substances. Those doses are so minute that, scientifically speaking, their effect is negligible. However, this is energy medicine: the tiny dose still carries the energetic effect (or spirit) of the substance. This form of medicine has several advantages: it is cheap and rarely causes side effects. Practitioners work in holistic ways and during a first consultation they will ask many questions about a wide range of things, varying from sleep habits to personality quirks. This allows them to identify the perfect match.

I have worked with people who have complemented mainstream medical interventions with shamanic healing. One example is of a person having chemotherapy but using spiritual techniques to reduce side effects and keep her spiritual and physical strength up. One simple spiritual course of action is using meditation to perform alchemy through prayer and spirit intervention. Spirit allies turn the chemo into a golden elixir but neutralise the toxic aspects. Another example is of people who suffer chronical pain calling on spirit allies and otherworld beings for help in managing the pain, often resulting in a significant reduction of medication.

A great immovable goddess called Insomnia

In shamanism we work with disease spirits. The spirits of diseases will take very specific forms because they are always trying to tell us something. I have run sessions where the spirit of the auto-immune disease Lupus appeared as a wolf (Lupus is the Latin word for wolf). In my own life I have worked with Insomnia as a mysterious but powerful teacher.[6]

Alchemy Therapy

It recently occurred to me (but I have not yet put this to the test) that people could work in a shamanic way with the spirit of a treatment or substance they cannot access. If you cannot travel to Germany to have a specific innovative treatment -then ask the spirits of that treatment to come to you and work on you instead. I have even wondered whether it might be possible to administer a "spiritual form of chemotherapy this way", that is less damaging for the human body (as chemotherapy destroys *everything,* including vital living organisms and systems).

- *When something isn't working it means that something is working on you!*
- *Things that are not fully resolved will keep on coming to attention (through crisis, ill health, accidents and other life events) until we extract all learning and finally put them to rest.*

For me it took years of agony to learn this, but I have come to trust the process.

Dialogue with disease spirits through active imagination

I have already recommended guided visualisation techniques but there are many ways of engaging the imagination in healing ways. The most engaging book I have ever read about this is Body and Soul: The Other Side of Illness by Jungian Analyst Albert Kreinheder[1]. He actively enters a dialogue with his ailments (some might call them demons) and successfully heals himself of several serious afflictions. His account also shows that such miracles can't be worked time after time because he still died of cancer at age seventy-six.

Another fascinating book is The Alchemy of Illness by Kat Duff[7]. She reflects profoundly on the role illness plays in the microcosm of a human life and the macrocosm of society. The most thought-provoking idea she raises is that through being ill some people might free others to be healthy and perform essential tasks in society. The thinking here is that chronic or serious illness is an act of service in terms of human shadow material. She is onto a profound insight here, something worth exploration.

There is a serious need for unflinchingly honouring all the people who handle shadow material in our society: undertakers, butchers, prostitutes, police officers, soldiers and so forth. By performing their service, they free the rest of us from having to deal with certain matters. There is a great mystery at work right there, in our collective psyche and energetic field.

A related issue is that we do not do enough honouring of those who lost their lives so that we can live in freedom. Immediately after typing this line, social media flashed up a notification saying that Steven Spielberg insists schools put Holocaust Education on the curriculum.

Recently a seven-year old Guatemalan girl died two days after she and her father were taken into custody along the U.S. border. Her name was Jackeline Caal and apparently, she had gone days without food or water. It is important to remember, cherish and continue to speak the names of the deceased. This is part of any shaman's or priest's Office for the Dead. (The Office for the Dead is a prayer cycle of the Canonical Hours in the Catholic Church, Anglican Church and Lutheran Church, said for the repose of the soul of a deceased person).

The Illness-wellness continuum

My perception of illness and wellness is less black-or-white than the dominant cultural lens. Healthy people carry the seeds (dormant potential) of disease within them – and equally some "medically diagnosed as ill" people I know have incredibly healthy souls and spirit. Their courage and commitment to healing and to Life opens portals for everyone around them.

In my years of focusing on one-to-one shamanic healing sessions I was sometimes shown by the spirits how illness hovered over someone as a possibility. It had not yet taken root, it could still be avoided and never take physical form, but it was there ... ready to materialise. In such cases I passionately urge people to make life changes.

To my professionally trained "x-ray eyes of the shaman" my own body carries many outcomes in potential and what actually happens ("gets activated") depends on how I manage the usual factors (diet, rest, stress-levels, exercise, a positive outlook) plus one additional thing: how I use my own imagination to walk around my own body and enter dialogues with the "demons" or dis-ease spirits I encounter. If I am willing to listen -they sometimes allow me to learn a lesson without a full-blown serious illness. Other times I am slow on the uptake, or I need rewiring, or I need a period of enforced rest. It is a creative dialogue and one that will certainly not help me "escape death" when my allocated time on earth is up – just as Albert Kreinheder did not elude death, after many narrow escapes and spectacular recoveries.

The illness IS the cure

Some authors have stated that "the illness is the cure" in the sense that any dis-ease is always a communication from our own bodies about balance and unresolved issues. In my own life the teachings of Gargoyle and Troll Child continue to amaze me. I continue to make changes and tweaks to the fabric of my life. If the fabric of my life is not healthy – my body won't stay healthy either. No amount of chemotherapy is going to do the inner work of balancing, forgiving, reconciliation and healing on my behalf.

> *If I were to name that intelligence, that deep knowing which operates through the agency of our dreams and flesh, I would call it soul, agreeing with philosopher Morris Berman, who once said: "Soul is another name for what the body does."*
> Kat Duff in *The Alchemy of Illness*[8]

Activity #17: Mirror, Mirror in the Street

Go for walk in an area used by many people. Bring paper and pen!

Make a point of looking at all the things that you normally "edit out". Some examples on our own London street are discarded chicken bones from a fast food restaurant which dogs stop to sniff at, dog poo (mostly cleaned up by their human "parents"), fox poo (no one feels called to clean up), autumn leaves, discarded shopping lists, beer cans and so forth.

Now *really* look at these items and accept them as a mirror: what are you being shown about yourself?! The chicken bones – one day I too will be reduced to bones. The fox poo: where do I leave energetic messes for other people to walk into? Wine bottles or beer cans: what is my relationship with alcohol and do I delude myself about my drinking habits? How do I behave after I drink some alcohol? Does this have any effect on the people around me? How do my children feel about their parents enjoying a bottle of wine at weekends?

Inner work is *not comfortable*! Drop the ego-attachment to yourself as a spiritual evolved clean-living person. Face up to how messy human life is and now messy and contradictory you yourself are. Then ask yourself: how can I harness my imagination to do better in some of these areas? Good luck!

Chapter 18

Cancer: Illness, Crab, Star Constellation, Mirror and Global Teacher

The disease was first called cancer by Greek physician Hippocrates (460-370 BC). He is considered the "Father of Medicine." Hippocrates used the terms carcinos and carcinoma to describe non-ulcer forming and ulcer-forming tumors. In Greek this means a crab

Cancer History[1]

Lung cancer is the most common cancer in the world, with more than 1.8 million new cases a year. In 2012, the World Cancer Research Fund International reported almost 240,000 cases of ovarian cancer and more than 14 million total cancer cases worldwide. This number is expected to increase to 24 million by 2035.

The problem with conventional therapy is most of it ends up in sewage.

Caleb Radford[2]

Instead of labelling them and making them feel like they are part of the mental health system, we reach them with these narratives. When they hear the pūrākau (stories) you see a little spark in them.

Michelle Duff[3]

Cancer -the illness

We often think of cancer as something alien that invades our bodies from the outside. We call it names. I have seen Facebook posts along the lines of: "Cancer, you bastard of a disease, you robbed me of my Dad.

The heart of the matter is that cancer is the result of uncontrolled cell growth. This means that it is part of us, it is our own body and system of cell-regeneration malfunctioning or spinning out of control. (There is no external "bastard"!)

Cancer Quest[4] explains it as follows: Our bodies are composed of trillions of cells, all working together. In cancer, one of those cells stops paying attention to the normal signals that tell cells to grow, stop growing or even to die. Cancer cells still share many of the same needs and properties of normal cells, but they become independent of the controls that make our body function smoothly. The process by which a normal cell changes into one that behaves so abnormally can take a long time and is often triggered by outside influences. The next few sections describe the differences between normal and cancer cells and outline the steps leading to the creation of a cancer cell from a normal cell.

Cancer is actually a general term that describes a large group of related diseases. Every case of cancer is unique, with its own set of genetic changes and growth properties. Some cancers grow quickly while others can take years to become dangerous to the patient. The many differences between cases of cancer, even of the same organ (i.e. different cases of breast cancer), is one of the main reasons that treatment is so difficult.

Since Gargoyle and Troll Child appeared, I have paid closer attention to cancer as a social phenomenon: what people are saying about it, what comes to attention through social media, what treatments the people I know (or knew before they died) choose and so forth. I have also been reflecting deeply on the following question: *what makes cells in a human body spin out of control after years of (apparently) functioning just fine?*

Cancer cells are cells gone wrong — in other words, they no longer respond to many of the signals that control cellular growth and death. Cancer cells originate within tissues and, as they grow and divide, they diverge ever further from normalcy. Over time, these cells become increasingly resistant to the controls that maintain normal tissue — and as a result, they divide more rapidly than their progenitors and become less dependent on signals from other cells. Cancer cells even evade programmed cell death and this, despite the fact that their multiple abnormalities would normally make them prime targets for apoptosis. In the late stages of cancer, cells break through normal tissue boundaries and metastasize (spread) to new sites in the body. (Scitable[5])

Cancer as a mirror

One of the principles I live by is looking in all the mirrors any given situation holds up. If Hippocrates named the disease, we can assume it has been around for a long time. Some of the earliest evidence of cancer is found among fossilized bone tumours in human mummies in ancient Egypt, and references to the same has been found in ancient manuscripts. Bony skull destruction as seen in cancer of the head and neck has been found, too.

> *Later Roman physician, Celsus (28-50 BC) translated the Greek term into cancer, the Latin word for crab. It was Galen (130-200 AD), another Roman physician, who used the term oncos (Greek for swelling) to describe tumors. Oncos is the root word for oncology or study of cancers.*
> Ananya Mandal MD[6]

If the phenomenon of cancer itself seems to be spinning out of control (in the sense of the number of people affected by it) we need to ask ourselves: what is a defining characteristic of the times we live in? One such feature undeniably is excess and unchecked growth. The world population has reached record (and unsustainable) levels. (As I am alive today and as we have three children, our family is part of that problem!) Personal consumption in western culture is out of control (our so-called consumer society). Western people use far more of the Earth's resources per capita than is fair on a global level. This has far-reaching consequences for both the inhabitants of developing countries today and for future generations .[7] The invasion and obliteration of indigenous lands, cultures and traditions is out of control.[8] Environment pollution is out of control.[9] The amount of plastic floating in our oceans beggars belief, and so forth.

An interesting question is what would happen if all the wealth in the world is redistributed equally to everyone. The idea is commendable, but world history shows that some countries have tried versions of this idea, with disastrous consequences.[10] Think of the collapse of the Soviet Union[11] or the Chinese Communist Revolution.[12]

Cancer as a global teacher

Humans are a plague on the Earth that need to be controlled by limiting population growth.

Sir David Attenborough[13]

Both humans and animals can develop cancer. During the research for this book I discovered that *even plants can get cancer*! For me this raises one extremely uncomfortable question: on a global level of eco-systems suffering while human "ego-systems" balloon and squash many life forms... *is cancer perhaps the cure?* Here I am speaking purely on the (impersonal and non-human prioritised) level of a planet forced to heal herself after incomprehensible levels of abuse and disrespect for her resources and life-giving powers.

Taking that question one step closer to home I cannot but ask myself: in what areas of life do we all fail to take the right action and observe the correct boundaries? We eat too much (the obesity levels themselves have become "an obese figure" in the statistics), we buy too much, we blame too much -and take too little personal responsibility, we use far more than our fair share of resources. Do our bodies unfailingly mirror back to us our own actions and life choices? Have human beings (especially the large concentrations of human beings with very harmful habits) become tumours rather than sacred earth keepers?

I am aware that I will make myself unpopular by even posing these questions, but can I live with myself if I do not ask them?

Cancer, the star constellation

When our youngest son was seven years old, he once asked why one of the most dreaded diseases known to humankind was also the name of a star constellation in the night sky. Conventional wisdom says that there is little connection between the two, other than the name crab. I consulted two astrologer colleagues, and both said that that there is no real connection. My son remained unconvinced.

In Greek mythology the second labour of Hercules was to kill the Lernaean Hydra. From the murky waters of the swamps near a place called Lerna, the hydra terrorized the countryside. It was a monstrous serpent with nine heads and attacked with poisonous venom. One of the nine heads was immortal and therefore indestructible.[14]

For each of the heads that Hercules decapitated, two more sprang forth. Assisted by Iolaus he applied burning brands to the severed stumps, cauterizing the wounds and thus preventing the regeneration of heads. During this battle he crushed a giant crab, which had come to assist the Hydra by distracting Hercules. Once the battle was over the goddess Hera placed both the Hydra and the Crab in the night sky as star constellations Hydra and Cancer where we can see them today.

As we know Hippocrates named the disease Cancer after cutting out an unnatural tumour that looked like a crab. When a tumour is surgically removed apparently there are veins and projections stretching out on all sides, just like the legs of a crab.

Doing some background research on this, I stumbled across a petition to rename the zodiac constellation because "cancer sucks".[15] The author felt sorry for the one out of twelve people who have Cancer as their natal sign and suggests we rename the zodiac constellation "Sebastian". For the record: his petition had eleven supporters.

What seems striking is how Cancer-the-illness appears to behave like the Hydra! To me the description of Herakles dealing with the beast reminds strongly of surgery followed by chemotherapy: first cutting and then burning.

The Moon in Cancer

Just as the moon cycles through each month every 28-30 days, its energy waxes and wanes through a person's life every 28-30 years in the same pattern, from new to full and back again. We experience the beginning of the cycle as a new start -perhaps a graduation, a marriage or divorce, a new home or job. The energy of this cycle waxes and builds for 15 years, peaking at the Full Moon, then begins to release over the next 15 years, finally reaching the Dark Moon phase. The seeds of the new cycle are planted here, and the next phase of life begins.

Susan Rossi[16]

In my own chart "the Moon is in the house of Cancer". In everyday language this means that the Moon was passing through the Cancer zodiac sign when I was born. The three astrologers who have looked at my natal chart have all commented on that placement. One called it a "magnificent cancer moon". As a non-astrologer I understand this to mean that I am a deeply maternal person, that my personality holds a strong desire to nurture and nourish new life (or life forms) and new visions.

People with a cancer moon sign are said to be sensitive, emotional and matriarchal, natural born empaths, pioneers and natural born guardians/protectors. And yes, I can recognise all those qualities in myself. I can also own the fact that it has been a learning journey to not take this to extremes: to operate healthy boundaries, to know when to step back, to remember that other people remain responsible for their emotions and life choices.

The next question arising then is: do the people who contract cancer have things in common? Other than a genetic disposition, are their personality traits that indicate a high risk of contracting Cancer?

The Cancer-prone personality

The research has been done. An article in Psychology Today, by Andrew Goliszek Ph.D. asks: Is There a Cancer-prone Personality?[17] The author says that how you think and act can put you at risk. He claims that *recent studies point to two personality types that seem to make us either cancer-prone or cancer resistant.* Unfortunately, this article does not provide the relevant citations, or links, but I found research into 'Mechanisms of cancer resistance in long-lived mammals'.[18]

Recent research[19] points to two personality types that seem to make people either cancer-prone or cancer-resistant. Speaking in very general terms, emotions such as depression, anger and hostility make us more prone to illness while positive attitudes such as hope, positive thinking and a focus on joy strengthen our immune system.

The Cancer-Prone Personality Type

- Represses both positive and negative emotions.
- Shows anger, resentment, or hostility towards others.
- Takes on extra duties and responsibilities, even when they cause stress and pressure.
- Reacts adversely to and does not cope well with life changes.
- Is negative or pessimistic.
- Becomes easily depressed or has feelings of hopelessness.
- Worries often and excessively about others.
- Feels the need for approval and to please others.

The Cancer-Resistant Personality Type

- Expresses emotions in a positive and constructive way.
- Controls anger and resolves anger issues positively.
- Knows when to say no.
- Copes well with stress and feels in control of situations.
- Is optimistic and hopeful (the power of positive thinking)
- Does not become easily depressed.
- Seeks out and maintains social support networks.
- Does not worry excessively.
- Likes to please but does not seek approval as an emotional crutch.

There will always be exceptions but from these findings we can extract pointers for balanced living and boosting our immune systems (ideally before things go wrong!)

Here we return to mind-body techniques such as meditation and guided visualization. These findings definitely do reinforce the need for keeping our relationships healthy and in balance.

One very important point I myself wish to make here is that cancer can be ancestral or environmental in origin as well. When babies or toddlers contract cancer we can't possibly claim that they repress emotions or have anger-management issues. We need to *use our imagination* to be extremely cautious with our words around people with cancer (or indeed any illness or severe life challenge). It is good to reflect on areas where we may be able to boost our health – but we must remember that in others (and in the final reckoning) we never see the full constellation of influences – therefore we cannot judge, only support from a place of love and compassion. In the final reckoning we don't ever see the full constellation of influences working *on us*!

Fighting Cancer

Just as Hercules did battle with the Hydra, we commonly speak of *fighting cancer*. Obituaries will say: "She lost her life after a long battle with cancer". Due to the awareness that cancer cells are produced by our own body I always get the image of *a person fighting themselves* when they "fight cancer" – and that saddens me.

I belong to the camp that believes that "the mind can heal the body" as opposed to the "mind doing battle with the body" camp. I am also in a camp that sees death as an ally and great life teacher, not an insult.

To my mind the way a medical doctor tells a patient about the diagnosis needs extremely skilful handling because the wrong words can set undesirable trajectories in motion. As a person trained in observing the energetic interactions between people, *cursing can be one shadow manifestation of diagnosing.*

From my own encounters with medical practitioners recently, I know that the way language is thrown around can be harmful. They all asked me to recount the history of cancer in my family (probably a fair question medically speaking, but it sets alarm bells ringing well before any diagnosis is made).

In an interview available on YouTube, Dr Glidden explains what he himself would do were he diagnosed with cancer.[20] He says that any tumour is not the disease, only a physical expressin of it, we need to find the *cause* of the disease. In the event of a cancer diagnosis he highly recommends a dialogue with medical professions about the following issues[21]:

- *Do I choose to proceed with mainstream medical treatment?*
- *What other options are available (that have been used successfully by others)?*
- *Speaking on a holistic level: what is going on in your life that your body manifests the uncontrolled cell growth we call cancer? Where in your life are the serious imbalances? What part of your habitual behaviour may be "out of control"?*
- *What are the success rates of surgery followed by chemotherapy or radiation for this type of cancer?*

Dr Glidden makes strong claims:

- All medical doctors know that surgery and chemo do not cure cancer -but it is the only remedy they can offer, plus it is a multi-million-dollar industry.
- Chemotherapy does not work in 97% of cases.
- Because of this fact, medical doctors have redefined the definition of "successful cancer treatment" as *living for five years after the initial diagnosis.*

My own Dad died just within the five-year-mark. (The five-year marker is viewed as an almost magical period. If you survive the first five years, chances are that you will continue to do well!) His life quality during those years was very poor because he was subjected to medical treatments that failed and left him physically impaired. The creation of a colostomy bag caused many complications and infections. He was an outdoors man who lived for his large garden and walks with his dog. He was not receptive to dealing with Cancer on any kind of holistic, alternative or symbolic level. The thought has often occurred to me that if the medical profession had not intervened, he might well have lived for the same five years (no longer) but with far better life quality than he had in reality. The medical profession could have provided palliative care and pain relief in the final stages of his illness.

The story my family chooses to tell is that "We could not have lived with ourselves if we didn't try all options". The story I tell myself is that the treatments he received failed desperately. Not only that, they affected his life quality during the years he had left and caused unacceptable stress (which permanently affected my mother's health in the form of a marked deterioration in both her memory and resilience). For me personally "trying all options" would have ranged from holistic treatments and deep reflection to death preparation work.

The cure for cancer –The Holy Grail of Science & Medicine

Each time a cell divides its genetic information must be doubled for the genes to remain the same. A cell that is about to become tumorous cannot make this genome replication and division without errors. To spot errors in the genetic material cells have evolved mechanisms to slow down or block cell division (so called cell-cycle checkpoints), promote DNA repair, or eliminate damaged, hazardous cells by engaging a cellular suicide program. How cells make the choice between life and death in response to DNA damage is critical not only for the fate of each cell, but also for avoiding life-threatening diseases such as cancer.[22]

In our times the "cure for cancer" has become a symbol for the unobtainable, the Holy Grail. I am a speaker on The Lost Wisdom of the Grail Summit this week.[23]

Recently there have been some interesting developments in the field of immunotherapy. Some patients have been effectively cured, with scans and tests unable to detect any trace of the disease.

A team of researchers at the Johns Hopkins University has formulated what is possibly the first universal blood test for cancer in the world. With findings published in the Science journal, the team details the new blood tests' ability to detect up to eight different types of cancers. These include ovarian, liver, stomach, pancreatic, esophageal, bowel, lung and breast cancers.[24]

My three children keep talking to me about stem cell treatment. They feel that this is the Cure-All and possible Holy Grail of future medical treatment. Time will tell! Having said that, the Medicine of the Imagination is and will always remain cheap, powerful, holistic and has no side effects!

Activity #18: Adversary-Ally-Teacher

Please go to a place where you can be undisturbed for a while.

Bring paper and pen. Light a candle.

Think of a person or situation in your life where it feels like someone is fighting you, or actively working against you. This could be an illness, but it could also be a colleague, neighbour, family member or other situation. Ask yourself with brutal honesty: what am I learning from this person? (The learning may be completely unintentional – but valuable!)

For instance, what I have learned from Insomnia is to keep spaces open in my schedule, to not be over-ambitious, to ask myself whether I am working from a place of joy or obligation, to develop good bedtime hygiene and switch off my computer and phone well before needing to sleep – etc.

Please write down all the small "gifts" you are receiving from this situation or person. Once you decide to view them as a *teacher* rather than an *adversary* – does that make you feel different about them?

Now return to the check lists for the cancer-prone and cancer-resilient personality types. Scroll through them and assess yourself. Identify where you need to make changes to increase your changes of long-term health.

For instance:

- I need to work on my emotional literacy and try harder to express my emotions (both positive and negative) in constructive and respectful ways *(Hint: use I Statements rather than You Statements, so "I feel..." rather than "you make me feel...")*
- I need to learn to say no when too much is asked of me or when people expect me to shoulder more than my fair share of any responsibility
- Actively try to find the gifts and learning in disappointments, rejections and vexing situations
- Meditate on the profound spiritual teaching that other people (for whom you have no official obligation of care

in the way you may have for young children or an elderly parent) remain responsible for their own lives, choices and challenges at all times
- Spend time reflecting on who my true friends are and ask myself on a regular basis whether there are some *near enemies* I may wish to step back from…

In the weeks to come, avoid getting sucked into reactivity and instead ask yourself constantly: what am I being shown right now? What am I learning? What skill am I developing? – Best of luck!

Chapter 19

When Lack of Awareness Becomes Toxic

Toxic people often make you want to fix them and their problems. They want you to feel sorry for them, and responsible for what happens to them. Yet their problems are never really solved, for once you've helped them with one crisis, there's inevitably another one. What they really want is your on-going sympathy and support, and they will create one drama after another in order to get it. "Fixing" and "saving" them never works, especially since you probably care more about what happens to them than they do.
Abigail Brenner[1]

Toxic People – Toxic Concept

The word "toxic" has unexpectedly gained popularity. These days we do not hesitate to say that people, situations or even emotions are toxic:

- "My mother-in-law, who is the most toxic person on the planet... *eyeroll...*"
- "The work environment in my office is toxic beyond belief! I take every sick day I am entitled to!"
- "Toxic Love"

I just ran a quick search and found the following examples:

Toxic childhood (how the modern world is damaging our children)

Toxic Love (a relationship where the participants can fool themselves and their partner into thinking that they are protectors, givers, nurturers or enlighteners)

Toxic parents (parents who do unloving things in the name

of love)

Toxic friends (they envy your success and you feel drained after hanging out with them or worse they are bulling you and actively poisoning your life – we already identified them as near enemies in another chapter of this book)

Toxic Adult Children (who hold you emotionally hostage by threatening you with self-harm or manipulating you in other ways)

Before we proceed let's arrive at a definition of what toxic means in a psychological/spiritual/emotional context. According to an article in Psychology Today[1] toxic people are manipulative, judgmental, take no responsibility for their own feelings therefore they project everything onto others, they do not apologise, are inconsistent and put you on the defensive.

That which hides outside awareness

You will not hear me refer to people as toxic. That is not to say that I have not met my fair share of people who are "not good for my health". I would go as far as saying that as a teacher of shamanism I meet more than my fair share of them because many unbalanced and deeply wounded people feel drawn to attending courses in healing. Tough![2]

Toxic is a handy word because it is short and crystal clear. The issue with labels like that is that they kind of "screw the lid on the jar" and leave little scope for a deeper exploration of what the genie in the bottle is trying to tell us.

I have reflected on this deeply. What makes ordinary people "toxic" (harmful to others) is *always something that remains outside their own awareness.*

If we say that our "mother-in-law is toxic", we cannot so easily walk away from her because we have married into her family. (Also meaning that she was around before we were... I was of a generation that was taught to respect my elders – maybe you were too?) One issue is that, by defining her as toxic, we deny any other achievements she may have to her name. People are multi-faceted and different people will activate (or bring out) different sides in all of us. Calling people slams a label on them and we are "done", we give ourselves permission to speak of them dismissively. Essentially, we dehumanize them[3].

Psychiatrist Brenner gives some very good examples of how toxic people behave and interact. She also acknowledges that relationships are complex and that familial relationships are especially difficult to handle because you cannot close a door on those people. I fully agree with her conclusion that the moment you feel bad about yourself as the result of a relationship with another person -it is time for deep reflection. They may be unlikely to change, but *you can change*, or rather: change your approach or attitude! Weigh up the pros (if there are any) and the cons, make the decision to limit your time with this person, (only as a final resort end the relationship) -and don't look back.

I have certainly walked away from friendships, relationships and even jobs that left me feeling utterly drained and depleted. Then there are also relationships or interactions in my life where "walking away" would cause too much damage or harm so I have gone for "option #2": I limit my time with these people, or time spent in certain types of situations. I appreciate that other people perceive this as "cold" or "uncaring" but it is preferable (by far) to paying with my energy (life force) and health (or peace of mind) for more interaction.

The archetype of The Wounded Healer

Human beings tend to externalise (*project out*, onto other people and situations) what they are not ready to own in themselves. This is what drives dysfunctional people (people with serious imbalances in their minds and lives) to attend courses in healing work. It is the need and soul desire-to-heal projected outward – rather than embraced deeply within. On some level they know that they need healing – but this yearning takes the more acceptable form of "a great desire to heal others". Now before thinking that you can "heal anyone", (and just for the record you can't, only Spirit or the spirits can do that!), take a moment to reflect on how hard it is to make lasting changes in your own life: to stop smoking, permanently keep off excess weight, or renegotiate a relationship/friendship that causes you pain, takes tremendous effort and commitment!! Now think again: does "healing others" *really* seem like an easier option than healing *yourself*?!

Once again, here a continuum opens up: no practitioner is ever fully healed. Our key wounds are like rivers or golden ore that will run through our flesh and the landscapes of our soul for life. Approached bravely we can mine for gold, profound insights, ever-deepening learning. I urge you to make sure you find a practitioner who does deep work on their own issues – they will be able to separate off their own "stuff" from your "stuff". Practitioners who believe that they can heal others without continuously working on themselves will engage you in a shadow dance where their own key issues are worked and repeated. Something will feel *off* and *you will be paying for the privilege*! Pay attention to that gut feeling!

The *perfect practitioner* does not exist and neither does *the perfectly healed or cured practitioner*. The same practitioner will have good periods (be well enough to work) and periods of retreat (needing to work on themselves), or good days and bad days. This is one of the reasons why tribal shamans will sometimes get guidance from their spirits that "today is not the right day" (this could also be for external circumstances, outside the practitioners' control. The spirits have the bird's eye view in a way that we humans in "Earth Arena" can't). Problems in the profession (I am speaking primarily about shamanic practice but the same thing goes for psychotherapy or counselling) are caused by *practitioners who focus on others as an escape from their own wounds and life challenges.* Be aware of this continuum and ask some pointed questions before you engage: does this practitioner have supervisor? Does this practitioner have time set aside for inner work and their own life journey? I personally think it is OK to ask for a yes or no answer on that (obviously not the details!), before putting our soul and psyche in someone's hands.

That thorny issue of our toxic selves

The thorny issue is that only very few of us grew up in truly non-dysfunctional (balanced, healthy, supportive!) families. Here I believe it is helpful to once again speak a continuum: some families are essentially strong and caring but there will be dysfunctional aspects to the way they operate. (I can personally think of one such family where everyone is in constant communication with each other and they all spend lots of time with each other -but any "outsider", think of a person marrying into the family, is dealt the card of "fit in or get out". There is no genuine willingness to get to know a new person and learn new ways of being in the world). At the opposite end of the scale we find families which are so dysfunctional that they are not families in any real sense of the word, other than the fact that the people involved are all related to each other through blood, birth or marriage.

All of us fall somewhere on the spectrum between two extremes. My own family of birth probably falls somewhere exactly in the middle range: our family is riddled with mental health histories (depression, phobias, mental breakdown) and different forms of physical/emotional/psychological abuse but there is a basic level of cohesion, meaning authentic commitment and communication between key family members. To this I could add that my own generation is doing far better than the generations preceding us -meaning that *our parents got something right and improved on the care they themselves received!!*

The thing is that anyone who grows up in a family with "serious issues" (unfortunately that is many of us!) will end up carrying pockets of dysfunction. When I read back diaries that I wrote in my early twenties, I cannot imagine how my husband (then boyfriend) put up with me! And, of course, I can say the same thing for him: thinking back to some of things we said and did then, I cringe. We have grown together as well as grown up together. We are more mature people for our partnership, the experiences we lived through, the children we are parenting together.

I will acknowledge (I hope that by leading the way I will unlock something for you) that my younger self was a well-meaning and talented but messed up person. After decades of healing work and self-improvement work, I am a better "deal" today. But I also know that at times of extreme stress I will sometimes revert to "older patterns" or childhood programming -meaning I need to commit to doing more work on myself. That work will not end until I die (and probably beyond).

People have dropped me from their lives because whatever I was presenting with (unacknowledged and unhealed) was not good for them. Today I feel no resentment about that: they did the right thing and those rejections powered my own healing journey (as indeed I hope that some of my own stepping-back will do for others). There is no point in acting as an enabler for other people's toxic material.

Having acknowledged that, one of my greatest issues with the Toxic People concept is that once again (as humans inevitably do) *we place the problem outside ourselves by projecting it onto others.* By calling others toxic we cling to the illusion that we are "clean". We can do better!

That which seeks healing through repetition (or acting out)

Anything that hurts, anything that "makes a noise", really anything that comes to attention in negative ways, is something that seeks healing.

When we exclaim "ever so toxic!" and slam doors shut there is one thing we fail to ask: "What seeks healing here?!" On occasion something needs healing and we can choose to be the person who brings the healing (this may be why the issue comes to *your* attention). This process mostly works through family and professional situations. When a member of my family presents with something unpleasant but does not give permission for healing work, I can still ask Spirit: what seeks healing? Is there anything I can or may do, honouring the free will of all people concerned? Sometimes that is to say prayers, sometimes it is to extract a "free floating ancestral soul (who is not at rest) from the family field". Sometimes it is to offer help in a different way again, a way that is more mainstream and therefore acceptable to the person concerned. Other times the answer is "no" there is nothing I can do at this time (without violating boundaries). Then I back off and hold the vision of the highest outcome. I also make a point of deeply honouring the fact that others have their own learning and healing journeys to make it is often not my job to play saviour and stand between them and their learning (fate/destiny/karma feel free to insert the term of your choice).

Having acknowledged that difficult truth: there is often much that "runs in families" (quite literally!) which can be resolved in an ancestral healing session if one member is willing to commit to the work (and gives permission for you to work through them and use them as a "portal"). Such work will take pressure off the whole family, even if other family members never know what was done or why it was done.

Interpersonal power

Most people are good and bad in equal measure. We all have a personal shadow. We cannot have interactions or relationships with people without encountering their shadow – and them encountering ours. *Make sure to marry someone whose shadow you can live with!*

Rather than shutting the door on all people whose shadow we have dealings with, we need to find ways of interacting in healthy (high vibration) ways with people who are dropping into lower frequency courses of action.

One book I recommend in this context is: Modern Machiavelli by Troy Bruner and Phil Eager[4]. It provides very practical guidance for anyone who experiences inter-personal conflict or "shark-infested waters" in their profession. The sub-title is "13 Laws of Power, Persuasion and Integrity". I was offered a review copy and the word integrity in the title was what convinced me to read it. I am glad I did! The authors explain why people behave the way they do and why all of us need to master a degree of strategy if we are to be truly effective in life. We need to learn how to manage conflict and how to understand both the overt and covert communications of others. The paradox is that only by understanding and accepting some hard truths about human nature can we handle the worst in others with a degree of grace. The book presents the material in the form of "laws" for social interaction, for instance "Law 7: Conflict is Inevitable and Selectively Advantageous." [4]

Shadows, Smoke and Mirrors

Where might you be a toxic presence in the lives of others? Where and how were you that in the past. Have you made amends? Have you done apology work on this?

It is by pulling all these things out of the closet and into awareness that we make a cauldron or crucible for ourselves. Absolutely anything can be an ingredient for soul alchemy and transformation if we engage with the images these dark mirrors hold up. These things lose their power to scare us, when we face them. It also frees up incredible amounts of energy when we release the notion that "we must hide aspects of ourselves from others to be loved at all".

The scariest yet liberating thing of all is that whatever we hide from ourselves is blatantly on display for others. People who know us well (or spend time around us) can easily tell us what our shadow is, where we dip into "the toxic spectrum" -if only we are brave enough to ask.... and creative enough to engage our imagination to dance with the information.

Spiritus or genie in bottle

Genies are magically confined members of a race of beings known as Jinn. Jinn are immortal indestructible creatures created before humans and after Angels. Long before the concept of biological matter ever existed. In fact they were created before any physical Universe as we know it existed. They exist in an indescribable realm in the same space as ours that is out of sync with our space-time so they and their Universe are not visible to us and ours is not visible to them. Ancient texts state that they are composed of "Smokeless Flame" or "Scorching Fire". However this might be ancient man's way of describing that they're made of light and energy fused together with the fundamental forces of the Universe
Unnamed author[5]

Ancient sorcerers and wizards devised magical lamps and bottles to trap these Jinn and these bottles were then placed in a special underground temple. However, over time these Jinns were able to use their mental powers to escape. Angelic forces apparently revealed that in order to keep the Jinn confined they need to be released, on occasion, in a tightly controlled manner. This manner resulted in the granting of wishes. Such lamps and bottles were also stolen and misused on occasion.

In following an example that my imagination threw up (the genie in the bottle) I discovered a story (and I guess no one can prove if it is true or not!) that tells us quite a lot about our own toxic self: we bottle it up, we hide it underground. However, over longer periods of time we can only make a pact with it, decide where and how it gets an outing and in doing so we achieve better life quality through better mental health. All of us are both genie and lamp!

The Holocaust

How could the Holocaust happen? How did the Nazis move from legalized discrimination to mass murder? How can we prevent future Holocausts happening?

> *"How can we make sense of this intentional killing of millions of innocent people?" is one of the most important questions asked during a study of the Holocaust. Many scholars have attempted to answer this question. Philosopher and Holocaust scholar Hannah Arendt argued that the Germans who carried out unspeakable crimes were ordinary people who simply accepted the conditions of their context as normal and the way things are done.*
>
> *... the bureaucratization of the Final Solution—the fact that Germans had specific responsibilities to perform as part of their jobs—made the process of killing seem routine. Hitler and the Nazis were extremely skilled at using propaganda and a deliberatively gradual process to make the isolation, segregation, and ultimate killing of Jews seem rational or justifiable.*
>
> Facing History and Ourselves[6]

Prominent Holocaust scholar Raul Hilberg explains that the Holocaust was made possible by means of small steps in the process. The (hideously named) Final Solution of the Jewish Question was a bureaucratic and strategically planned process designed as a systemic way to rid Europe of 11 million European Jews. The word holocaust means "complete destruction by means of burning". In 1944 Raphael Lemkin, (a Polish Jew who fled the Nazis, coined the word *genocide.*[7] He believed that the world might be in a better place to prevent such atrocities if the crime had a name. (Tragically, this proved not to be so: the world has witnessed genocide since and continues to do so).

It has been claimed that many ordinary people did not know what was unfolding and on what scale. Other sources claim that people did know very well but that they were too scared, (or brainwashed), to protest.

A related question is how the Germans who carried out these unspeakable acts and crimes against humanity, could accept these actions as normal and "routine".

We have already come across the concept of The Other (or "Us and Them" as we say in colloquial English). In a less far-reaching context, we all engage in this by calling other people toxic or undesirable. What history shows is that if such thinking goes unchecked (and becomes implemented on a large scale politically and socially speaking) a moral landslide will occur, and everyday values become compromised beyond redemption.

Another obvious element is brain washing and propaganda: if we hear something stated as truth every day for years on end, we will end up believing it unless we make a strong decision to step back and think for ourselves. (This book tries to provide the toolkit for this!)

Yet another issue is peer pressure and herd behaviour. When our peers shame us for cowardice or threaten us with exclusion from the group, self-preservation kicks in and this often leads to a drop in moral standards in a larger number of people than we would like to believe (this has been tested and demonstrated by psychologists). Just look at any in-group of teenagers in any secondary school and how they (commonly) deal with less popular peers.

I am writing this in London UK, in the period where Brexit remains controversial. I have spoken to many foreigners (like myself) who considered themselves proud Londoners up to that fateful day of the vote. Many of those people have since set plans in motion to leave the UK and a major talent-drain is underway. One shadow looming large (and one fear easily named) is that "those foreigners take jobs that belong to us natives". Research shows that historically this is not true: people were attracted to the UK to do jobs no one wants to do (cleaning or taxi driving) or to fill shortages in highly skilled jobs such as nursing, medicine and teaching. However, once a public mood takes over and people sense the freedom to voice opinions that were not perceived as "politically correct" before, major landslides of public opinion can occur quite rapidly. In a similar way terrorist attacks have eroded tolerance for people of a Muslim background. There is nothing fair about this, but has become an everyday reality in the UK, as well as most Northern European countries. It demonstrates that as a nation we are less far (and less safe) from what happened in Germany in the 1930s and 1940s than we prefer to believe. Here is yet another example where engaging our imagination may literally save lives.

Activity #19: Taking an unflinching look at the Holocaust

Go to a place where you can be undisturbed for some time. Bring paper, pen, a recent newspaper and electronic device (phone, iPad or laptop).

Take some deep breaths. Within yourself access the quality of courage and blow it up like a balloon until it fills you completely!

Now Google the Holocaust… We have all seen those images before. They are not comfortable to look at. We prefer looking the other way. These were people like you and me: leading ordinary lives, raising their children, doing their jobs. They were deported to concentration camps. Look them in the eyes – *really look them in the eyes.* They do not live in a place called "History" -they live on deep within all of us. They live on in our ancestral field. They lived a terrible fate that human nature made possible. There is no sugar-coating or denying that fact.

Scan the newspaper. Is there any feature in there that has

echoes of what happened in Germany during WW2? Is there a description of genocide, any mention of human beings locked up in cages or treated worse than criminals? Are there pictures of starving children in war zones looking just like the inmates of WWII concentration camps?

All these people were, are and will always remain members of The Human Family. Even those who died still live on in our collective ancestral field. We are all related to all other human beings, the only difference being a matter of degree.[8] All human beings have Deep Ancestors in common. Take a deep breath and take a hard look at the human phenomenon that is YOU:

- Have you ever followed orders (or the instructions of an authority figure) and done something you now regret?
- Have you ever resorted to dehumanizing another human being – if only in your own mind? Have you ever referred to other people as "vermin"? Have you heard others do this?
- Have you ever seen an injustice committed but not spoken out for fear of your own skin?

If you are truly brave, take a moment to connect with your Inner Nazi. The part of you that is capable of all those things and more. If you can do this, you will know how the Holocaust could happen. Stay with the discomfort and write down some notes for yourself: what needs to happen if humankind is to avoid creating holocausts and genocide? How can you yourself make a small contribution to that cause? Make a pledge to doing this… And thank you for doing this!

Chapter 20

Narcissism & Imagination

There can be no other gods in an extreme narcissist's world, regardless if they say they believe in God or not. In practical terms, a narcissist is God in his/her own imagination

Extreme narcissism is an egotistical preoccupation with self. It focuses on personal preferences, aspirations, needs, success, and how one's self is perceived by others. Some basic narcissism is healthy. This kind of narcissism is better termed as responsibly taking care of oneself, or what I would call "normal" or "healthy" narcissism

Samuel Lopez De Victoria[1]

The narcissist has a very vivid imagination. Most of the drama takes place in the paranoid mind of the narcissist. His imagination runs amok. He finds himself snarled by horrifying scenarios, pursued by the vilest "certainties". The narcissist is his own worst persecutor and prosecutor. Let his imagination do the rest.

Dr San Vatkin[2]

Narcissus -the myth

The moral tale of Narcissus and Echo comes from Greek mythology. In Ovid's version, Narcissus was a hunter, the son of river god Cephissus and the nymph Liriope. He was a handsome young man and many people fell in love with him. He despised them for it. As a child, Narcissus had been prophesized by Teiresias, the blind prophet of Thebes, to 'live to a ripe old age, as long as he never knows himself'.[3] One day Narcissus was out hunting in the woods. A nymph called Echo spotted him and lost her heart to him. Narcissus sensed someone following him. Echo decided to reveal herself and embrace him -but he pushed her away and told her to leave him alone. Echo roamed the woods in despair and faded away until an echo sound was all that remained of her. Nemesis, the goddess of retribution and revenge, decided to punish Narcissus for his cruel behaviour. She took him to a pool where he could see his own reflection -and fell in love with it. Once he understood that is was only a reflection and therefore hopeless, he committed suicide. In the place where he died a narcissus flower appeared. Some say that Narcissus still admires himself in the Underworld, by staring at the waters of the river Styx (representing the boundary between the realms of life and death).

In another version of this myth, recorded by Lydian geographer Pausanius, Narcissus has a twin sister who is exactly alike in appearance -and Narcissus falls in love with her. She dies and the grieving Narcissus goes in search of her.[4] Different perspectives can offer a golden grain of "truth", a *timeless wisdom*.

Just as the word toxic has gained a new life in modern usage so the adjective *narcissistic* is not lagging far behind. It appears everywhere! Articles inform us how to spot a Narcissist and remind us that this condition is incurable: "Five Early Warning Signs You're with a Narcissist"[5] or "Is Your Ex a Sociopath or Narcissist?[6]"

What is a narcissist?

The word is now commonly used to refer to any person with a marked degree of self-involvement. At a social event you may get stuck with a person who talks about themselves all night without even asking one question about you. They used to be called *a bore* or *hard work.*

The term is also used deliberately in character assassinations of high-profile individuals. Often the word narcissistic does not seem to be enough on its own and words such as malignant or out-of-control are added for extra measure. Any word that is over-used and thrown around carelessly will lose its power and rightful meaning. Using language that way impoverishes language! *Malignant narcissism* is a diagnostic term taken from psychiatry. It refers to superiority, exhibitionism and, exploitativeness.[7]

According to expert Elisabeth Lunbeck[8], pathological narcissists are abusive, manipulative, cunning but often very successful. They can be quite seductive. They draw people into their ambit, and then exploit and discard them. If someone's just a brute, they're not going to be very successful; it's the seductive brute that's the problem! On the other hand, there is such a thing as *healthy narcissism,* and this is necessary for doing well in life. The healthy narcissist – the productive narcissist can marshal that high self-esteem and put it to good use, to be a leader. Leadership literature practically assumes that a good CEO is a narcissist!

Lunbeck makes the related point that the term *self-esteem* has now become "an object of ridicule". The power of the concept of narcissism really lies in its paradoxical nature. It can refer to and explain both what we value the most and what we despise the most—it covers an incredible range of human behaviour from normal functioning to pathological destructiveness.

One of my issues is that my parents never took my side, *ever*. If got into a conflict with anyone it was assumed that I was at fault and my child self was treated as a perpetrator in a kangaroo court. No one sat me down and said: please tell me what really happened, what does your side of the story look like? Why do you feel wronged or upset? I received no guidance on navigating my way through issues. No one told me that I needed healthy boundaries and the ability to communicate those calmly, to survive the "rugby scrummage" that passed for life in a grammar school in The Netherlands in the 1980s.

Today I understand fully that parents cannot teach or model what they have not received or developed themselves. This tells me a lot about the childhood experiences of my parents and that is a precious gift, it helps me understand them. However, I also know that this reversal (this treatment coming from the people who were supposed to stand up for me) was so extreme that through hurting me, it forced me to raise my own awareness. For one thing it forced me to really hear criticism and learn from that – which is a good quality.

A childhood like mine puts a person at extreme risk of falling into the claws of a narcissist, because abuse is the "default setting". Feeling compassion for the abuser is part of that default setting. (Instead of knowing when to "cut your losses and run for safety" you have been conditioned to "try even harder and blame yourself"). My life got interesting! I met my fair share of narcissists along the way. I met a far larger number of people whom had suffered serious *narcissistic wounds*: their sense of self has been so profoundly wounded or harmed that today their lives involve around staging dramas that force others to lavish love/listening and support on them -but no amount of love and attention lavished ever heals anything (because they do not transmute the core childhood wound).

Pain is a hard taskmaster. Human beings spend a lot of time and effort avoiding pain. From small pains toddlers learn to avoid bigger pains or life-threatening scenarios. From broken hearts adult humans learn about discernment, healthy boundaries and not giving their soul away

Pain is not only about "triggering avoidance". There is more to it:

Pain often is something coming to attention because it seeks healing!

Human beings try to avoid pain, but it always catches up (sooner or later). Sometimes it catches up at a considerable delay, meaning that unresolved issues will surface again in the descendants of people long dead. Pain does not evaporate when a person dies. It is either healed (transmuted, balanced and any wrongdoing forgiven) or, if not, it pools in the ancestral field. Someone, one day, *must* carry it again – *because it needs healing and working through.* In mysterious ways certain types of pain are *impersonal.* We often carry the pain of people we never met. The pain of our ancestors lives on in our bodies. Their terror lives on in our nightmares.

When we engage with deep-rooted pain in meaningful ways we nearly always find ancestral pain too. We enter a layered landscape that interacts with both dreams and mythology. C.G. called this The Collective Unconscious: '...it is made up of a collection of knowledge and imagery that every person is born with and is shared by all human beings due to ancestral experience. Although individuals do not know what thoughts and images are in their Collective Unconscious, it is thought that in moments of crisis the psyche can tap into the Collective Unconscious.[9]

Through healing my own pain, I understand the pain of my parents, my forefathers and foremothers. I gain precious insights into the forces and limitations that shaped their lives: the abuse that was passed on, the wars they lived through, the children they lost, the medical care they did not receive. *This makes me love my family and ancestors more!!* Not only that, I gain the opportunity to heal some of these things. I can do apology work, where an apology is due. I can ask healing spirits to unravel and transmute unhealthy entanglements. I can make amends for things my ancestors did. If I do not undertake this work – who will?

Traumatised people often traumatise others in turn. What this really means is "making others carry our pain for while" because it brings the illusion of relief, of having shifted it. However, this sensation is short-lived. Only too soon, pain and trauma will be singing in our blood, bones and dreams again. And not only that: there is now another person who carries this trauma. *Trauma breeds and spreads – when it goes unchecked.* This is one the most powerful motivations for engaging in ancestral healing work! Healing, balancing and transmuting such imprints, memories and issues can clear the family line. We free future generations from being affected and burdened by this. By clearing ourselves we also reduce the chance of us inadvertently hurting (or even traumatising!) those around us. Those are major gains, in a culture where mental illness has reached epidemic proportions!

I once asked my shamanic practitioner students to do a piece of work on finding their "inner Donald Trump". Everyone in the group was able to do this – but most people said they ended up time travelling to their two-year old self having a tantrum. See March 2017 blog titled Trump's Teachings.[10]

Clinically speaking the term Narcissism refers to a condition called Narcissistic Personality Disorder (NPD). Perhaps we fear narcissism because we are all so acutely conscious of how much we present ourselves to the world. We bear witness to selves under construction, in virtual space. In the comments sections, we now react to others at lightning speed, on a scale greater than ever before in human history, judging others as fake and evil.[11]

Narcissists perceive themselves as so uber special that no one else matters. Their behaviour unfailingly creates a minefield of suffering and trauma around them.

Extreme narcissism is an egotistical preoccupation with self. It focuses on personal preferences, aspirations, needs, success, and how one's self is perceived by others.

Psychologists say that egotistical narcissists are typically created in one of two ways. One way is through excessive pampering on the part of the parents. Parents create an attitude in the child that he/she is better than others and entitled to special privileges. This creates an arrogant child who lacks a healthy dose of gratitude and humility. It describes the proverbial brat that no one likes.[12]

Another way that extreme narcissists are created is when a child receives a significant emotional wound or a series of them culminating in a major trauma of separation/attachment. It creates a dysfunction in the ability for the narcissist to connect emotionally to others. No matter how socially skilled an extreme narcissist is, he/she has a major attachment dysfunction and wound. This wounded person constructs one or more false fronts in order to survive and insulate themselves from people because of distrust and fear (Lopez De Victoria, 2008).[1]

I recommend the following books: Dangerous Personalities - An FBI Profiler Shows You How to Identify and Protect Yourself from Harmful People[13] and The Gift of Fear.[14]

Using our imagination – listening to the warning signs!

Our culture expects us to "rub along" with others and often this means dismissing our gut-instinct, which will tell us (accurately) that something is off. Narcissists are confidence tricksters! They will sweep you off your feet and take you by storm with dramatic gestures and seductive moves. They can be surprisingly "popular" on first acquaintance (they are experts at making a good first impression!) Their dubious charisma consists of four ingredients.[15]

- Attractiveness (flashy, neat attire)
- Competence (self-assured behaviour)
- Interpersonal Warmth (charming glances at strangers)
- Humour (witty verbal expressions)

As these positive vibes cannot be sustained, narcissists tend to operate in the short-term zone: new people, new situations, short flings because they become addicted to both the positive social feedback and emotional rush.[16] *Research shows that people make decisions within the first few minutes of a relationship that determine the long-term nature of the relationship.* We fare better if we learn to look beyond superficial impressions and see a person in a variety of different situations and contexts before we make up our mind. (Romantic culture actively promotes the dream of being swept off our feet!)

Another way that the narcissist's ego gets special attention is through the role of being a victim. Welcome to the *victimized extreme narcissist.* Most people recognize ego as arrogance. At the same time, they fail to see the subtle deception of ego when it takes the role of a being a victim. As kind and compassion-driven human beings, we easily are fooled by this form of extreme ego.[1]

If we cannot imagine how narcissism plays out and what the driving forces of such a person are, we become easy prey. About 0.5 – 1% of the general population is formally diagnosed with NPD (Narcissistic Personality Disorder) but obviously there is a far larger number of people displaying key traits and behaviour without ever being diagnosed.[17]

Activity #20: Recipe for cooking a Narcissist:

If you are *not a narcissist,* you may well have difficulties spotting the wiring in others! Your own life experiences may have taught you that narcissism is real and how it manifests.

Go to a place where you can be undisturbed for half an hour. Light a candle. Allow your awareness to drop down deep inside your own body. Move from the brain, as the seat of thinking, to your heart, as the stronghold of deep inner knowing. Try to hold a relaxed yet alert state of consciousness (this gets easier with practice!)

I invite you to enter a Portrait Gallery where the narcissists who have had an impact on you are represented. This may be in the form of an oil painting, sound installation or names called out, a scent you associate with them, memories of a place you associate with them – and so forth. Talk a walk down this "hall of infamy". Acknowledge that these people have their talents, but that they do not have your best interests at heart.

Call in the Greek goddess Nemesis – but ask her to arrive in her *compassionate manifestation* (not in full fury!) Nemesis is said to direct human affairs in such a way as to maintain equilibrium. Her name means *she who distributes or deals out*. She is The Leveller. Ask Nemesis to level the playing field between these people and you – so their manipulations no longer fool, trap or ensnare you. Nemesis is often depicted as a winged goddess. Ask her to take you under her wing. Another interpretation of her name is "dispenser of clues". Ask her to be your guide for the minefield that is future encounters with Narcissistic (or scheming, self-involved) people.

Ask her to transmute any feelings of inadequacy you may hold from occasions when these people made you feel lacking, in the wrong, or cold for imposing boundaries. Observe her pulling these feelings and memories out of your body and energetic field. Next observe her pouring the elixir of discernment and healthy self-love into you.

Thank her and return to everyday consciousness. Continue to connect to her and express gratitude daily: speak a brief prayer to her, leave her an offering or perform a kind act in her name that balances a situation for someone else.

Chapter 21

Doors of Perception

Imagination plays a number of important roles in mental health. The ability to contemplate things that are not actually happening can contribute to mental health problems such as anxiety and delusions. But imagination can also play a powerful role in healing.
Imagination, Good Therapy[1]

Sensory deprivation and imagination

Tribal shamans have always entered altered states of consciousness by means of fasting, through extreme feats of physical endurance and through extreme isolation (to the point of dehydration and physical danger). One technique used by tribal shamans for initiating their apprentices was sensory deprivation. In today's world of social media and 24/7 stimulation and demands we still have a means of experiencing that: sensory deprivation tanks.[2]

We are all in 24/7 communication with the world around us. So, what happens to a human brain when all sensory input is eliminated? One article frames this as *the default state of the brain.* We only have speculative theories at this point but one such theory claims that this is the place where we find the imagination. What is the default mode network doing? It could be responsible for planning, hypothetical ideas, beliefs, and maybe even the imagination. It might be the basis of conscious experience, by forming a 'dynamic core' of neural activity that anchors the interpretation of sensory input.[3] In a sensory deprivation environment, the brain receives no concrete input on which to ground the stream of consciousness. Without a sensory anchor, the brain's free association processes have only themselves to build on, with no point of reference to stabilize beliefs. Meanwhile, the brain's perceptual machinery, which tries to construct a model of the world, has no 'ground truth' to use as a filter. The results over time are hallucinations and eventually delusions, probably due to the default mode network reaching increasingly tenuous but mutually-reinforcing conclusions about reality, with nothing external to cross-validate it with.[3]

When an individual enters a sensory-deprived state, the brain begins to exhibit "psychosis-like" symptoms such as anxiety, altered states of consciousness, hallucinations, and delusions. Prolonged exposure to a deprived sensory environment has significantly more severe effects, which can result in significant cognitive impairment, disorganized speech and suicidal thoughts and actions.

Even just depriving one of the five senses can induce a hallucinogenic effect. As a teacher of shamanism, I often blind fold my students for certain tasks. I also impose periods of silence, where they are not allowed to talk to each other.

Immersion into an environment of total sensory deprivation has been shown to cause hallucinations such as visions of shapes or faces, auditory hallucinations of voices and sensing an "evil" presence in the chamber in as little as fifteen minutes. In contrast shorter periods of sensory deprivation in flotation tanks have been demonstrated to show significant therapeutic effects! This phenomenon has given us a new acronym: REST (Restricted Environmental Stimulation Therapy).[4]

People enter a waking dreams state (this increases the theta waves in the brain, the same way shamanic drumming does!) Apparently, this brings an immediate reduction in stress hormone and this reduces anxiety, pessimism and sleeping problems in people. The notion of the human imagination floating in the velvety void at the heart of REST resonates with me.

Finding creative ways of saying no

I was conditioned to prioritise mind over body from an early age. Many a time did I have a "bad feeling about something" (manifesting as extreme reluctance, pressure over the chest or persistent stomach ache), but I would push on because I thought that this was what was expected of me. Unsurprisingly this never ended well. The situation invariably got worse, *making it easier for me to say no or operate a different boundary* (but the backtracking obviously caused resentment). Eventually I learned to listen to my body and say *no.*

I actively make it a focus to observe closely how others say "no". Some people do this incredibly lovingly and creatively. I think it is a talent some people have! I do not have the talent and I was born in the Netherlands -where super direct people speak their minds all the time -so I really need to work at it... However, recently one of my students made my day by saying: "I need a well-boundaried teacher and I found that role model in you!" Hallelujah -me as a role model in personal boundaries?! I feasted on that compliment for days!

The key to saying no is making it a positive thing: "I will not take this on because I cannot give it my full attention right now".

Saying no to others is often a healthy form of saying yes to self-care.

Seer, Sage, Shaman

The word seer comes from the word seeing but it refers to what we see with our eyes shut. One definition from the Online Etymology Dictionary is "one to whom divine revelations are made". In a culture where perception is tied to the material and physical dimension, having the gift of sight is a mixed blessing. In our culture we are way more familiar with "sight-seeing" than "seers and the gift of sight".

Research has demonstrated that the ways people form mental images (and the ability they have to do so) seems to vary significantly. In 1880, Francis Galton published his classic paper "Statistics of Mental Imagery" [5] after asking a series of subjects about images summoned by their minds. Other people have since built on his pioneering work.

In her article in The Guardian, Mo Costandi asks a key question[6]: *If you can't imagine things, how can you learn?* In everyday speech we often say: "I will need to see it before I believe it" and let's remember the "fantasy-prone person"! However, often we need to see something clearly in our imagination before we can understand it or make it happen.

> *Never underestimate the power of visualisation. It may sound like a self-help mantra, but a growing body of evidence shows that mental imagery can accelerate learning and improve performance of all sorts of skills. For athletes and musicians "going through the motions," or mentally rehearsing the movements in the mind, is just as effective as physical training, and motor imagery can also help stroke patients regain function of their paralysed limbs.*
> Mo Costandi[6]

According to Costandi, neurologists refer to the inability to form mental images as *"congenital aphantasia"* – from the Greek words a, meaning "without", and phantasia, meaning "a capacity to form mental images" – and they believe it affects approximately 2% of the population (one in 50 people). Remarkably, aphantasics do experience visual imaginary in their dreams, so it seems that only intentional visualisation is affected.

As a teenager I actively used my imagination for learning. In maths I would perceive numbers as personalities and play around with number sequences before falling asleep. In German class I would construct my own mental shortcuts for the grammar rules my teacher explained and then use those as a roadmap in exams.

My Latin teacher made our class memorize one page of

new Latin words a day, for six years. I generally did that over breakfast, and it became a habit I followed with other languages I learned. Commit a page of new words a day to memory and your vocabulary will grow fast – it is a good workout for your brain. Optimal learning occurs in the place where joy, imagination, repetition and good structuring/sequencing all come together.

Perceiving = believing

Things we do not perceive exist outside our field of awareness, and lack of awareness can have harmful consequences. However, the things we *do* perceive are not necessarily the "truth", as our perceptions are coloured by personal history and personal experiences. In recovery from addiction circles the following phrase is used: *feelings just are*. It is true that feelings just are -but feelings are not facts.

For all of us lenses of perception are in operation: for some people this is a very scientific lens (*I will need proof before I believe this statement!),* a highly intuitive lens (*I just know that this is so!*), a shamanic lens (*the spirits told me!)* and so forth.

Perception is a tricky thing indeed. Some people believe that a medical doctor always knows what is best for our body. Others trust law-enforcement 100%. Some people believe that vaccinations save children's lives while others believe that refusing vaccinations saves children from autism. Please remember The Confirmation Bias!

> *There are things known and there are things unknown, and in between are the doors of perception.*
> Aldous Huxley[7]

> *Let me focus on imagination. It appears to be a romantic invention which, however, had survived Romanticism with its cult of the poet's personality and self-expression, and was later developed in modernist aesthetic thought (such as I.A. Richards's Coleridge on*

Imagination, 1934, or the archetypal criticism of Maud Bodkin or Northrop Frye). At the same time, it can be said that the notion of imagination is a product of a development which lasted for millennia and on whose beginning there is Plato's notion of maniā or madness, which, according to the dialogue called Phaedrus, drives divinely inspired artists (but also bacchants, lovers and soothsayers) to grasp the ideal, divine beauty.
Professor Martin Procházka[8]

Activity #21: Captives of our own perception

Go to a place where you can be undisturbed for a while. Bring paper and pen. Light a candle.

We are all the product of previous experiences and the way we have chosen to interpret those experiences. Young people are not aware that they have such choices, "things just are". As people grow older (and often while they attend higher education), they become more able to think about the way they think (while others never reach that stage of reflection and re-evaluation).

Today's exercise is about mapping how and where we might be captives of our own perception.

Please write down a brief description of key events that happened in your personal life yesterday. Also write a brief description of how you perceived these events.

For instance: yesterday was a Monday, never a great day. I got stuck in traffic and arrived late for an important meeting. The day just went on from there: that comment my colleague made about me really annoyed me. The best part of the day was a game of squash with one friend but, annoyingly, he always wins…

Now take that same description and use your own words as "modelling clay". Use your imagination to call up people you know who have a completely different take on life and/or temperament from you. Behave as if they were someone else's observations. For every line or event, now write own a completely different "take".

Yesterday was a Monday. I drove to work reliving a great weekend, I got stuck in traffic but that allowed me to call my elderly mother and have a longer chat with her. Of course, I arrived late for a meeting, but my mother is more important! One colleague made a silly joke about my dress sense. My younger self would have felt hurt, but today I am proud of looking a little eccentric. It makes people perceive me as an individual! Joe and I met for a game of squash and of course he always wins. It is hard to find the time but at least I have avoided that spare tyre many men my age acquire!

Go for extreme:

- *I lost my job and it was the greatest gift because I would never have left of my own volition.*
- *I spent a night sleeping rough on airport bench after my flight was cancelled and it gave me such appreciation of the challenges that homeless people face every day!*
- *Someone tried her best to offend me, but I was able to extract a compliment from her words....*

If you feel up to it: repeat this exercise with key events in your life. Look at the life-changing events. Did adversity bring you gifts? Can you see the same events through the eyes of another person? If you can – what do you see? What do you take away from this exercise?

> *OK... so stress is always an invitation and perfect opportunity to improve one's ability to handle stress -right? I am abundantly blessed today!*
> Imelda Almqvist, Facebook post, 2 April 2019

Chapter 22

Dreaming

Marie Louise von Franz, a scholarly colleague of C.G. Jung, once wrote that
dreams "are the voice of nature within us."[1]

> *... in dreams we put on the likeness of that more universal, truer, more eternal man dwelling in the darkness of primordial night. There he is still the whole, and the whole is in him, indistinguishable from nature and bare from all egohood. It is from these all-uniting depths that the dream arises...*
>
> C.G. Jung[2]

Dream Interpretation

There are many different schools of thought for interpretation of dreams. Philosophers discuss whether dreams should be described as hallucinations or illusions. In shamanic traditions all over the world dreams are often viewed as vessels carrying meaning: omens, signs, warnings and divine guidance.

When I do dream incubation work with students, I make the distinction between three different types of dreams, based on thirty years of keeping a dream journal:

- Composting dreams *(processing everyday occurrences)*
- Personal dreams full of symbolism and spirit guidance *(I think of those as healing or therapeutic dreams the spirits create for me personally)*
- Archetypal or mythological dreams that are not about me as a person but about the larger forces that shape and animate the cosmos *(there are the dreams I use as a seed or starting point for articles and workshops).*

The science behind dreaming

There is a discipline dedicated to the neuroscience of dreams. Sander van der Linden offers the hypothesis that dream stories may be stripping the emotion out of a certain experience by creating a memory of it.[3]

There are five stages of sleep: most dreaming we do, and also our most intense dreams, occur during the REM stage. For that reason, people are more likely to remember their dreams when woken directly after REM sleep. Vivid, bizarre and emotionally intense dreams (the dreams that people usually remember) are linked to parts of the amygdala and hippocampus. While the amygdala plays a primary role in the processing and memory of emotional reactions, the hippocampus has been implicated in important memory functions, such as the consolidation of information from short-term to long-term memory.

He explains that one neurobiological theory of dreaming claims that humans construct dream stories on waking (just to make sense of things) but dreams are actually electrical brain impulses that pull random thoughts and memories from our personal database.

Our dream stories try to strip the emotion out of a certain experience by creating a memory of it. This way, the emotion itself is no longer active. This mechanism fulfils an important role because when we don't process our emotions, especially negative ones, this increases personal worry and anxiety. This would mean that if you are experiencing emotional trauma or severe stress, dreaming can be a form of overnight therapy or self-healing! When our brains work through such events at night, essentially it performs the "elegant trick of divorcing emotions from memory, so it's no longer in itself emotional".[3]

There is experimental evidence that mammals (other than humans) also dream so dreaming is likely to serve a purpose.

The proposed link between our dreams and emotions is also highlighted in a recent study published by Matthew Walker and colleagues at the Sleep and Neuroimaging Lab at UC Berkeley, who found that a reduction in REM sleep (or "less dreaming") influences our ability to understand complex emotions in daily life – an essential feature of human social functioning. Scientists have recently identified where dreaming is likely to occur in the brain. A very rare clinical condition known as "Charcot-Wilbrand Syndrome" has been known to cause (among other neurological symptoms) loss of the ability to dream.[3]

Dream Diary

Many people claim not to remember their dreams. This does not mean that they do not dream! My husband "risks his life" if he speaks to be before I have written my dream diary because I cannot "thread dreams back into my memory" once other content takes centre stage.

> *Last night I dreamed that I lived in a society which was organised differently from real life London reality: young people were given a room in the house of an elderly person, so the one would have a home and mentor and the other the opportunity to impart wisdom. In the dream I was visiting the house where a brilliant young French student lived, hosted by a rather grumpy elderly man. She was out when I arrived, but the man showed me he had given her his front room, where the piano lived. She was composer. He explained that she composes music by using the wand a conductor uses to direct the orchestra. She points it at different stars in the night sky and those stars then send her music her brain downloads. The man explained that this is why, in popular images, a magic wand is often shown with a small star on top....*

I once had another dream where states of mind appeared as actual "states" -in the form of different countries I visited, so I became a tourist taking a tour of my own psyche. Sometimes I have a connected series of dreams (serial dreaming!) were every night I receive a new instalment until all aspects of a specific topic, have been covered.

Dreams and imagination

Are dreams and the imagination essentially the same thing? Both refer to mental processes and states of mind. Imagination happens in a conscious (or waking) mental state while dreams make use of the same sensory abilities, but no conscious effort is involved. We also make a distinction between dreaming (when we are asleep) and daydreaming (while we are awake).

Sigmund Freud called dream analysis the "royal road" to the unconscious. He believed that dreams (along with slips of the tongue) were the result of unconscious wishes and desires in an individual.[4]

Philosophers have also looked at dreams. Descartes famously suggested that "dreams pose a threat towards knowledge because it seems impossible to rule out, at any given moment, that one is not dreaming".[5]

Carl Jung took a more far-reaching approach. Jungian analysts try to decode dreams by viewing characters in dreams *as aspects of the dreamer*.[6]

The people of Ancient Greece practiced dream incubation.[7] The general idea was to receive guidance or healing directly from a god. The underlying assumption is that diseases were caused by displeased deities but that divine intervention could also heal them.

Joseph in the Old Testament in the Bible was a gifted dream interpreter and that made him a powerful figure.[8] His skills made him a prophet.

In the 16th and 17th century, (the era of the witch trials), Father Gracian, who was St. Theresa's confessor, wrote that "it is a sin to believe in dreams".[9] In that period the sexual content of dreams was linked to Satan and temptation.

Shamanism teaches that the spirits use dreams to communicate with us.[4]

We all dream the world into being

Many indigenous or tribal peoples go one step further. They teach that dreaming is the ultimate state in which creation is always occurring. The world has not just been created once upon a time, but *the world is always being created.* The aboriginal peoples of Australia call this The Dreaming or The Dreamtime:

All creatures — from stars to humans to insects — share in the consciousness of the primary creative force, and each, in its own way, mirrors a form of that consciousness. In this sense the Dreamtime stories perpetuate a unified world view. This unity compelled the Aborigines to respect and adore the earth as if it were a book imprinted with the mystery of the original creation. The goal of life was to preserve the earth, as much as possible, in its initial purity. The subjugation and domestication of plants and animals and all other manipulation and exploitation of the natural world — the basis of Western civilization and "progress" — were antithetical to the sense of a common consciousness and origin shared by every creature and equally with the creators. To exploit this integrated world was to do the same to oneself.[10]

If one accepts this key principle, then the correct use of our imagination is a key quality, one that survival of the human race may well depend on! Ultimately this teaches *reverence.* We lose our human-centred perspective.

One of the most famous dreams in the history of science came to German chemist Kekulé. He had a vision of a great serpent, or Ourobouros, biting its own tail, revealing the shape of the benzene ring.[6]

The aboriginal peoples of Australia also knew a great serpent: The Rainbow Serpent! When they saw a rainbow in the sky, they interpreted this as their Divine and cosmic creator being, The Rainbow Serpent, moving from one waterhole to another![12]

Dream interpretation books
Dream interpretation is a deeply personal issue. Engage in the hard graft of keeping a dream journal and learn from your own dreams! For guidance I recommend the work of international teacher Robert Moss.[13]

Day Dreaming
Not all dreaming occurs while we are asleep. Human beings also engage in daydreaming. This can be a negative thing when one drifts of during an important meeting. We all know people who "have their head in the clouds". Yet day dreaming can be a positive thing: research shows that it is associated with greater creativity in children.

What seeks expression through me?

I believe that our mainstream Western concept of "ourselves as completely separate units that function independently from others and our surroundings" is one of the great delusions of Western culture.

Here are some examples of what might be moving through me (or indeed anyone) at any given time:

- Needs and imprints from the ancestral continuum (or larger family field)
- My own unconscious desires and yearnings (so called "phantasies")
- Daydreams and conscious fantasies that colour my perception
- Karma and/or soul contracts that date back to previous incarnations, (which I do not remember in this lifetime)
- Parental, cultural and educational conditioning
- The land I live on, or walk on, may murmur and make requests through my own psyche and emotions
- I may have an overshadowing being with me, seeking

to have its needs and desires met through me (this is a common spiritual problem in addictions)
- I have spirit allies whispering in my ear making suggestions and challenging my own thoughts and decisions

Fantasy and Phantasy

There is also something that psychotherapists call Phantasy (*unconscious fantasy* as different from conscious fantasies and daydreaming). Those kinds of phantasies can rule (and even destroy) our lives unless we work hard to become aware of them.

Psychoanalyst Julia Segal wrote a book titled: Phantasy in Everyday Life: A Psychoanalytical Approach to Understanding Ourselves.[14] She defines phantasy as *the unconscious fantasies which control our assumptions, thoughts, emotions and indeed our behaviour*. Often another person and I are coming from a place of "opposing phantasies" (assumptions of what might happen or should be happening).

One example is of two people having sex. One assumes that they are having recreational sex (with no strings attached) while the other one is unconsciously hoping for procreative sex (pregnancy). Such crossed wires can destroy lives... Holding vastly different phantasies about friendship or marriage can also make daily life very challenging. I just opened the book at random and read this: *Feelings not recognized in ourselves are attributed to others -with many and far-reaching consequences*

I have referred to this phenomenon as *projection* in this book. It can (partly) be viewed as an attempt to do away with internal conflict. For instance, the conflict between being selfish and acting unselfishly is a real one, which can cause us trouble. Sometimes we try to set this conflict up in the outside world rather than bearing it (and resolving it within) ourselves.

Segal explains that in marriages people frequently carry different sides of a conflict. What then happens is that they are pushed into entrenched positions where all nuances are lost. Someone not giving an inch and apparently threatening something cherished (such as the status quo or a long-standing dream) pushes us on the defensive. Couples can completely exhaust themselves (and drain the reservoir of goodwill between them) dancing around the mulberry bush like this.

Gatekeeper of Unlived Dreams

I once made a painting titled Gatekeeper of Unlived Dreams. I mention it in the presentation titled: *Gods of Portals, Life Transitions and Liminal Spaces,* filmed by the Gatekeeper Trust.[15] My painting is based on the awareness that a human life consists of a very long sequence of choices. In my dreams I sometimes see glimpses of lands, cities and rooms where the choices we did not make continue to exist.

I once had a dream where I was in a very large house with many rooms. Those rooms all represented dreams that I had had on previous occasions and there were connecting doors and hallways! From one room (dream) I could step into the room just behind it and find myself in another room (a dream my waking mind had long forgotten). This was the Master Library of Dreams!

Is our universe unique? Might there be other universes out there, besides our own more familiar one, where all the choices you made in this life play out in alternate realities? This idea is often explored in science fiction because it provides scope for amazing story lines. The concept is known in popular language as a parallel universe.[16] In astronomical terms it is a facet of the astronomical theory of the multiverse.

Robert Moss recommends using a technique called dream re-entry[17]: undertaking a meditation or shamanic journey to return to the dream and allowing it to play out fully. This way we can retrieve information or insights we would have missed otherwise.

The Multiverse

One big question regarding the Multiverse theory is: are we the only universe out there? With our current technology, we are limited to observations within this universe because the universe is curved and we are inside the fishbowl, unable to see the outside of it (if there is an outside).[16]

Other universes could have very different laws of physics from our own, as they are not linked to ours. Might the spirit world be such a parallel universe? Might it even be the sum of all parallel universes?

Activity #22: Becoming a Dream Hunter and Dream Collector

Please commit to keeping a dream diary for a week (several weeks is better!)

Please do the following things:

- Write down all dreams as faithfully as you can, even tiny snippets and fragments
- Give every dream a unique title
- Write a brief reflection as well – you were the dreamer: what do you think or sense that this dream means?
- Read this chapter again and work out for every dream if it was a composting dream, dream of personal significance or archetypal dream of large collective significance?
- Put your general focus on dreams for this week: ask the people around you if they remember last night's dream, pay attention whenever and wherever dreams are mentioned. Become a Dream Hunter and Dream Collector!

After a week, read back your hoard. How did you get on? Was it valuable? What school of dreaming thought do you now subscribe to (if any!)? Will you continue?

Chapter 23

Imagination and Interpretation

Imagination refers to holding in mind a representation that may not be (yet) 'true' and does not necessarily reflect the facts about the external world or the Reality as of now. The act of imagination may use previous memories and a general knowledge of the world to recreate past memories or to imagine novel future events.
Sandeep Gautam[1]

Human faculties involved in the use of imagination?

In Chapter 17 we looked at autism-spectrum disorders and concluded that in those people the faculty of social imagination is limited compared to neurotypical individuals (in varying degrees, depending on the individual), however they may well excel at divergent thinking and use their imagination in unique ways. We have also seen that in some forms of mental illness the imagination becomes enlarged or grandiose and spins out of control.

In this context the work of Simon Baron Cohen[2]: the biology of imagination is often quoted (though it must be noted that not all parents of autistic children or adults who self-identify as autistic, agree with his findings!) Cohen makes a distinction between:

- *The contents of the imagination (which are culturally determined)*
- *The capacity for imagination (which is biologically grounded)*

In addition to this he focusses on the imagination as a false or distorted representation of Reality, as opposed to mere imagery. The imagery is a mental representation[3] but it may still (more or less!) represent the world accurately. Psychologist Alan Leslie (working in London in the 1980s) proposed that imagination involves three steps[4]:

1. A "primary" representation (an image that has "truth relations" to the outside world)
2. Making a copy of this primary representation (so called "second order representation")
3. Introducing elements of change to the second-order representation (playing with its truth relationships to the outside world without jeopardising the important truths that the original or primary representation needs to preserve)

This may sound rather abstract, but it reminds me of an exercise my co-teacher Susan Rossi set our sacred art students in the US recently:

A. Take a photograph of yourself (the primary representation)
B. Make several photocopies of that photograph (the secondary representation)
C. Draw or paint (*any* material!) over these images and run wild. The resulting image will be *you* and *not-you* at the same time. *(This task was inspired by an exercise Susan was set once by teacher Jenafer Owen).*[5]

We used this exercise specifically to get our group of (as it happened) female students to explore and unveil manifestations and expressions of their inner masculine aspect or force.

Gautam[1] says that a similar process (or sequence) is in operation when we make predictions, or plans for the future, based on what we have experienced in the past:

1. Past events and life experiences

2. Constructing plausible future events and scenarios
3. Navigating: this means making changes from the first person to third person perspective (a device often used in novels!) and so seeing things from another person's point of view
4. Theory of Mind, (a Jean Piaget concept, often abbreviated to ToM) as in constructing a representation of "another" or "the other" as opposed to self. Here the focus shifts but the procedure carries a risk that the new representation may not be true (only represent our perception).

Gautam also makes a distinction between two types of spatial-point-of-view awareness: one involves tracing and the other perspective-taking. More recent tests by Michelon and Zacks[6] argue that there is substantial evidence that we use at least two different methods to understand the perspectives of others:

When we are trying to decide whether someone else can see what we can see, these experiments suggest that we use the line-tracing method, but when we're trying to understand the relative positions of objects, we use the more cognitively demanding perspective-taking approach.

Another way of saying this is that we need to arrive at a Cognitive Map (where the other person becomes "the territory we are mapping", so to speak!)

Gautam[1] next addresses the meta-representational capacity essential for mind-reading. By mind-reading is meant here the ability to put yourself in another person's shoes and look at the world through their eyes: *Leslie's deeply interesting argument is that when you mind-read, you again need to quarantine your primary representations.* Here's how his argument goes. Just as your mental picture of a fish has 'truth relations' to a real fish in the outside world, so a belief, or a sentence, has truth relations to real events in the outside world."

Gautam uses the example of a statement such as:

"John is having an affair with a female colleague" *(primary representation)*

This is then copied to produce an identical version allowing us to "play around" with this statement.

"John is having an affair with a female colleague" *(statement, piece of information, may or may not be correct)*

Thirdly a prefix is added: "Mary believes that John is having an affair with a colleague"

This final statement may or may not to true, an element of doubt or uncertainty is introduced, but if Mary believes it, it is true for Mary in that moment.

We may never find out if this fictional John was having an affair or not, but the point is that Leslie[4] borrowed this insight from standard views in philosophy of mind because they have such unique (and useful) logical properties. When we mind-read we may well be busy employing such second order representations. It also allows us to maintain our own knowledge base *("I know that John is not having an affair")* yet communicate someone else's different (even opposing, if false!) belief." *("but I know that Mary believes he is!")*

Simon[7] contends that children with autistic spectrum disorders lack this imagination circuit or network and have deficits with ToM in particular, and Imagination in general. Thus, as per this hypothesis, they must also have problems imagining future autobiographical events, problems with episodic memory and problems with perspective taking approach to spatial navigation.

Let me now say this one more time in plain English: children on the Autistic Spectrum face challenges reflecting on their own (past or present) behaviour or interpreting the behaviour of others. From this follows that they have even greater difficulties conjuring possible future scenarios for themselves (many of which may never come to pass) and predicting what another person might do next (if they are not following a routine or familiar pattern).

To sum things up: theories have been proposed for how the human imagination works in the neurotypical mind. Other authors have examined how the imagination operates in the mind of atypical individuals. These authors focus on psychological and biological points of view. I have attempted to map the human imagination by providing a brief summary of these theories but adding a spiritual perspective and dimension.

Celestial Catechism

Celestial mythology, distilled to its essential core, does the same thing. The informal tale we tell of the lives of the stars is a metaphorical narrative. It is intended to inform us about the forces and processes at work in the universe, but it relies more on poetry than scientific precision.

E.C. Krupp[8]

In indigenous cultures the interconnectedness of everything is always emphasized and prioritized: Community takes priority over Individual, Ancestors and spirits over the limited human mind. Symbolic language acts as the grammar of myth and takes priority over logical thinking: everything always stands for something else and through those rich layers of symbolism Reality manifests Itself.

To my mind this is best illustrated by the field of ethnoastronomy (the astronomy of non-Western cultures and peoples). We will let E.C. Krupp speak again[8]: The term non-Western is not a geographical designation; it is a cultural one. We use it to describe people outside of the Euro-American sphere, including the native cultures of the Americas. The power of European and American colonialism is evident in the fact that the majority of the world's population is defined by what they are not.

As for defining science, if we wish to study science in non-Western cultures, we need to take several intellectual steps. First, we must accept that every culture has a science, that is, a way of defining, controlling, and predicting events in the natural world. Then we must accept that every science is legitimate in terms of the culture from which it grew. The transformation of the word science as a distinct rationality valued above magic is uniquely European. It is not common to most non-Western societies, where magic and science and religion can easily co-exist. The empirical, scientific realm of understanding and inquiry is not readily separable from a more abstract, religious realm.

Our night sky was the first storybook for our ancestors, as they sat around the fire and told stories.[9] The night sky also acts as a giant projection screen for cultural preoccupations. Through the patterns of the stars and the movements of the planets (the ancient Greek word *planetoi* means wanderers) we attempt to understand ourselves; not just our personal selves, but the human condition, the mysteries of human existence on earth.

The night sky demonstrates the eminence of the imagination in human existence, cultures and communities. However, researchers have found that our imagination changes our perceptions of reality: it can play tricks on us!

A Swedish study[10] consisted of a series of experiments using illusions in which sensory information from one sense changed or distorted one's perception of another sense. You can choose to look at the world either through optimistic 'rose-colored glasses' or through a cynical and pessimistic lens. This alters your perception of reality. Christopher Bergland[11] says that 'mental imagery and visualization can alter how we perceive the world around us. To a large extent, your mind can create reality at a neuronal level. By choosing to look on the bright side, and see the proverbial glass as perpetually half-full, the world around you will seem more hopeful and full of possibility.'

The world is not only as we collectively dream it, the world also shapeshifts and mirrors our imagination. This finding means that many New Age books are right: we can (to a considerable extent) create our reality. We may start off by changing our perception of reality, but once our reality changes and tangible outcomes start occurring, we are not only talking about perception any longer: we are dealing with manifestation. (However, please note that I am not saying that *we can manifest anything we like*!)

To achieve the maximum balance between imagination and analytical mind-set we need to be able to weave between the two mind-sets, according to Christopher Bergland.[12] If you tend to overthink and be hyper-analytical all the time, current research shows that you might want to "unclamp" your executive function throughout the day and let your mind wander more. Conversely, if you tend to be spacey or always daydreaming, your mind and brain will benefit by consciously making an effort to dial-in your focus and force your mind to wander less at some point throughout the day. It's important to stay cognizant and vigilant about constantly mixing up your explanatory style and perceptions of the world. This will prevent the neural networks of you mind and brain from getting stuck in a rut that blocks a healthy flow of information in all directions.

Imagination and Divination

This same principle (of mirroring and interconnectedness) is the underlying key principle in divination work. As the whole Web of Life is connected and every thread co-vibrates with other threads in the great Song of Creation it means that one can use a snapshot of one place in the Web to give a reading of what is going on at other places in the web. Omens, portents, animal behaviour and the placement of random objects – all these things can provide a staggering amount of information if your imagination and hotline to spirit are in gear.

Memory and the neuroscience of imagination

Not unlike most modern electronic devices, the human imagination requires memory capacity. One researcher wondered if they are even separate or if imagination just means taking memories and combining them in fresh or different ways to create something new, kaleidoscope-style. However, research involving an MRI scanner showed that there are distinct areas of the brain responsible for each activity.

Neuroscientists have pinpointed where imagination hides in the brain and found it to be functionally distinct from related processes such as memory.

Mark A. Philbrick[13]

Losing our memory, slowly but certainly, strips us of our identity. This is an issue people with dementia or Alzheimer's face (and arguably their families and carers bear the greatest impact of this). Without memory we have no identity but if we create all our reality from memories and past experiences, we remain stuck in old perceptions and old patterns. This is the paradox! By now we know that anything that exists – *has a shadow manifestation.*

False confessions and imagined crimes

For some well-publicized (but unsolved) crimes several people have come forward and made a deathbed confession. This is true for e.g. the (so called) Zodiac Killer.[14]

Not all memories are reliable (earlier we discussed repressed memory syndrome). One researcher called Julia Shaw[15] studies how false memories arise in the brain and she applies her skills to the criminal-justice system. She is quoted by Emma Bryce: 'Contrary to what many believe, human memories are malleable, open to suggestion and often unintentionally false. "False memories are everywhere," she says. "In everyday situations we don't really notice or care that they're happening. We call them mistakes, or say we misremember things." In the criminal-justice system, however, they can have grave consequences.'

Shaw points out that before the age of three our brain cannot form memories that last into adulthood (meaning that such early memories are suspect or at least unreliable). She also believes that a limited awareness of memory research in the context of therapy contributes to systemic failures (such as miscarriages of justice). She is campaigning for this because only very few people read academic journals, yet the information can save or destroy lives!

Post-traumatic stress disorder can mess with people's memories. Hypnosis and regression techniques are considered an unreliable source of information by US and UK courts.

The key issue here is *suggestibility*. In the same article[15] cognitive psychologist Elizabeth Loftus is quoted as explaining that:

- Often, false memories develop because there's exposure to external suggestive information.
- People can also suggest things to themselves – this is called autosuggestion. People draw inferences about what might have happened. Those solidify and act like false memories.
- In police questioning the subtle ways a question is pitched can affect what a witness reports; the feedback you give to a witness can modify how confident they are in their memories and they can shape those recollections.
- Ultimately, poor interrogation methods can lead to mistaken eyewitness accounts, baseless accusations and even false confessions.

Why do people confess to things they never did? I think the most fascinating examples aren't because of torture or because they felt like they had to, but because *they actually think they did it,*"

Shaw says[15]. To understand this, we need to look at the way that the human brain stores information. That's encapsulated by a concept called Fuzzy-trace theory, first described in the 90s by American psychologists Charles Brainerd and Valerie Reyna.[16] The theory suggests that our brains lay down memories in two forms: gist and verbatim-memory traces. Gist traces record broad features of an event; verbatim traces store precise details. "The verbatim is exact, and the gist is general," Shaw says. So, verbatim traces record a person's eye colour and name, while the gist traces register how well you got on and whether you liked them.

As a general rule, memory is a reconstructive thing," says Deryn Strange[17], associate professor of cognitive psychology at the John Jay College of Criminal Justice at The City University of New York. "So we are not able to play back any moment in our past and expect it to be an accurate record of what happened."[15]

Their survey has also revealed several features that allegations have in common: usually the accuser is known to the accused; the claims principally involve alleged sexual abuse; and most accusers are undergoing questionable therapy. People seeking therapy are vulnerable, and they're looking for answers, Shaw[15] says. So, if the therapist says: 'You must have repressed something,' they say: 'Let's go find it!'

This is something I keep an eagle's eye on with my own shamanic practitioner students: be very diligent about not planting suggestions or memories. This is easily done when the spirits show us an event in symbolic or metaphoric language. Taking that too literally we may plant suggestions and do active harm (while thinking we are healing someone!)

There are so many therapies and treatments available now that we easily lose track of where certain boundaries need to be drawn for the health and safety of all involved. There is a very good reason why only people who complete years of medical training can call themselves medical doctors. People working with mental health issues need a lot of training and experience too, to do so safely and competently.

In shamanic practice I actively warn my students about taking on clients with advanced mental health issues. When these things progress too far, people need a full team of professionals, not just one practitioner running a few sessions (however helpful). Then there is the issue of doing work that is so powerful that it destabilizes a person who may not be held by a cohesive team of specialists, or who may not have the required support in their local community. These things present a knife's edge: wishing to help and serve yet knowing our own limits and the limitations.

In 2016, London's Metropolitan police force was criticised for adopting a policy stating that anyone who made a sexual-abuse allegation would be believed. "Referring to people as victims when you're not sure victimisation has taken place has huge potential to influence the legal process," Shaw[15] says. She agrees with Elizabeth Loftus's suggestions in 2008, that courts should adopt a new oath: *"Do you swear to tell the truth, the whole truth, or whatever it is you think you remember?"* [18]

The word victim invokes pity (and with it that sense of disconnection described earlier). We read newspaper articles about the victims of a plane crash or terrorist attack. The issue I have with this (and I have posted and blogged about this) is that those people who died unexpectedly were vibrant human beings, often in the full of life. It does not seem right to remember them as *victims* – it is surely far better to mourn the tragedy of their death but remember them for their gifts to the world, their quirks, at their "most vibrant and alive"?

True crimes and false confessions

Right, so why do a surprising number of people confess to crimes they did not admit?

One of the biggest arguments against torture - besides the

fact that it's inhumane - is that the information and confessions received during torture are often unreliable or untrue (this certainly holds true for the transcripts of the witch trials in Europe)

Sometimes, an innocent individual can become so convinced of their own guilt that they end up actually believing that they committed a crime. The guilt usually refers to something connected to, but actually not part of, the crime. (If you, say, find your elderly father dead you may feel guilty for not getting there sooner – but that is not the same thing as actually killing him!)

Possible reasons for a false confession[19]:

- Sometimes, confessing is presented by the authorities as the easy way out, perhaps the difference between a jail sentence and parole. However, once spoken a confession is not easily retracted and cannot be deleted from history altogether
- Violence was used during the interrogation or people are completely worn-out by many hours of non-stop abusive questioning meaning they will stop it the only way they know how (confess)
- They want the fame...
- Children are more likely to give false confessions than adults (they are more vulnerable and their memory may not yet be functioning at adult levels)
- Some people will go much farther to protect their loved ones than they will to protect themselves
- Mental handicap, mental illness, learning disability (or similar, not of sound mind and obviously the so called "insanity defence" is based on this principle)
- They are under the influence of alcohol or drugs

This list certainly and tragically maps many shadow aspects of the human imagination. However, remember that we use our imagination to create our *perception of reality*:

We will end this chapter with more cosmological wisdom from E.C. Krupp[20]: According to Campbell (1983: 8), the first function of mythology is 'to waken in the individual the sense of wonder and participation in the mystery of this finally inscrutable universe.' It is Campbell's second function, however, 'to fill every particle and quarter of the current cosmological image with its measure of this mystical import' that leads us to speak of the sky. We construct a congruent reality out of nature that we believe reflects the structure of the cosmos. Our vision of the cosmos is an exercise in ordered space and time. That mythic cosmic order is imposed by and revealed by the sky. What happens in the sky is therefore inextricably linked to the maintenance of society and culture, which to be valid must appear to conform to cosmic order. Finally, because the pattern of each individual life should adhere to the broader pattern of nature, myths of human destiny echo myths of cosmic order, sharing the rhythms and trajectories of the greater universe. The mythic adventure or hero's quest inserts the individual into the social order, and to survive there, that character must align himself or herself with the will of the gods and the inclination of the cosmos.

Activity #23: Undercover Detective

Go to a place where you can be undisturbed for a while. Bring paper and pen. Light a candle.

Try to remember some vivid childhood memories. Write down everything you remember: location, colours, smells, words spoken, who was present, any feelings you had, your age.

Then contact people who might be able to confirm or challenge your memories (siblings, parents, people who were present). Talk to them *and do not expect them to back up your own take on things.* Hear them out! Do not argue with them or tell them that they are "wrong"!

Write down their take on the same incident, period or event. Compare: do these stories add up? Did others add information that enriched your memory or placed it in a broader context? Did others challenge your memory? Is it possible that you misremembered something or that extreme emotions coloured your memory of an incident?

This exercise may leave you feeling dizzy or disorientated. How will you move forward with the memories you are adding to your memory bank every day? Will you keep a journal? Will you talk to others more often to get their interpretation of things?

How does this affect your relationship with yourself? Will you trust your memory in quite the same way from now on?

Chapter 24

Karma, Projections, Fantasy and Delusion

This deeper understanding of karma rests upon our essential identity as souls — spiritual beings who are animated by a vital and divine force. As souls we are spiritually held accountable for what we create, promote, and allow in our lives. We are constantly in the process of accruing and/or balancing out karmic debts of responsibility for our creations. Karma is not physical, it is spiritual, and we carry karma forward through time within a given lifetime or, as some believe, from one lifetime until the next. Once accrued, the balancing action of karma plays out on the stage of our everyday lives through our bodies, thoughts, feelings, relationships, circumstances, and experiences. The name of the game of life is to pay off our karmic debts rather than accruing new ones so we can come to know ourselves and others as divine beings and enter into the consciousness of God. Just as gravity is a law of the physical world, so is karma a law of the spiritual world.

Judith Johnson[1]

Moon cycles and personal mythology

When we explored the mythology of illness and the zodiac constellation Cancer, we learned that: "when a tumour is surgically removed it comes out with both veins and other projections protruding in all directions". To me the word *projections* (as in physical protuberances) here is highly significant and symbolic.

Susan Rossi[2] introduced us to the fact that just as we observe moon cycles from Earth there is also a larger cosmic moon cycle in operation in our natal chart. It is interesting to check what the phase of the Moon was when you were born. For me it was the first quarter moon, which looks like a "half-moon". One half of the moon is luminous and visible while the other half is invisible, cloaked in darkness.

I can relate to that! I balance being visible, on call, and operating in the public eye with retreating from the world for lengthy periods. Switching to silent retreat mode allows me to hear the voices of the spirits more clearly.

However, there is also a cosmic moon cycle that unfolds in our life (and astrology chart). This means that all of us move through the cycles of new moon, "half-moon", full moon, disseminating moon and so forth, during our lifetime.

Victims of our own success

It is the job of movie stars to carry the projections of the audience. When we lose ourselves in a good film we identify with characters in the movie. Some actors, playing the role of the villains, are subject to verbal abuse in the street or supermarket. This is because they do their job so well that people forget that they portray a role, but they are not the character they play. They are victims of their own success!

Another thing that happens to movie stars is that people project all kinds of things on to them: deluded people entertain fantasies that actors or actresses are sending them secret messages because (in some parallel universe) they are soul mates and lovers. Sadly, many big screen names have been stalked and harassed.

Less disturbingly they carry other projections too: who does not remember the film stars or musicians that were famous during one's teenage years? These people are a bit like "coat hooks" – we hang things up on them: memories, yearnings, moods, our first love, our first kiss. We hear that song again and wham! We are right back in the school disco!

Does this mean that movie stars have karmic issues with all the people that project onto them? I don't think so! *Our projections remain our own responsibility*. (And if we do not own them and work through them: *our psychic litter*).[3] I accept that there is such a thing as collective karma affecting whole groups of people and movie stars or politicians may well be involved in some expression (collective working out) of that. But this does not make them personally responsible for the actions of every unhinged person who sees them on TV or in the cinema.

Projections do not karma make

Now think of doctors or teachers. We project heavily onto those people as well. Perhaps in a positive way: we believe that our medical doctor is always right but the reality may not be so black and white. Or maybe our teacher reminds us of an uncle we do not like – so we tend to interpret their actions or professional advice in a negative light. We have all been there. Is this karmic in nature? Not necessarily! It is projection: expecting others to carry the hidden content of our own mind for us. It will weigh those others down – and ideally any professional will learn how to deal with that and clear themselves of it. To my mind *projections made from a low level of self-awareness do not necessarily karma make*.[3]

When a police officer arrests a criminal – is that karma? No, it's doing a good job! Imagine a police officer having karmic issues with every single person they ever cautioned, arrested or had other dealings with – who'd ever want to be a police officer? Then again, there is a grey zone in operation here: some people get wrongfully arrested. Others are subjected to uncalled for physical abuse while an arrest or police interview occurs. Does that carry karma? I think that the latter scenario does because it is no longer a person *just doing their job*. There is a personal agenda and violation occurring on an inter-personal level. People may well join law enforcement because of karmic issues with others, justice or the law – but I perceive this as more abstract and less personal (not personal karma between you and every single teenage offender on your patch). However, *I do believe that every single teenage offender holds up a mirror for a policeman on his beat* – and I hope that shadow work is built into law enforcement training.

Medical doctors messing up

Whenever a medical doctor makes the wrong diagnosis or treatment decision – does that carry karma? This is tricky. I suppose a lot depends on whether it was intentional, whether they observed the correct protocol, whether it was the right decision based on the information available at the time, whether their work schedule had allowed them enough sleep and so forth. Do doctors earn high incomes because there is a hidden karmic cost to their work?

I believe that when our time to die has come, fate will work through others around us to make it happen. This sometimes comforts the relatives of murder victims a little: "if their death had not been ordained, it would not have happened". This links back to earlier explorations of a benevolent or random and unpredictable (stochastic) universe. It also touches upon magic and something we call "Changing the Weave" in Northern European Tradition shamanism. Can we petition the Norns (the Norse equivalent of the Greek Fates) and avoid death?

There are doctors in war zones or developing countries making impossible decisions on no sleep and even less equipment. There are junior doctors on duty in emergency rooms in city hospitals, facing scenarios beyond their current ability to handle. Human beings learn through making mistakes. Yet there are some professions where we all like to believe no one ever makes a mistake.

We already looked at the multi-million-dollar pharmaceutical industry selling the illusion that chemotherapy is an effective form of treatment. What is the karmic deal for all parties involved?

The Law of Cause and Effect

Some people say that karma is the spiritual version of the Law of Cause and Effect.

The Law of Cause and Effect is better known as the Third Law defined by Isaac Newton: *"For every action there is an equal and opposite reaction"*[4]

This is certainly true in physics, but it also applies in shamanic healing work. Some people want to improve their lives without making changes (not going to happen!) and other people think that they can implement major life changes without this affecting the people around them in any way (they soon find out...)

Entanglement, fantasy or delusion

I do not doubt for one moment (and I see a lot of evidence of this professionally speaking) that we all have karmic issues that keep us entangled with many other people but it is also true that all of us project and fantasize in near-demented ways when it comes to the people who cross our path. When I see a handsome actor on the big screen, then fancy myself in love and in with a chance – but get angry when the phone call never comes, that is not karma, that is *pure fantasy*! The infatuation and anger may feel 100% real, but they are based on illusion (if not total delusion).

When I attend a life-changing course in shamanism I may entertain fantasies about the teacher or workshop leader becoming my friend for life – but the amazing teacher carries no such obligation. This teacher will be carrying powerful projections from all people present in the room.

This is the reason why we can clean up our relationships with others hugely by taking our projections back and no longer burdening them with an unspoken request that they carry our psychic rubbish for us! Those assumptions can become so heavy that they actively destroy relationships. Sadly, we see this happening all around us every day.[3]

Delusions

Delusion

An idiosyncratic belief or impression maintained despite being contradicted by reality or rational argument, typically as a symptom of mental disorder

We usually think of delusions as something people with mental health histories are prone to. They are fixed beliefs that do not change, even when the person is presented with evidence of a conflicting truth. People can have delusional disorder without their general functioning being impaired. Their behaviour is not distinctly odd, the exception being their delusion.

One article on this subject[5] informs us that there are several types of delusional disorders and each type captures a particular theme within a person's delusions:

- *Erotomanic:* An individual believes that a person, usually of higher social standing, is in love with him or her
- *Grandiose:* An individual believes that he or she has some great, but unrecognized talent or insight, a special identity, knowledge, power, self-worth or a relationship with someone famous (or even with God!)
- *Jealous:* A person believes that their partner has been unfaithful (but without supporting evidence for this belief)
- *Persecutory:* An individual believes that he or she is being cheated, spied on, drugged, followed, slandered or mistreated in other ways
- *Somatic:* A person believes that he or she is experiencing physical sensations or bodily disfunctions, such as foul odours or insects crawling on their skin
- *Mixed:* A person presents with a mix of several of these delusions where no theme dominates
- *Unspecified*: those delusions do not fall into well-described categories or they cannot be clearly determined.

Many powerful delusions are rooted in things that can, at least potentially, happen in reality. When two people fall for each other it is not a delusion, it is called falling in love! When you fall deeply in love with someone, but the other person isn't feeling the same way -then the difference between those two scenarios is only the width of a hairline crack. Balanced people know whether their feelings are unrequited and when it is time to move on. Less balanced people cannot always tell. Some people become mentally imbalanced through the shock of discovering that falling in love so deeply is no guarantee for reciprocity.

Delusions can start leading a life of their own. If you believe for long enough that your husband is cheating on you (when he is not – remember the fictional John?) the sheer pressure and weight of suspicion may ultimately drive him to it -as he may practically feel forced seek relief and confirmation of his sanity elsewhere. This principle holds true for many human failings: our own desperate focus and fear-based repetition forces the other into the behaviour we most dread and wish to avoid (the most obvious example being that excessive clinginess and neediness provokes the dreaded outcome of abandonment in others – because they cannot take the behaviour any longer).

Priests have a special relationship with God but only some (aggressively atheist) people would describe them as deluded. Shamans have a special relationship with the Spirit or the spirits, but some people call them deluded charlatans. It is all a matter of perspective, private beliefs and dominant culture.

From shamanic healing work I know extremely well that people can have physical pain and sensations for which the medical profession finds no evidence or cause. Energetically speaking those things are *real* and can be dealt with.

Having had a stalker on two occasions in my life I was not deluded in thinking someone was "out to get me" (because some people were). In one period of receiving death threats, I was once shoved in the back while queuing for a train and nearly fell off the platform onto the tracks. Until today I do now know whether that was an accident or deliberate – but I do know how it felt at the time!

We need to engage our imagination when we encounter individuals who display bizarre behaviour. Don't judge too soon – have you never ever had a deluded moment? In addition to encouraging an individual with delusional disorder to seek help, family, friends, and peer groups can provide support and encouragement. It is important that goals be attainable, since a patient who feels pressured or repeatedly criticized by others will likely experience stress, which can lead to a worsening of symptoms. A positive approach may be helpful and perhaps more effective in the long run than criticism.[5]

Collectively anything that falls outside normal range scares us -we can learn a lot (and ease distress in others) if we become more willing to step outside our comfort zone. This takes correct use of our imagination harnessed to compassion, married to healthy personal boundaries and a keen perception of true danger.

In previous chapters, I have provided examples of our own imagination working against us: conspiracy theories, implanted memories and false memories. Projection and scapegoating mostly work against "others" and in the final reckoning *those others are we. We all do this to each other. For every action there is an equal and opposite reaction!*

Activity #24 Double take!

Go to a place where you can be undisturbed for a while. Bring paper and pen. Light a candle. Take some deep breaths and focus on feeling how the earth supports you, how the element air has unfailingly brought you vital oxygen since birth.

Think back to a moment when you saw someone behaving oddly. Be brutally honest with yourself: have you ever behaved oddly in a place where others could see you? Have you ever walked around in a state in inebriation or despair?!

Write down five reasons that might just have caused this person's behaviour (they do not need to be correct, but they need to be plausible!)

Examples:

- The person had just received bad news
- The person suffers from anxiety disorder
- The person is homeless and has probably not had a straight night's sleep or a straight meal for weeks (etc.)

Accept the mirror that this person holds up: how do I behave when I am in shock, agitated or sleep-deprived? See yourself in them… allow the boundary between self and other to dissolve, for just a few minutes…

Next time you are in a public location and someone acts strangely, go back to this exercise and see if you can find some compassion for them. Rather than turning away or avoiding them, see if you can offer something positive instead: a smile, an offer of assistance, a listening ear for five minutes….

(However, stay clear if your intuition tells you that the person is dangerous. Call the emergency services if necessary).

Chapter 25

Collective Karma

Instead of labelling them and making them feel like they are part of the mental health system, we reach them with these narratives. When they hear the pūrākau (stories) you see a little spark in them.
Mark Kopua[1]

Whanau (noun, New Zealand)
An extended family or community of related families who live together in the same area.[2]

Recovery from Colonisation

Just as individuals have karma (unfinished business on the level of soul) with each other, groups of people (nations, tribes, clans, families) often have karma with each other too. One example of such collective karma is the devastation of indigenous cultures we can easily observe in many locations through colonisation, imperialism and plundering. The enduring effects of these actions and the profound suffering caused by this are almost beyond comprehension. People were pushed off their land, ridiculed, converted to Christianity against their wishes, had their children stolen and put in boarding schools (The Stolen Generation in Australia, the same thing happened to the Sami people in Scandinavia and so forth), they had alien education and health care systems forced on them… . *How can we, collectively, use our imagination to apologise, make amends and somehow balance at least some of the harm that was done?!*

Some ground-breaking and deeply inspiring work is being done in New Zealand just now. Māori knowledge and mythology (creation stories) are being used to heal people in distress.

Mark Kopua is using Māori knowledge to heal whānau in distress.

The boy sits there, his head down. He feels stink; he knows all the adults are there to talk about him, about what's wrong with him.

He's always been told off for being so fidgety, for not paying attention. He knows it's a bad thing. But when the talking begins, it's not about how to fix him. They're telling a story about atua, the gods, and one of them sounds exactly like him! He's called Uepoto, and he's always curious. He's full a mischief, a tutū.

The boy looks up.

"That's where the healing starts, with an exchange of words," says Poutu Puketapu, 25, a mental health worker at Gisborne service Te Kūwatawata. Only, that's not his title here -in this space he's a Mataora, or change-maker. And the boy isn't a patient, or client, or even a consumer. He is simply whanau

Michelle Duff[1]

In Western culture we love labelling people. Not just that but people soon *become the labels.* We describe them as "a psychotic" or "an addict" or a "sad case of PTSD". Every time we use such a label, we reinforce the message that there is something wrong with them, that there are two groups of people: the sick and the healthy (implying that those labels do not apply to us!)

As I have tried to demonstrate in every way I can conceive of, this is not a tenable position. Even "healthy" people have areas of dysfunction and they carry disease agents in their bodies. Just as "sick" people can be luminous and profoundly inspiring in their spiritual wisdom, courage and honesty. It might be better to describe the illness-wellness situation as a spectrum or continuum, where all of us are always in motion, never fixed in one place.

Mahi a Atua is a form of narrative therapy that focuses on recovery from the trauma of colonisation. Māori creation stories are used as a form of healing, connecting alienated Māori to their *whakapapa*. The pilot programme began in August 2017 as a response to the disproportionate mental health issues among Māori, and is backed by the Ministry of Health's innovation fund and Hauora Tairāwhiti District Health Board.[1] Māori youth are two-and-a-half times more likely than non-Māori to commit suicide. Māori in general are more often underdiagnosed and once in the mental health system are more likely to be secluded and imprisoned.

At the time of Creation, everything came into existence humming with the vibration of divine perfection. By reciting creation stories, we are chanting something back into that original state. As a practitioner of Seidr I often chant the names of the runes for people and situations that are imbalanced in the hope that these ancient cosmic blueprints will pull things back into balance. *Creation is always happening and unfolding,* it was not a one-time event in the past!

The Global Apology Project

I run a closed group on Facebook called The Global Apology Project. Members share causes in need of apology work as well as prayers and rituals that work well for them. Find and join us if you wish.[3]

Our explicit aim is to work Outside Time. There are many people long dead who are still owed an apology and healing attention. We owe many animal species an apology from the human realm and this includes animals now extinct because of human actions or over-hunting.

Land all over the world holds trauma from historical events that occurred as well as *things happening right now* (war, trauma, starvation, famine, torture, genocide - to but mention but a few). Long after human beings, animals and even the plants or trees die – trauma is held deep in the land. In geomancy (shamanic work with land) such trauma shows up as layers in the memory of the land, often stretching back to mythical time.

Cultural appropriation is always unfair, often profoundly offensive and sometimes downright illegal! However, when we live in a cultural melting-pot as many people do today, living in multi-cultural communities we cannot avoid being touched and shaped by those other traditions. It cannot be any other way (the other way would be segregation and who wants that!)

Our own children used to attend a very creative inner-city primary school. One day our youngest son came home with a garishly painted orange clay candle holder. I thought it would please him to see it in use, so I put a tea light in it and placed it on the dinner table. He was horrified: "Mum!! That is a special candle holder for Diwali, the Hindu festival of lights! It symbolises the victory of light over darkness. You must not light the candle on the wrong day!" At that point I gave the artefact a place of honour on a shelf because it doesn't feel right to me for a Dutch-Swedish family to celebrate Diwali. Instead our family follows the Swedish custom of celebrating the feast day of St Lucia[4] on December 13th, but I fully support the school teaching my children about different faith traditions as part of a multi-cultural curriculum!

Imperialism and Colonialism

These terms are often used interchangeably but they have distinct and different meanings:

As both colonialism and Imperialism means political and economic domination of the other, scholars often find it hard to differentiate the two.

Though both the words underline suppression of the other, Colonialism is where one nation assumes control over the other and Imperialism refers to political or economic control, either formally or informally. In simple words, colonialism can be thought to be a practice and imperialism as the idea driving the practice.

Colonialism is a term where a country conquers and rules

over other regions. It means exploiting the resources of the conquered country for the benefit of the conqueror. Imperialism means creating an empire, expanding into the neighbouring regions and expanding its dominance far.

Colonialism is termed as building and maintaining colonies in one territory by people from another territory. Colonialism can altogether alter the social structure, physical structure and economics of a region. It is quite normal that in the long run, the traits of the conqueror are inherited by the conquered.[5]

In terms of etymology: our word colony comes from the Latin word *colonus*, which means farmers while our word imperialism comes from the Latin word *imperium*: command. It is a common Western misperception that imperialism dates back to Roman times and The Roman Empire. The Roman Empire was officially founded in 27 BCE, but the Chinese Empire was founded much earlier, in 221 BCE. During the copy-editing process of this book my editor Andrew Wells helpfully pointed this out and explained that the Akkadian Empire is probably the origin of imperialism in the 24th to 22nd centures BCE.

Tens of millions of people from Western European states spread out all over the world, pushing native peoples off their land, bringing lethal diseases, and often eradicating local cultures and customs. They treated the "new land" that they "discovered" (think of Christopher Columbus) as empty and uninhabited (despite much evidence to the contrary!) Also think of the way British people settled in Australia and New Zealand. In the 18th century Australia was used by the British as a conveniently distant penal colony for convicts. How would we feel if some superpower sent all their criminals to live on our ancestral land? And now British people have voted for Brexit and a majority wishes to stem the flow of foreigners settling in the UK. Exactly the same dynamic is occurring in many European countries right now, the mood is grim the tone is rude! There undoubtedly is collective karma playing out in our times (the early 21st century). Awareness of this would help us make political decisions from a different place (and a different level of compassion and accountability).

Almost incomprehensible harm was done and many indigenous peoples (in the case of this example the Aboriginal tribes of Australia and the Maori of New Zealand) struggle until today with poverty, identity issues, alcoholism and many other problems directly related to the history of colonisation. We cannot delete or eradicate the past. We cannot apologize enough for the crimes our ancestors committed. However, we can create a better future by engaging our imagination and acting from a place of compassion and awareness of ancestral debt to these peoples.

Whatever is not healed and acknowledged will seek attention through repeating itself

Story Medicine or Narrative Therapy

Diana and Mark Kopua are driving *Mahi a Atua,* a trial alternative mental health programme for Māori in Gisborne[1]. Since Te Kūwatawata opened six months ago, the number of urgent callouts to the traditional psychiatric and assessment treatment team has halved. Referrals to the DHB's child and adolescent mental health team, a specialist service, have dropped from an average of 70-90 a month to between five and 10. "This is because we are seeing families without the need for any wait time, and seeing them intensely and supporting them to overcome their problems without the need to refer them," Kopua says.

In our desire to do better, one thing we need to realise is that the western health care system is not in alignment with traditional medicine teachings. This means that when Maori individuals struggle -they are often given treatment that amounts to cultural or emotional maltreatment. Please note that I am not saying that the individuals employed in this system actively set out to do this they are only a doing their job as they perceive it, as they were trained to do it -but it is obvious that western psychiatric care completely fails to help these people (as indeed it fails most western individuals as well in my opinion).

After taking a year out to learn Te Reo Māori, Kopua began developing Mahi a Atua. Working with troubled teenagers, she would re-tell them pūrākau, the stories of various atua, or gods. Whānau were involved in these sessions, where it was discovered which atua the teen related to, and the challenges they shared. With a role model from their own genealogy to compare to, the teen could anchor themselves to a positive identity.[6]

ADHD and the gods

This therapy flips the Western format on its head. Instead of a one-to-one diagnosis focusing on the diseases' cause, Kopua and her Mataora focus on helping the person and their whānau find culturally relevant meaning.

We use Māori knowledge systems to give Māori a different lens and language to understand problems. We aim to get a lot of feedback when we're in the room, and we don't ever talk about that whānau without them present.

Te Kūwatawata doesn't look like a mental health service. It looks like an art gallery, and some of the Mataora, like Puketapu, are artists. They will pair up with a qualified clinician to work in a session with a whānau, breaking down the power dynamic of a typical client-doctor relationship.

I really hope that someone will apply these techniques in the field of autistic spectrum disorder. Is there perhaps a Maori God who excels at divergent thinking? Or are there inspiration gods with autistic traits to be found in other pantheons?

Maybe we need to cast our net even wider. I observe that young people absorb a lot of concepts from mythology and shamanism through characters in contemporary films and video games.

Ron Suskind[7] *writes in the New York Times about his [autistic] son, Owen, who has an encyclopaedic memory for Disney movies. Owen uses these movies to understand and communicate with the world around him. To communicate fear, Owen acts like the rat in Ratatouille. To show strength, he acts like Gaston from Beauty and the Beast. The real world doesn't make sense to Owen, but the world defined by Disney does.*

Cameron Doolittle[8]

Shamanic Healing in a multi-cultural setting

In shamanic healing sessions with people from very different ethnic backgrounds I have often been guided to work with stories or myths from their own culture. Privately I call this *mythology therapy*. Many (western) people believe that mythology is a collection of ancient stories that has no relevance for modern life but I have found the opposite to be true: when I am stuck in my own life (in either a difficult situation or on an art project) a myth or ancient tale will often provide the key that unlocks the situation. Modern stories can do the same thing!

Honouring the issue of cultural appropriation, we must tread with extreme sensitivity here too. However, if I have a Japanese client in the room and she tells me a story about a powerful Japanese warrior goddess who possesses all qualities that she lacks then I have just been given an important key to unlocking the innate healing forces within her.

To be able to work this way one needs to step away from the dominant western cultural perception that there is only one god and that He is male. One also needs to release the notion (from same cultural lens) that God is only good and all-loving. Non-Christian deities often span a far wider range of qualities.

With "Doctor Di", the whole family are involved. Her son, previously withdrawn and angry, has shown more progress in five sessions than the past five years, Erena says. Whiro, the god of anger, is his favourite. "My son loves it. He says 'I love getting told the stories mum, I understand my feelings'. "He can relate them back to characters and realise he's not the only one out there who has to go through these things. He said to me: 'I like Whiro, because he's in a dark place like me'.

"It was sad for me as a mum, but it was healing for me to hear my son start letting some things go. He's bubbly, he's starting to be more outgoing, his confidence is lifting, he's more engaged with the family."[1]

For me as a teacher/practitioner this is one of the main reasons why believe so strongly in the power of Pagan or Heathen gods. Because they do not play by any rules written by the early Christian Church Fathers, they can offer pathways for expressing difficult emotions or making difficult choices. These are things that all human beings face and must navigate at some point. My personal belief is that orally transmitted myths were used to map and teach those pathways long before organised religions arrived on the scene.

In this context let's not forget that scholars have stated that the Aztec people believed the Spaniards were gods when they arrived and that a similar thing happened with Captain Cook in Hawaii.

> *Through studying the Hawaiian returning god myth it is clear that a distinction between the initial contact of native empires and the Europeans with the end of the empires should be made. Differentiating these two separate events, allows historians to focus on the true importance of the prophecies: the peaceful welcoming of the Europeans into the kingdoms. Furthermore, although indigenous cultures welcomed the Europeans as deities, these receptions were short lived. Through the Europeans' actions, the aboriginal nations realized their visitors were not divine.*
>
> Lucie Johnson[9]

The gods and goddesses of the future

One of the most inspiring dreams I have ever had occurred in April 2017:

> I had been invited to spend the day with a group of teenagers. They were unknown to me (meaning that they were not friends of my own three teenagers). Their intention was to show me The Ways of the Future. They put me in a classroom (there was a whiteboard!) Then they started telling me how working with ancient gods and goddesses is no longer good enough. We need to actively create the gods and goddesses of the future. If we do not do this, we will continue to create a future shaped and delineated by the past. As I have a very great love for (and intimate relationship with) many ancient gods and goddesses I felt some resistance rising. I felt I had to speak out in support of those ancient deities. The teenagers laughed and gently pressed me back down on my chair. It is simple! They said. The future will not resemble the past. We young people live in a time of unheard-of opportunities and dangers. We need gods and goddesses that patrol the internet, Gods and Goddesses invigilating social media. Facebook needs a Face Goddess and Twitter needs a Bird Goddess. We also need a True Face God and gods in charge of the drugs that teenagers use at parties... As our concept of reality expands (reality has never been what we think it is anyway!) ever more gods and goddesses can enter and fill our consciousness. We conceive them just as they conceive us! The teenagers said: Gods and goddesses are shapeshifters and Reality is the greatest shapeshifter of them all![10]

Activity #25: Mythology Therapy

For this activity you will need a computer or iPad. Write a brief description of yourself: your good qualities, any fears or dislikes, your quirks and peculiarities. Also write down some key events that shaped your life.

Read back this description and lift out the key words. Type those into your browser and search for a "deity characterized by" ... Do the same with a condensed version of the story of your life.

Is there a deity that you have much in common with?

Is there a tale in world mythology that has striking resemblances to your life?

There are apps that will do this for you. I found one: https://www.allthetests.com/quiz29/quiz/1311342252/What-deity-are-you

The disadvantage is that all answers are going to be Greek deities and it is way more interesting to do a DIY job!

Once you have found your match – read up on the deity and/or the myth. Sit with it. Tell people the story. What qualities does this strengthen in you?! HAVE FUN!

Chapter 26

Soul and Imagination - Sacred feminine and masculine

Our soul's craving for wholeness drives the unfoldment of all stories. A profound mystery teaching is found at the heart of a collection of myths from ancient Sumer, such The Descent of Inanna and the sacred marriage of Ereshkigal and Nergal. The language may be archaic, but the message is timeless: the sacred marriage between divine feminine and masculine principles is what animates and revitalizes the cosmos This phenomenon needs to occur within our own psyche (on the level of soul and archetypes) as much as in the world around us. I invite you to take a journey of initiation into these mysteries by means of this art video.
Imelda Almqvist[1]

Animus and Anima as archetypes

C.G. Jung was a Swiss psychiatrist and psychoanalyst (1875 -1961).[2] He lived and worked at a time when gender roles were divided and delineated in a traditional way. He revived many old concepts from alchemy and ancient mystery school teaching. He gave them a modern name and application. He did not invent those things, he revitalized and personally defined/interpreted them – but he did so in a visionary way, giving the material "a new coat" for modern times. Based on his work with many clients, as well as his fearless descents into the darkest (most inaccessible) regions of his own personal psyche, he concluded that our human psyche embraces both the masculine and feminine. This is always the case, regardless of what the actual gender (or gender identification) of the person concerned is.[3]

Many articles and books have been written about both gender development and gender identification. It falls outside the scope of this book to summarize this body of work (others have done this far better than I ever could). What I will say is that anthropologists have reported that indigenous shamans are often *"psychonauts"* (Intrepid explorers of the human psyche) and that they deliberately blur the gender distinctions that apply to the local culture they live in.

Northern Tradition author Raven Kaldera[4] says that if you look at the research on shamanism worldwide and especially that of the subarctic circumpolar shamanisms, from Siberia to the Inuit you find, over and over, the disturbingly frequent presence of spirit-workers who transgressed gender roles and indulged in unusual sexual practices. In some cultures, just showing evidence of these behaviours was considered a sign that a child was bound to be a spirit-worker of some sort. Interviews with these "transformed shamans" report that the spirits informed the shamans in question that they were required to put on the clothing and take up the jobs of the opposite sex; in some cases, they lived their whole life in this way, including taking lovers appropriate to their role, and in some cases the male-to-female shamans would ritually mime childbirth.

In nearly all courses that I teach the issue of "balancing the sacred feminine and masculine within us" comes up, for both women and men (though courses in shamanism generally attract more women than men).

Essentially Jung taught that the human personality identifies with the gender a person is born with. Today that is being challenged by many groups in society and for good reason. The work being done to raise awareness of this is stretching both our ability to connect to all we are in potential plus it stretches the human imagination in much-needed ways.

The most interesting component of Jung's teachings in this context is that the human psyche is wired to compensate for the gender role a person spends most of his/her time actively living out. I personally know people who live as a man some of the time and as a woman the rest of the time (it may change from day to day or from hour to hour depending on activity and mood). Now, it may be the case that the people doing this, and therefore modelling this fluidity, are expressing a more universal unease or uncertainty (ontological dilemma) in the human psyche – in doing so they hold up valuable mirrors for all of us.

In the psyche of women, a masculine principle is active and Jung calls this the Animus. The equivalent feminine principle in the psyche of men is called *the Anima.* For 21st century purposes we could perhaps step away from gender-identification and simply state that these *larger cosmic forces are active within the psyche of any human being and they strive to balance whichever aspect we embody more actively in our everyday life.*

Jung concluded that within all human beings there is a "transpersonal psychic structure" which transcends the personal: An archetype is like a Platonic Ideal. It exists as a Universal or an Idea which is common to all of mankind. The Jungian mathematician Robin Robertson[3] refers to this as a *cognitive invariant,* meaning it has universality, a commonality which is evident across multiple individual psyches.

So whilst the anima/animus will naturally have a personal colouring in each individual it will also have an archetypal or transpersonal component.

Following the above it appears that the child has this latent archetype or capacity in the psyche prior to birth. Under normal circumstances the masculine and feminine will be modelled on the first imprint in the child's life of the masculine and feminine – the father and mother.

This parental relationship then is the prime imprinter of the anima or animus, as the case may be. Whilst it is not the sole imprinter, it has (as can be imagined) the single biggest influence.[3]

Culture heroes and celebrities as "the new gods"

The animus or anima can have many different faces or wear many different masks, if you like. (The classical Greek word *persona* means mask!) This is where culture heroes and celebrities come in. They often embody an aspect or manifestation of these archetypes. We could use the examples of Mahatma Gandhi and Mother Theresa. Leaving aside what they were really like as people, in the contemporary cultural imagination we often use their names as shorthand (or icons) for *peaceful protest* and *selfless giving* (respectively). Another good example is Nelson Mandela who represented integrity in leadership, wisdom, and forgiveness.

Where things get interesting is that anything that is out-of-balance will seek attention and healing. This means that if either animus or anima is displaced/ignored/side-lined, it will start acting up. I think we all know women who outdo the average man in (so called, *as defined in our culture*!) uber-masculine behaviour. We can all think of men too who outstrip women in (so called) uber-feminine behaviour and speech.

In astrology a distinction is made between the higher octave and lower octave of a quality. Another way of saying this same thing is to speak of the healthy expression and dysfunctional expression of that quality. Earlier in this book we have already discussed the Buddhist terms "far enemies and near enemies".

Some "animus" examples

Golden quality: strong leadership

Lower octave or far enemy: bullying

Near enemy: a narcissist pretending to be a compassionate leader

Protective – controlling – manipulative in the disguise of protection

Spiritual warrior -trouble maker or gang member – terrorist who believes he/she is a spiritual warrior in service to a great cause

Full of ideas and initiative -lack of stick-ability//flighty – charismatic person who drags others down with her/him into hare-brained or financially or spiritually destructive schemes

Rational or clinical thinking -cold-blooded/uncaring -psychopath

Some "anima" examples

Nurturing – smothering – uber-controlling in ways that stalls the growth of others or enabling dysfunctions (e.g. addictions or perversions) in others

Emotionally literate -emotionally incontinent – outwardly caring but coldly manipulative

Self-assertive, can express anger – bitchy – destroying others by means of attacks veiled as constructive criticism

Healthy boundaries -cold and uncaring – claiming to know what is best for others yet violating their boundaries or controlling them

Rites of Passage and Mystery Rites

As a teacher of shamanism, sacred art, Mystery School work and rites of passage material, my job is to take groups of people through deep processes. I create crucibles or spiritual containers, where alchemy on the level of soul can occur. Here are some of my conclusions, based on *empirical observation*:

There is a place where our inner world or psyche touches the transpersonal and even the world of spirit

Because of this transpersonal aspect we meet expressions of cosmic blueprints in work with individuals and groups (meaning gods and characters from myths come out to play!)

Any imbalances will desperately seek attention and healing

Personal pain, life wounds and serious trauma will present as very serious imbalances (so serious that they affect all people

around us)

Once we have awareness of that, we can actively work with these characters (or spirits, deities, divine beings, depending on your point of view) in therapeutic/healing/balancing ways

If this work is not done a person will live out their whole human life repeating certain core dramas that represent re-enactments of core wounds and formative experiences. Only personal growth and an active commitment to greater awareness and shadow reflection can break this cycle.

Sacred masculine and sacred feminine

As this work continues, I often ponder how our contemporary expressions "sacred (or Divine) feminine" and sacred (or Divine) masculine) relate to Jung's animus and anima. What I do know is that they represent timeless essence, cosmic principles active within all of us -no matter whether we believe in them or not and no matter what our gender or identity is.

I also know that a sacred marriage of opposites needs to occur. This is the alchemical marriage or *hieros gamos*: the marriage of sun and moon, of yin and yang, of feminine and masculine, of light and darkness. From this union then arises the birth of a Divine Child: the new. This child is not necessarily human in nature, it can also be a new paradigm, a new idea or a new culture.

We live in very exciting times. By and large (depending on where we live, the leaders of our communities, our age and our upbringing etc.) we have gained the freedom to engage in far broader expressions of true self. We have access to a very wide range of clothing, accessories and services.

In Western culture we are also very fortunate to live in (relatively) liberal times. Here in Europe there currently are no 17th century style witch hunts in progress, but I still wish to acknowledge that we all see plenty of prejudice, intolerance, trolling and even hate crimes. Sadly, the phenomenon lives on wearing a different coat.

Lesbian/Gay/Bisexual/Transgender/Queer/Intersex and Asexual communities flourish and thrive in many locations (especially many big cities). There are in-person communities as well as on-line communities, forums and focus groups. Those communities all have their own sub-cultures. (Cultures are porous and many-headed like the Hydra, they are rarely as cohesive and straightforward as descriptions of them appear to paint them – something to bear in mind when we study history!)

These groups and individuals act as teachers and mirrors for the rest of us. They hold up a different set of values. They stretch our imagination and the cultural range of possibilities/ expressions. They invite all of us to journey deeper inside ourselves and ask ourselves: *what seeks expression through me?*

Jeremy Poore[5] reports: Our men's and women's circles set out with a simple purpose: Discover the divine qualities of male and female energies. Through meditation, practice of qigong, shamanic journeys, study of Kabbalah, and dialectic conversation, we found ourselves seated at the fire feeling and describing these opposed yet complimentary energies.

What we uncovered was that we needed to disassociate with ideas of male and female. The divine masculine is an energy of action, courage, power and the abstract. The divine feminine is an energy of patience, wisdom, flexibility, and nurturing. The combination of these energies allows motion when blended. Perhaps we had it all wrong by separating into men and women's circles.

We learned our genders, whether physical or by identification, are not what defines the divine.

We also learned we were not universally strong in all of these qualities. As any human seeking wholeness, we must journey toward our goal. Knowing of the existence of these energies and their qualities is perhaps the first step. We need to nurture our strengths and grow where we are weak. This is evolution.

One spiritual mystery teaching is that the world has her own soul, the *anima mundi* or world soul. For the Anima Mundi to be in balance, all of us need to find balance.

> *Straight away all the gods and goddesses gathered to discuss how they could recover Thor's hammer.*
>
> *Heimdall, the fairest of the gods, like all the Vanir could see into the future. "Let us dress Thor in bridal linen," he said, "and let him wear the necklace of the Brisings. Tie housewife's keys about his waist, and pin bridal jewels upon his breast. Let him wear women's clothes, with a dainty hood on his head."*
>
> *The Thunderer, mightiest of gods, replied, "The gods will call me womanish if I put on bridal linen."*
>
> *Then Loki, son of Laufey, said, "Thor, be still! With such foolish words the giants will soon be living here in Asgard if you do not get your hammer from them."*
>
> *So they dressed Thor in bridal linen, tied the necklace of Brisings around his neck and housewife's keys about his waist. They pinned bridal jewels upon his breast, and dressed him in women's clothes, with a dainty hood on his head.*[6]

Activity #26: Norse God Thor's Bridal Dress

For this activity I invite you to spend some time exploring gender fluidity.

For a day (or part of a day) dress in a way that is unusual for you. Depending on what you usually wear and how you normally style your hair, do something different. Here I will mention that a star student of mine once walked around London wearing a bridal dress. This was inspired by the Norse myth about the uber-masculine god Thor dressing as a woman, as he is a Viking at heart!

If you always wear black – wear hot pink for a day.

If you always wear a dress or skirt, go for jeans and a hoodie, note how people respond when your hoodie is up, and they cannot see your hair.

Alternatively wear a pinstripe suit and tie for a day.

Observe closely how people respond to this different self. Do you get different reactions? Are you approached by people who normally pay little attention to you? Is it the other way around, do you perhaps receive no attention at all from quarters where you have come to expect this? Do you even see apprehension or fear on people's places (one female student reported this when she went for the black hoodie impersonating a delinquent teenager!)

Make up the balance: *how much of your identity depends on others mirroring back a specific version of you? What happens when that confirmation drops away or is challenged?* How does it feel to be "not you" or "a different you" for a day? What did you learn? Will you do this again?

Chapter 27

Culture, Subculture and Disability Culture

The world remains a great enchanted garden
Max Weber[1]

Ableism (noun)
Discrimination in favour of able-bodied people.[2]

Sacralization (noun)
Disenchantment is related to the notion of desacralization, whereby the structures and institutions that previously channelled spiritual belief into rituals that promoted collective identities came under attack and waned in popularity [...] Thereby disenchantment can be related to Durkheim's concept of anomie: an un-mooring of the individual from the ties that bind in society.[1]

While writing this book I kept an eye out for ways in which the human imagination is forever innovating contemporary life.

Disenchantment and re-enchantment

In contemporary Pagan Culture (a fast-growing sub-culture in western society) one expression that is gaining popularity is *re-enchanting the world.* If a considerable number of people feel that the world needs re-enchanting, this really means that there is a lot of disenchantment around. Now what does that mean exactly?

In social science this seems to be a translation from the German *(Entzauberung)* and it refers to rationalization and the devaluation of mysticism that is apparent in modern society.[1]

Pagan (or Heathen depending on self-identification) people will put it more succinctly: the world has lost its magic!

However, my own personal perception is that the world is as full of magic as ever, but our own blinkers and filters stop us from perceiving and receiving the magic! Therefore, I do not believe that we need to re-enchant the world. I believe that we need to change our settings and engage with the magic that is ever present. Not because everyone needs to convert to paganism or heathenism (that is not going to happen and would be a loss of precious diversity) but because *an enchanted life is so much richer.* Disconnection does not appear to make people very happy. We are disconnected from our ancestors, from our traditions, from the land we live on, from the stories our tribe used to tell around the fire, from the stars and so forth. The ancestral fire has been replaced by TV's and gaming stations, the night sky by a computer screen.

We cannot create what we cannot imagine -instead we will keep on creating the same dysfunctional realities generations before us did. (So called) New Age people are forever urging us to *not impose limits on what we believe is possible.* In truth I feel that they go too far. It is *through accepting certain limits that we can go much deeper working with what we have* (and this teaches us discipline!), but their perception has value.

> *I do not believe we create our own reality – that's a naïve conceit of the privileged. If we want to live in a truly enchanted world and not just in our little corner of it, enchantment has to become the new consensus reality.*
> John Beckett[3]

Consensus reality and Tribe

I have come to believe that all subcultures come into existence out of a deep desire for a group of people to share *consensus reality*. The need for community is wired into human beings. Without our tribe we lose our identity, our sense of belonging, our anchor in the world.

When the spirits demanded that I embark on training in shamanism, I literally did not know even one individual following this specific path. One great thing about attending workshops is meeting kindred spirits so this situation soon took care of itself. Until today I hammer on the value of community spirit and peer support with my own students. Today my key friendships and connections are with the people who share this path and soul commitment, they are my Tribe. This calling is an intense one and to me conversations with non-shamanic people often seem bland or boring. (They still live in a disenchanted world. It is unbelievable how much they do not see, even though it is swirling all around them!)

What is culture?

Blogger, author and mother of three children on the spectrum, Kim Wombles[4] explains that culture is an obvious concept, one that is easy to recognize. While easy at the conceptual level, it is much more difficult to define a unique culture and who belongs to it. It may be easier from the outside to pigeonhole people into distinct cultures than it would be for individuals to self-identify as a member of a specific culture and then specify the distinct beliefs, values and customs of that culture. Some individuals may exist within a culture as seeming members, and yet internally reject all that a culture represents to them.

Gardiner and Kosmitzki (2008)[5] present the concept of culture as containing several characteristics involving the beliefs, values, and rituals, among other things, that members of a group hold in common. This becomes an externally placed system rather than a self-identified and agreed upon culture, especially when cultures are assumed along national lines. Much like Bronfenbrenner's ecological system[6], cultures exist in layers, but with porous, malleable boundaries that change both imperceptibly and explosively, depending on the stimulus.

It could be argued that any culture consists of multiple smaller micro-cultures within it. It can also be argued that our family of origin (birth or adopted, conventional or atypical, cohesive or fragmented) is a micro-culture that shapes us. It shapes too how we allow ourselves to express our emotions and needs (and experience them within ourselves).

In my family of origin, the setting was that the needs and emotions of only one family member mattered and that the rest of tiptoed around this volcano-about-to-erupt. This is a common pattern in dysfunctional families. It has taken me decades to give myself permission to feel all my emotions (without censoring and without guilt or feeling "that I should not be feeling this" – as feelings *just are*) and listen properly to my own needs.

Communities are like overlapping circles. Most of us have local communities but are also members of our chosen communities or ethnic communities. Those may evolve around a religion or belief system, gender-perception, professional or other interests.

Disability Culture

Disability culture is a widely used concept developed in the late 1980s to capture differences in lifestyle that are caused or promoted by disability. Disability cultures exist as communities of people around topics of disability.[7]

Essays exploring different faces of disability culture could fill a fascinating book. However, for reasons of space and focus, I will limit the focus to disabilities that have already had a mention in previous chapters.

In addition to people forming sub-communities in person, the internet has facilitated an immense rise in on-line support groups, forums and communities. While doing some research on the subject of psychopaths, sociopaths and evil, I discovered that there are on-line forums where people who self-identify as psychopaths or sociopaths (some have been medically diagnosed and others have self-diagnosed) swap experiences and support each other (and sometimes argue with each other).

People on the autistic spectrum find each other on-line and form communities and sub-cultures too. They define themselves in opposition to the dominant culture and refer to this as the culture of the NT's or *neurotypicals* (meaning people who are wired the mainstream way). This network and phenomenon are continuously growing more complex. Modern technology has had a huge impact in these areas, and it has opened up many opportunities, unheard of when I was a child.

As many individuals and many (sub) cultures do, individuals on the spectrum define themselves in opposition to what they may perceive as the dominant and domineering culture. This blending between cultures leads to social, psychological, and cultural (ex)change. This process brings us to the phenomenon *acculturation*.[8]

Historically speaking, acculturation is a direct change of one's culture through dominance over another's culture through either military or political conquest.

The effects of acculturation can be seen at multiple levels in both the original (native) and newly adopted (host) cultures.

Kim Wombles[4] poses an excellent question in her online article: *"When does a group of people become members of a culture?"* Is it when the group members decide they have a distinctive culture? Or is it when the outside world decides the separate group represents a distinct and separate culture from the dominant culture? Where culture is concerned, it appears that this is a divisive issue, and there will be non-disabled individuals who argue that disability does not represent a cultural entity. However, many people have argued, both from the perspective of the disabled and from the perspective of the caregivers, that *disability can represent a distinct and separate culture from the mainstream, dominant culture.*

As Wombles puts it in her own words: True disability culture embraces people who have been marginalized by society because they are perceived *as defective, not valid ("invalid"), or somehow in need of pity.*

According to Hall[9], disability culture has several key values that include accepting human differences, a pragmatic approach to help ("helping others as a natural and right thing to do"), a humorous approach to disability that may often be seen by the mainstream culture as dark, and a *sophisticated future orientation* that looks forward to potential difficulties in order to work around them or prevent them entirely (p. 146). An identification and acceptance of membership in the disability culture can have distinct advantages for the disabled person, providing acceptance, support, and positive feedback for the individual

Autism and Asperger's Culture

People with autism spectrum disorder face a range of challenges:

- an impaired ability to perceive the mental states of others
- difficulties in grasping abstract concepts
- sensory overload
- a tendency to disconnect from one's surroundings

None of these things make social interaction straightforward!

I do not have a diagnosis of Autistic Spectrum Disorder but I can definitely relate to the sensory overload and to the yearning to disconnect from my surroundings and escape into solitude. I can often perceive the mental states of others so well that they overwhelm me. In terms of everyday life this is almost as dysfunctional as not perceiving them! I am certainly in touch with my Inner Autist and not ashamed of admitting that she exists. Yet I cannot say that I belong to any disability subculture.

Just as American culture, European culture or British culture is not one cohesive whole, disability culture is not a monolithic entity either. Distinct and separate cultures are found under this umbrella.

A great deal of time and effort has been spent on the theory that people with autism spectrum disorder have impaired theory of mind (abbreviated to ToM). This issue is contentious in autistic culture and in adult autistic on-line communities. Members often show a hostile reaction to the Baron-Cohen theory, as explored in previous chapters.

The thought occurs to me that neurotypical people often show a complete disregard for the feelings and thoughts of others, outside their own peer group or social group. How do we collectively treat elderly people, homeless people, differently able people, to mention but a few groups?! -For that reason, it could be argued that *neurotypical people too demonstrate blatant displays of lack of a theory of mind!* Earlier we looked at Temple Grandin's achievements (and Greta Thunberg's activism) and the term *diverse thinking,* which rightfully shows autism in a far more positive light.

The ToM model is that a person understands the idea that not only does he or she possess states of mind (feelings, thoughts, and beliefs) but that other people also possess states of mind and that these might differ from his own. An inability to conceive of this state of mind is what sets an autistic person apart from those who can.

The degree of impairment in the ability to form mental representations varies not only between individuals with autism but within the individual himself, as he develops throughout time, although even people with autism who achieve second-order representations still tend to misunderstand bluffs, sarcasm and all but the most obvious of jokes. There is no such thing as "an average autistic person" and even neurotypical people vary in their ability to conceive of states of mind in others, depending on age, education, circumstances and level of pre-occupation. This is not fully developed (yet) in teenagers and wanes again in old age or at time of serious illness (including mental illness).

It is important to point out that ToM is not dependent on intelligence levels as autistic people can have a very high IQ that is not matched by a high EQ or emotional intelligence level. (This phenomenon can also be observed in people who do *not* have a diagnosis of autism!)

Theory of Mind is *not* the same thing as emotional expression. Children diagnosed with autism or Asperger's are distinctly different in their ability to relate emotional states, most pronounced was the *manner in which* children recounted their remembered experiences.

Children with autism were able to discuss contextually appropriate accounts of simple emotions but their strategies for interpreting and conveying all types of emotional experiences differed from the strategies used by children developing along neurotypical lines.

The thing to note is that while the ability to reflect on and communicate emotions may be impaired in individuals with autism, especially when the emotions move towards complex and self-reflecting, the physiological response in emotions is not impaired and normal (meaning it is the same as in neurotypical children). In plain English: they feel joy, anger and sadness, just as neurotypical children do!

What may appear to be an impaired theory of mind may therefore reflect language difficulties instead. Wombles reports that the biggest difference is in licence for emotional display. There is none of the subterfuge or subtlety we find in (what she calls) the *exoculture* or *macroculture* of neurotypical individuals. The intellectually disabled do not tend to focus on time, or on using time in the same manner; there is no sense that time is passing them by, that time is being wasted: *Time is not something that can be run out of for my son and many of his peers. Time is abundant, and they do not sense that life is passing them by. There is not the same discussion of time or of regrets because of time used poorly. It is, I think, in many ways a preferable way to be; ever in the present, in the moment, and I often think that some folks who turn to Buddhism spend years of effort trying to do what my son does effortlessly: exist in the now'.*[4]

Neurotypical and other communities can also learn a great lesson from disability culture where errors are perceived as great wisdom lessons.

Wombles[4] continues to explain that "because grey areas may not exist for individuals with autism, and rationalizing behaviour is also not something easily or well done by individuals with impairments in theory of mind, it has been insightful to watch my son's reactions to injustices. I have come to believe, through watching him as he has aged chronologically but remained cognitively impaired, that moral reasoning at its base is affective in nature. *Harm to others causes a physiological reaction that is visceral enough for the individual with autism to react personally and emotionally. The bandied-about lack of empathy, at least with my experience with my children, is not based on an inability to feel deeply, keenly, another's pain. They first have to notice the pain is there; they then feel it in a deeply personal way.* Injustices rip at them; hurts shred their hearts, and they want to help, they want to fix. On the other hand, getting them to realize the consequences of their actions, when they have caused harm, can be incredibly difficult; connecting the dots and recognizing the harm is a consequence of their actions can take some time and effort. I think that there is reasonable evidence to argue that moral reasoning where it relates to actions that cause harm to others is affective in nature rather than cognitively based." *(Italics inserted by the author of this book)*

Speaking as a mother of three neurotypical children and teacher of shamanism (working with all age groups) I would add that it can be very difficult getting neurotypical children (and adults!) to admit that they were in the wrong and did harm. I will go even one step further and say that *the ability to admit wrongdoing, apologise wholeheartedly and make amends is not fully developed in an alarming percentage of our adult population!* This contributes to the state of our planet and world affairs: we have narcissistic leaders and collectively we continue to make decisions that harm individuals, land, groups, animals and the whole Web of Life.

Moral reasoning

We will now return to the concept moral reasoning. The psychologist Lawrence Kohlberg[10] was an American psychologist best known for this theory of stages of moral development. He formulated a theory which opened up a new field within psychology by formulating stages of moral development, adapted from a theory conceived by Jean Piaget[11], a Swiss psychologist known for his work on child development.

Essentially, Kohlberg says that moral reasoning, which forms the basis of ethical behaviour, has six identifiable developmental stages and each stage in increasing degrees of "adequate response to a moral dilemma". These can also viewed as three levels of two stages each. Stages cannot be skipped and regression (dropping back to a more primitive mode of functioning) is rare:

Level 1 (Pre-Conventional)

1. Obedience and punishment orientation
   (How can I avoid punishment? The morality of an action is judged by its direct consequences)
2. Self-interest orientation
   (What's in it for me? Understood in a narrow way which does not consider one's reputation or relationships to groups of people)
   (Paying for a benefit)

Level 2 (Conventional and typical of adolescents and adults)

To reason in a conventional way is to judge the morality

of actions by comparing them to society's views and expectations.

3. Interpersonal accord and conformity (good intentions as determined by social consensus)
   (Social norms)
   (The good boy/girl attitude)
4. Authority and social order maintaining orientation

If one person violates a law, perhaps everyone would—thus there is an obligation and a duty to uphold laws and rules. When someone does violate a law, it is morally wrong; culpability is thus a significant factor in this stage as it separates the bad domains from the good ones. Most active members of society remain at stage four, where morality is still predominantly dictated by an outside force

(Law and order morality)

Level 3 (Post-Conventional)

Post conventional moralists live by their own ethical principles – principles that typically include such basic human rights as liberty and justice. People who exhibit post-conventional morality view rules as useful but changeable mechanisms – ideally rules can maintain the general social order and protect human rights. Rules are not absolute dictates that must be obeyed without question. Because post-conventional individuals elevate their own moral evaluation of a situation over social conventions, their behaviour, especially at stage six, can be confused with that of those at the pre-conventional level.

5. Social contract orientation

A key principle is the focus on the greatest good for the greatest number of people. This is achieved through majority decision and inevitable compromise.

Democratic government is ostensibly based on stage five reasoning.

6. Universal ethical principles (Principled conscience)

Moral reasoning is based on abstract reasoning, using universal ethical principles. This involves an individual imagining what they would do in another person's shoes.

The resulting consensus is the action taken. In this way action is never a means but always an end in itself; the individual acts because it is right, and not because it avoids punishment, is in their best interest, expected, legal, or previously agreed upon. *(Although Kohlberg insisted that stage six exists, he found it difficult to identify individuals who consistently operated at that level).*

Kohlberg suggested that there may even be a seventh stage—Transcendental Morality, or Morality of Cosmic Orientation—which links religion with moral reasoning. *(As he had great difficulties finding empirical evidence for stage 6, Kohlberg claimed that stage 7 is speculative).*[10]

Neurotypical people process through these stages as they grow older and their awareness evolves. Some (a small number of) individuals might reach higher levels at younger ages and less educational attainment. Most reach the conventional morality level. A distinction needs to be made here between morality and *social conventionality*. It seems that master criminals or psychopaths break only certain laws (not all!) where there is a great pay-off for them to do so. They are often hard to spot because of the conventional lives they lead. They perfect the art of not attracting unwanted attention to themselves.

Despite impairments in ToM, (and consequently a difficulty inferring mental states), many individuals with autism are able to distinguish in the school setting between social convention violations, "conventional transgressions" and moral violations (where one results in potential censure and the other in potential harm done to another person). The difficulty arises for individuals with autism where the recognition of appropriate social behaviour (either as a witness or potential instigator) also requires the representation of mental states. Where rules are explicit and known, individuals with autism are equivalent to neurotypical peers, but where the rules are situational specific and implicit, impairments in language and theory of mind create difficulties in being aware of social rules and potential difficulties.

In plain English: the greatest difficulties lie in the fact that community life and all social interaction are incredibly multi-layered and some of those layers are nebulous and subtle. They are not consistent either; they vary greatly between groups in society. A set of teenagers will operate different norms from a group of mums attending toddler group. I have often been baffled by the things my eldest son perceives as socially rude (such as not responding to a social media message within seconds). This following conversation occurred when he was eighteen:

> Me: "Just say your phone ran out of charge, which also happens to be the truth!"
>
> He: "It is still rude!"
>
> Me: "But how do any of you A Level students (the American equivalent is High School exams) get any work done if you are constantly pinging each other messages on social media?!"
>
> He: "Oh Mum, you just don't know what you are talking about. The fact that your generation can't do it, does not mean that *we can't do it*!!"

Even within one year-group of a school attended by neurotypical teenagers we will observe a continuum: those young people who are popular and socially confident will essentially inhabit a "different world within a world", where social interactions are an exciting and joyful part of life. For our eldest son every stranger is *a friend he has not yet met!*

There is also a group of less confident young people who tend to keep their head down and follow the trendsetters or in-crowd, for a socially secure and peaceful life. Then there are young people with unusual interests or skills -they are sometimes referred to as nerds and geeks.

People with anxiety disorder will perceive all social interactions as a minefield. For young people with more serious mental health issues, or atypical wiring, school life can be exponentially more challenging again.

We find circles within (and around) every circle, and worlds within (separate from or partially overlapping with) the dominant world. This happens in every age group, social group in society or work situation. In a very real way, the "world" we live in shapes what we perceive as reality. This also explains (at least partially) why it can be so hard to understand where other people come from (or what place they are talking from). We can live near-identical or parallel lives yet perceive reality in vastly different (or even opposite ways). One "reality" can literally be an adventure park for one person (our eldest son) and a nightmare for another person (my teenage self).

The suicide statistics for teens (aged 13 – 18 years) have doubled over a period of eight years. A recent article linked this especially to social media and cyber bullying, the proliferation of self-harm and DIY suicide websites.[12]

Wombles[4] argues that Kohlberg's moral development theory is not perhaps applicable in the same way for autistic and intellectually disabled individuals in as it is neurotypical individuals. Instead, where it involves moral transgressions where harm to a victim can occur, both neurotypicals and individuals with autism and intellectually disabilities react not cognitively, but affectively – meaning that they respond from a place of feeling and fellow feeling (psychopaths and sociopaths are not included in this discussion of affective response). This statement is based on the research of Velez Garcia & Ostrosky-Solis.[13]

For an individual to be accepted into a specific culture or community he/she needs to adopt (at least outwardly) the values and customs of that community. (Perhaps we all know people who go to church every Sunday for the social/community aspect but, when pressed, admit that they do not believe in God). This is referred to as the process of enculturation and socialisation.

As individuals with autism struggle with social relationships and communication, socialization is not innate. Children with intellectual disabilities other than autism generally absorb cultural values and beliefs quite easily, by a process of cultural osmosis.

Children with autism are inward-directed and often unaware of not only subtle and unspoken values but even values that are obvious. Because of this difference in awareness of one's surroundings and an inability to read the subtle/unspoken significance or meaning of underlying events can lead to a lack of enculturation in people with autism. They may not be aware that these things exist and even if they are aware, there is no sense of compliance, of needing to cooperate with them. – Only very few of us cooperate with things that we neither understand nor perceive the value of!

There are two sides to the autism coin. One side is how individuals with autism respond to norms and values in their community or culture. The flip side is how cultures and communities respond to people on the spectrum. A case has been made for viewing autism and Asperger's Syndrome as a *difference not a disability*.[14]

As a person and parent based in Britain, I was not entirely sure whether British culture generally has a more positive perspective. I did some research.

Autistic and/or authentic

Autism may represent the last great prejudice we, as a society, must overcome. History is riddled with examples of intolerance directed at the atypical. We can sometime fear that which diverges from the "norm", and sometimes that fear leads us to frame those who are different as being in some way lesser beings than ourselves.
Nikki Stevenson[15]

Stevenson suggests that intolerances generally take generations to overcome and heal. She cites both racism and gay people being diagnosed with "sociopathic personality disturbance". Autism is framed as a disability, she says, via deficit models (meaning a focus on things individuals *cannot do*). The current estimate is that 1 in 100 people is "on the spectrum" (we will remember that this is the same percentage as for the diagnosis of narcissistic personality disorder – but please note that no connection is assumed or made here).

Much current autism research as well as medical treatment research into drugs, cures and pre-natal screening is funded by the pharmaceutical industry. This takes us back to issues discussed earlier: the vested interest in a "disease model" and continuation of the problem (for reasons of financial profit). One percent of the human population is a very large number of people indeed!

Very high functioning people with autism will never even be diagnosed. Stevenson feels strongly that an autistic person knows they are different and has the right to know they belong to a distinct minority group. (The issue here then is, as with LGBTQQ choices) *self-identification*.

The autistic spectrum is exactly that: a spectrum or continuum. It ranges from people so intellectually brilliant and socially high functioning that they are never even diagnosed while neurotypical individuals will perceive them as slightly odd or awkward. At the other end we find children and individuals so profoundly autistic that their parents/families/carers are forced to act as "involuntary 24/7 prison guards", just to keep them safe. No one wants that for their child or loved one. No one starts a family hoping for (or even imagining!) that scenario.

Acceptance is a marvellous quality in human beings, but will we ever accept an autistic child visitor smearing faeces over our walls or smile at a child masturbating in public? *Acceptance tends to have a spectrum of its own*. The range of that will vary widely between individuals, families and communities but acceptance is rarely a 100% unconditional deal. For relatively high-functioning individuals, acceptance (and social awareness of the needed for greater acceptance) may work but in the most severe cases I very much doubt that this is viable. Few people and families would literally accept all forms of culturally deviant behaviour in their social circles and homes. Decorate the house after every occasion X visits and smears faeces all over our walls? The uncomfortable reality is that we have neither time nor funds for the inconvenience.

Stevenson[15] says that currently it is believed that autistic people are more prone to mental health issues than the general (neurotypical) population. Despite mammoth efforts by parents and teachers many autistic people go through life as outsiders and social misfits. *Apathy is the enemy of progress and whilst we sleep, big business may pre-natally diagnose, abort, treat and "cure" an important human group out of existence. Human rights seem to not matter when the human in question has a disability label pinned to them.* We must stand together to oppose this injustice and define autistic people as a minority group. *(Italics inserted by the author of this book).*

This brings us back to moral law and moral lines. I asked earlier whether it is right that many people choose termination after a diagnosis of Down's syndrome in early pregnancy. What if (one day) we master testing for autism as well and the phenomenon fades out because of that? What will be the loss? What will be the moral price?

Another shadow needs naming: the fine line between celebrating difference and glamourizing disability. Not every autistic person is a Temple Grandin just as not every person with motor neurone disease is a Stephen Hawking. Making disability look easy or heroic is *not helpful* to the families who live with this reality every day: from adults in nappies to carers never managing an uninterrupted night's sleep.

> *There's nothing gallant about everyday life with a significant disability.*
>
> *Great stories need conflict and struggle. Imaginary conflict is romantic and heroic. Fictional pain and terror are exciting and glamorous. Make-believe tragedy rivets our attention. Conflict-free stories are boring and lifeless.*
>
> *It's a great metaphor, but we must remember that it's a metaphor.*
>
> Rich Dixon[16]

This chapter, as do most chapters in this book, raises more questions than it answers. Cultures are not always separate and distinct, and most individuals belong to several, if not many, different communities. In a, non-existent, utopian world individuals with disabilities would weave between communities, finding acceptance and support in both. In everyday life many of us, (even those without an obvious disability), do our very best to function in mainstream culture but we run to our subcultures (safe communities) for a higher level of being understood, seen and not judged.

If we collectively agree that it is acceptable to abort embryos (individuals in the making) with certain conditions and genetic configurations, then over time that dividing line will move. I have already described what the Nazis set out to do and how they got away with it. To my eyes this looks like a slippery slope and once again I call on all readers to fully engage their imagination (married to compassion) for deep reflection on this. I also invite you to use your imagination to understand what living with (or caring for) a serious disability is like. Read up on this and ideally visit a person you know who lives with disability. Walk in their shoes for an hour, if you can – you will learn an extraordinary amount.

As a closing comment I will mention that there are now websites that provide detailed instructions for teens on ways of committing suicide.[17] All 21st century parents need to be aware of this. I already said in an earlier chapter: the death drive (and Death's appetite) cannot be denied. We need to educate ourselves and be in an active relationship with the mystery that is Death. We ignore the more frightening things in live at our own peril.

Activity #27: Give a carer a break!

If you know someone who is the 24/7 carer of a partner/child or parent with a disability, offer them some time out. You may need a lot of instructions and even training to even cope for *one hour*. Babysitting an autistic child (or children plural) takes things to a whole new level, even for experienced parents.

Talking to a person with profound dementia can be shocking and draining, if you are usually surrounded by individuals at the height of their intellectual powers.

Offer a carer some respite, insofar as you are able. Have the child of single parent on sleepover for 24 hours so they can enjoy some rare adult time out. Move into the home of a carer for 24 hours so they can enjoy some normal movement and uninterrupted adult interaction with other humans.

When you see disability around you, look the person in the eye. See them as an individual -not a condition, label or disability. Make that person-to-person connection rather than rushing past. Try to see their timeless sacred soul behind the limitations.

Try to stretch your own level of acceptance and look at situations with a fresh perspective. If a child misbehaves spectacularly in public, allow the notion that this child may be an autistic individual suffering from overwhelm (don't assume you are seeing bad parenting in action!)

Go deep within yourself. You may not have any mainstream disability, but can you identify areas where you are less able than most?! We are all disabled in ways no one notices. We all have areas where our abilities fail spectacularly. Some of those failures are psychological or spiritual in nature. Acknowledging those makes it easier to really *see* and connect with disabled people.

Chapter 28

The Next Fix: Addiction

Quitting smoking is easy, I've done it hundreds of times.
Mark Twain[1]

At first, addiction is maintained by pleasure, but the intensity of this pleasure gradually diminishes and the addiction is then maintained by the avoidance of pain.
Frank Tallis[1]

Addiction

Addiction is so rife in western culture that I often wonder if there is a person alive today who is truly free of any and all forms of addiction. Here I include common (but less publicized) phenomena such as sugar addiction, co-dependency, love addiction, social media addiction, exercise addiction and internet addiction. Are we always looking for our next fix?

Addiction is an illness (literally dis-ease) of excess. A person is driven by a craving for more-more-MORE. It is never enough. Addiction never heals itself. Addiction is, truly, a monster of a disease. In previous chapters (especially Chapter 10) I have already linked addiction to Wetiko.

New discoveries also create new addictions. Addiction to the internet and social media did not exist when I was a child, as those phenomena did not yet exist. For my two brothers "playing" meant playing outside in the street with friends (even as teenagers) – not playing on an Xbox or games console. For me "playing" at that age meant playing my violin!

One of the hardest lessons I ever learned in my own life (in my early twenties and in active recovery from co-dependency) is that addictions are like onions or Russian nested dolls. The moment you peel off one, another one appears underneath it. All people suffering from alcoholism also suffer from co-dependency (all their relationships are seriously messed up). Meaning that if they stay dry, there is more work to be done (and that can be a rude shock after putting in the hard work of achieving sobriety!)

Sugar addiction is extremely common in our culture. So is addiction to being on-line 24/7. When you really search your own soul and fearlessly scrutinise your own habits, you will find addictive patterns (if not full-blown addictions). Our family has people arriving at our house saying (still standing in the hallway!): "Hi how are you – what is your Wi-Fi code, please? -You don't mind me asking do you – I just need to pop off one urgent message!" Actually, I do mind.

Wherever I am (no matter the country, continent or language) I observe people reaching for their mobile. A lull in the conversation occurs, or a companion walks away to collect a coffee – quickly check notifications... I do not allow my children to bring their phones to family meals. I take days (and most of the summer period) off from the Internet. I unplug my phone.

Recovery

The Twelve Steps program created by the founders of Alcoholics Anonymous[2] has become the standard for recovery from pretty much any type of addiction. The work is done through supportive self-help groups where everyone works the program and volunteers for some leadership duties (such as hosting, moderating or being a guest speaker for one session). There is no question that the Twelve Steps are heavy on spirituality (which may frighten off some people). However, over a lifetime of working on both myself and with other people I have come to believe that this could never be any other way: *addiction is a spiritual disease, therefore only a spiritual cure will succeed.* This spiritual cure brings a total rewiring of values, focus and principles for living an honourable life.

One core teaching is: *once an addict, always an addict.* Recovery is a commitment for life. The moment people think they don't need to work those principles or steps any longer a relapse or slide back into disease-behaviour occurs.

Another key teaching is that as part of cleaning up their lives, people need to stay clear of addicts who are still actively practicing their addiction, as temptation is a serious pitfall. A focus on recovery and sanity often means a whole new circle of friends and only very limited exposure to family members who are still on the addiction frequency. It is obvious that this poses extremely painful dilemmas and difficult choices that loved ones will not always support (or comprehend).

The Twelve Steps

Just for the record, here are the 12 Steps as defined by Alcoholics Anonymous[2]. For other addictions (and other belief systems) there are some words that need substituting (Please note that the suggestions in cursive script are my "tweaks"):

Wherever the word God appears, please feel free to adapt as you perceive this Higher Power: Goddess, Buddha Mind, Krishna, Universal Love and so forth

1. We admitted we were powerless over alcohol *(food, other people, gaming, gambling, social media, sugar....)* – that our lives had become unmanageable.
2. Came to believe that a Power Greater Than Ourselves could restore us to sanity.
3. Made a decision to turn our will and our lives over to the care of God.
4. Made a searching and fearless moral inventory of ourselves.
5. Admitted to God, to ourselves and to another human being the exact nature of our wrongs.
6. Were entirely ready to have God remove all these defects

of character.

7. Humbly asked Him *(/Her/It/The Universe etc).* to remove our shortcomings.
8. Made a list of persons we had harmed and became willing to make amends to them all.
9. Made direct amends to such people wherever possible, except when to do so would injure them or others.
10. Continued to take personal inventory and when we were wrong promptly admitted it.
11. Sought through prayer and meditation to improve our conscious contact with God as we understood Him *(Her/ Them/It etc.),* praying only for knowledge of His will for us and the power to carry that out.
12. Having had a spiritual awakening as the result of these steps, we tried to carry this message to alcoholics *(addicts in the most general sense, people addicted to anything)* and to practice these principles in all our affairs.

I have seen this program work for people where years of therapy failed. One common saying is that *"it works if you work it!"*

Addiction is our Inner Monster, the Minotaur at the heart of our psyche. Like the Minotaur it is a hybrid: half divine and half "Other". We return to a theme we have encountered before: The God Demon or Demon God. When we engage in the right way this monster will heal our lives and set us free. When we don't – it will devour us. We will drown in alcohol, our own tears or other people's fears.

I will briefly return to the creepier content of this book: yes, disembodied spirits feed on addiction. They attach themselves to (e.g.) alcoholics and urge them on. They whisper in their ears: "one for the road", "just one is not going to hurt", "You have your addiction under control, so you can now enjoy a drink in the pub with friends!" They gather and cluster around pubs and watering holes. They drive addicts back to their fix.

Recovering alcoholics would do well to see a shamanic practitioner and have such entities (they are really lost, suffering or overshadowing beings) removed and sent to the right place in the Hereafter. The same goes for *any* addict.

Wetiko Revisited

Earlier we made a distinction between personal transgressions and (larger scale) Wetiko. We pondered this quote:

> *It is always very difficult to live in this life so as not to be a damaged person or one who damages others*
> Jack D. Forbes[3]

The demon we all really need to wrestle, (as Jacob did in the Bible), is not the serial killer or mass murderer (those are best left to law enforcement and the FBI) but the toxic belief that there are "two kinds of people": good people and bad people, superior races and inferior races, people like me and people different from me: "Us and Them". That way of thinking has caused some of the greatest atrocities in human history. It marks the beginning of dehumanising other people.

Unless we do serious shadow work and cleaning-up work around this, we all carry within us the seeds of such things occurring again!

Forbes calls this, the disease, (expressing itself as imperialism, colonialism, torture, rape, slavery, terrorism, brutal violence, greed etc.) *cannibalism or Wetiko cannibal psychosis.*

Paul Levy wrote a related book titled Dispelling Wetiko.[4] His book examines the psychic epidemic, collective psychosis or cancer of the human soul called Wetiko and he explains why and how it is highly contagious. This "virus" operates through blind spots in the human psyche, rendering people oblivious to their own madness.

During the process of writing this book, (a steep learning curve!) it has become very clear to me that there is a relationship between consumerism-gone-mad, the way addictions proliferate in our world and Wetiko.

We do not only consume more than our fair share of the Earth's resources, we also act as parasites consuming the life force of other beings (some human, others non-human and all have their undeniable place in Creation, the Web of Life). This is not sustainable. One key principle in shamanism is the concept of *fair energy exchange*. When that principle is not honoured, things flip out of balance: harm is done and imbalances (even grave injustices) occur. An increase in life-threatening diseases also occurs.

> *Those afflicted with Wetiko consume, like a cannibal, the life force of others – human and non-human – for private purpose or profit and do so without giving back something from their own lives.*
> Paul Levy[4]

This book has explored both healthy states of mind and the consequences of imbalanced or diseased (dysfunctional) states of mind. Forbes uses the word "psychosis", as in *Wetiko cannibal psychosis*. The other word he uses is cannibalism. Levy uses the word *virus*, and also the phrase *cancer of the human soul*. Wetiko gets in through our blind spots. I refer to those as "areas where we lack in awareness". We do not actively need to intend harm, for harm to occur! We are all "good and bad" people at the same time. Externalising that uncomfortable fact and "splitting" the people around us into "goodies and baddies" is not a mature state of mind, nor will it help solve the crises our world faces today.

> *We are always, thanks to our human nature, potential criminals.*
>
> *In reality, we merely lacked a suitable opportunity to be drawn into the infernal melee. None of us stands outside humanity's black collective shadow.*

Whether the crime lies many generations back or happens today, it remains the symptom of a disposition that is always and everywhere present – and one would therefore do well to possess some "imagination in evil," for only the fool can permanently neglect the conditions of his own nature.

In fact, this negligence is the best means of making him an instrument of evil.

Carl Jung[5]

Healing our addictions and being 100% supportive of other people recovering from their addictions therefore must be a top priority, collectively speaking.

Is Wetiko simply evil, or is it a disguised form of the divine that is literally helping us awaken?

Paul Levy[6]

Is Wetiko (working on us through our addictions and our propensity for excess), a virus, vampire, parasite, cannibal, disease or is it a teacher? Is it perhaps all those things and more?! In this book we have explored the concept of the "God-Demon": the god-in-us, the demon-in-us. In addictions we fill the "god-place" within us with semi-gods – the substances or fixes we can no longer live without.

For diseases of the imagination – the cure is also found in the imagination

We need to use our imagination to understand darkness and demons. If we don't, they will rule our lives and, ultimately, the world.

Activity #28: Meet the Minotaur

Please go to a place where you can be undisturbed for a while. Light a candle. Bring notepad or sketchpad and some pens or felt tips. Read these instructions in full first.

Move yourself into the mindset of an intrepid explorer or *psychonaut*. Set a strong intention to meet your Inner Minotaur. If this brings on a state of anxiety, instead try scribbling or sketching your way through the process!

Look at yourself from a place of self-love and compassion. Be fearlessly truthful with yourself: is there a force or presence within you that feeds on your behaviour?

You may tell yourself that you don't have an issue with alcohol yet drink most nights. When were you last unplugged for more than an hour? Do you rely on other people for meeting nearly all your emotional and self-esteem needs? What do you use to plug "black holes" in your psyche?

Ask this question… Walk around the landscape of your own psyche… Use your imagination! These black holes may appear as craters, wormholes or in a completely different way. The most important thing is for you to admit to yourself that they exist.

Now ask to meet your Inner Minotaur. Tell this Minotaur that you are going to feed him/her/it love from now on, not alcohol/food/drugs or other "highs".

That was not too bad, was it?! Maybe he/she/it could even be adorable, *an ally* even, if fed the correct diet? If you agree with this, please make a commitment to returning and feeding your Minotaur love and affection – using your imagination.

Chapter 29

Medicine of the Imagination

When I examine myself and my methods of thought, I come close to the conclusion that the gift of imagination has meant more to me than any talent for absorbing absolute knowledge.

All great achievements of science must start from intuitive knowledge. I believe in intuition and inspiration.... At times I feel certain I am right while not knowing the reason.

Albert Einstein[1]

Imagination Meets Intuition

We have explored the imagination but not yet met all her sisters: intuition is one. For Einstein, his brilliant insights did not come from logic or mathematics – they came from intuition and inspiration.

I am a profoundly intuitive person. I often start with a deep inner knowing about something and then I go and research the facts. Most people would consider that an upside-down approach!

Intuition is commonly defined as a way of accessing information without a tangible means of doing so. In this context we speak of a gut reaction or "just knowing". I constantly tune into things. Almost immediately I will have a good feeling, bad feeling or other feeling (deep distrust, the strongest sense that the information is not accurate or a person not honest and so forth) and I will then make a decision based on that. This often means making decisions that make little sense to others.

For me intuition is closely linked to dreaming as well. I often receive my best insights through dreams. I have written many courses and sacred art retreats using a dream as the "seed concept". I have also made dozens of art video that had a powerful dream as their starting point[2]. My intuition often speaks through dreams.

Music

Another sister of Intuition and Dreaming is Music: Einstein said that he used images to solve his problems and found words only later.

Michele and Robert Root-Bernstein[1] report that: *In other interviews, he attributed his scientific insight and intuition mainly to music. "If I were not a physicist," he once said, "I would probably be a musician. I often think in music. I live my daydreams in music. I see my life in terms of music.... I get most joy in life out of music."*

We need to harness all these amazing processes/faculties when we want to train the muscle that is our imagination!

Nine Muses

> *Since ancient times, the muse has often represented the synthesis of imagination. She and her sisters have always walked the path between a thing that was old and the thing that could be reborn. Poets asked the Muses for guidance in the telling of their songs and stories, and the goddesses personified poetic forms as well as inspiration. They represented the first whispers of a story— the moment of epiphany when a new story was discovered or rebuilt. And they stood in the place between memory and imagination— emphasizing both production and reproduction.*
> Alissa Cook[3]

The Muses from Greek mythology were (are!) nine young women or goddesses embodying (or personifying) Science, Literature and the Arts. They were the daughters of Zeus and Mnemosyne (the goddess of memory). Here is a list of their names and arts:[4]

- **Clio:** The Muse Clio discovered history. History was

named Clio in the ancient times, because the name is derived from "kleos" the Ancient Greek word for the heroic acts. Clio was always represented with a clarion in the right arm and a book in the left hand.

- **Euterpe:** The Muse Euterpe discovered several musical instruments, courses and dialectic. She was always depicted holding a flute, surrounded by other instruments.
- **Thalia:** The Muse Thalia was the protector of comedy; she discovered comedy, geometry, architectural science and agriculture. She was also the protector of Symposiums. She was always depicted holding a theatrical – comedy mask (a symbol we still commonly use today).
- **Melpomene:** Her name literally means to sing, or "the melodious one". Her name was derived from the Greek verb melpô or melpomai meaning "to celebrate with dance and song. The Muse Melpomene was the protector of Tragedy; she invented tragedy, rhetoric speech and Melos (a succession of musical tones constituting a melody).
- **Terpsichore**: Terpsichore was the protector of dance; she invented dances, the harp and education. She was called Terpsichore because she was enjoying and having fun with dancing ("Terpo" in Greek refers to being amused). She was depicted wearing laurels on her head, holding a harp and dancing.
- **Erato:** Muse Erato was the protector of Love and Love Poetry – as well as wedding. Her name may well be come from the Greek word "Eros", which refers to the feeling of falling in love. She was depicted holding a lyre as well as love arrows and a bow.
- **Polymnia:** The Muse Polymnia (her name literally means "the one of many hymns") was the protector of divine hymns, mimic art, sacred poetry and eloquence as well as agriculture. She invented geometry and grammar. She was depicted looking up to the Sky, holding a lyre.

- **Ourania:** The Muse Ourania (whose name means Heaven or Heavenly) was the protector of sky objects and stars; she invented astronomy. She was always depicted bearing stars, a celestial sphere and a bow compass. She is sometimes identified as the eldest of the divine sisters.
- **Calliope:** The Muse Calliope (a musical instrument named for her creates sound by sending air or steam through large whistles) was the Chief Muse. She accompanied kings and princes in order to impose justice and harmony or serenity. She was the protector of heroic poems and the rhetoric arts.

I love the fact that astronomy is viewed as one of the arts and that justice is one too! In twenty-first century astronomy there are nine asteroids named after the Muses.

One way of viewing the lasting influence of the Muses is by saying that Divine Beings come forward to work with us when we flex our imagination and do creative work. If we take into account all the subjects we have covered so far, how and where can we make the best possible use of our imagination?

Harnessing and sharpening our imagination

To arrive at a perspective on this I think it is helpful to divide the use of our imagination up into four areas:

- The personal realm (our life, our work, our relationships, our relationship with ourselves…)
- The realm of personal and collective shadow (pockets of narcissism, addiction, co-dependency, projection, illusion, delusion)
- The realm of mental illness (stating clearly that once people's minds have fragmented, what they need most of all is compassionate help with a spiritual dimension)
- The realm of Wetiko and evil and how we cannot create a

better world without educating ourselves about the way these things operate within all of us.

Ontological Dilemmas
I perceive two great ontological dilemmas:

- Living beings must eat other living beings (life forms) to stay alive
- Leading even the most ethical and disciplined life will not stop us from hurting other human (and non-human) beings (often inadvertently, often without realising it).

However, please note that the fact that one person is hurt or feels angry does automatically mean another person did something wrong…

Ontology is the philosophical study and examination of what is meant by "being"[5]

This field studies the nature of being, becoming, existence and reality. Traditionally it is listed as a branch of philosophy called metaphysics. It addresses issues concerning the existence and grouping of entities (gods, angels, demons, Muses).

All genuine moral dilemmas are ontological.

Both opponents and supporters of dilemmas acknowledge that there are epistemic conflicts.

Epistemology[6] is the theory of knowledge, especially regardings its methods, validity, and scope, and the distinction between justified belief and opinion.

The personal realm

(Our life, our work, our relationships, including our relationship with ourselves)

I observe that it is quite common for people to get through life without ever *thinking about* the way they think. This then means that every thought which pops up in their head is perceived as reality. What is not perceived at all is how that stream of consciousness creates a very large part of that same reality. It also dictates how we view our reality. We have already said earlier: we cannot avoid pain in life, but suffering is "optional".

Here is a summary of what we have gathered and learned about the use of imagination so far, *in a very personal context*:

- We need to be more mindful and develop a far greater awareness of what flourishes (and festers) in our own imagination. We need to own the basic fact that we are constantly creating our own reality (through choices, decisions and interactions with others and collective bodies or groups)
- We have learned that we all tell ourselves (and each other) stories. The next level is to put more focus on telling medicine stories, healing narratives and uplifting messages. Next time you meet a person who has had bad news, it is your choice whether you say: "Poor you! I would never survive that!" (or worse: cross the road to avoid the person) or "It breaks my heart to hear and see you struggling, -but I see the strength and courage in you! I am there for you!" *(And obviously you must come through on that, only saying it is not enough!)*
- We have seen that we all have a personal shadow: inner saboteurs and even Wetiko work through us in all the areas where we are not aware, commit excess or have our own needs met at the expense of other people. Unravelling that through constant vigilance can only be done by individuals working together fearlessly. (I recommend the work of Tsulstrim Allione[7] and Debbie Ford[8]). This work involves releasing the notion that "I am a good person but others 'out there' are bad people". *(There are bad people out there, just as there are extremely altruistic and saintly people out there, but based on statistics we have provided earlier, about 93% of the population clocks in as a fairly balanced mix of good*

and bad).

- We have seen how active imagination can be used to tackle even health problems and serious medical conditions.
- We have observed how overcoming our fear of Death makes us far better people who can become true elders and pillars of our communities.
- We have looked at curses and cursing.
- We have looked at the concept of finding safe expressions for our shadow so we can avoid some of the more devastating (or unconscious) expressions of an undeniable and indelible presence.
- I have invited everyone to question their human-centred and even anthropomorphic perspective and projections *(does everything in Creation need to have a human face before we will consider its needs in decision making?)*
- We have even looked at karma and the possibility of previous incarnations. We have looked at the ancestral field and Knowing Field that cradles The Human Family.[9]
- (Last but not least) I have invited you to truly honour and respect the people who perform shadow tasks in our society: soldiers, bin men, law enforcement officers, undertakers, prostitutes....

The realm of personal and collective shadow

(Pockets of narcissism, addiction, co-dependency, projection, illusion, delusion)

It is so easy to watch the news or read the papers and feel utterly dispirited and powerless. How could I personally ever make a difference? Isn't that only the tiniest drop of change in a vast ocean of suffering?

We need to accept the mirrors that our external world holds up about our internal world (and that process works both ways). Only "dirty" minds could create such a "dirty" world (think of whales choking on plastic, child soldiers and prostitutes, and babies in nappies teargassed at the US-Mexican Border).

So rather than exclaiming that the world is a Vale of Tears, go to work! Curb your excesses. Actively check yourself for pockets of narcissism and self-serving behaviour. Admit to your addictions and commit to working a spiritual program (such as The Twelve Steps). Co-dependency is an addiction – not a virtue! Wrestle with your illusions and delusions, your "god-demon". Your demon may just turn out to be a god (or God) as it was for Jacob in the Old Testament. Failing that, developing the right relationship with your demon might make him/her an ally over time. There is an art to this: I highly recommend the book Feeding Your Demons: Ancient Wisdom for Resolving Inner Conflict by Tsultrim Allione.[7]

Your personal power to change the world lies in the accumulation of a lifetime of choices and interactions with both yourself and beings other than yourself.

The realm of mental illness

Let me first state unequivocally that once people's minds have fragmented, what they need most of all is compassionate help with a spiritual dimension.

People with serious mental health histories need expert help, including highly skilled spiritual help. I believe that medication has its place. It can be a life saver in specific scenarios, but it also stalls and suppresses much which genuinely seeks healing.

The field of mental health needs more research into spiritual interventions (spirit release work is one powerful example of this, soul retrieval is another) and we actively need to learn lessons from powerful shamans in other cultures. We are fortunate in that many authors are now writing books about these tricky subjects.

The realm of wetiko and evil

(And how we cannot create a better world without educating ourselves

about the way that these things operate within us)

In a very real way, all of us have an 'inner serial killer'. We are all mass murderers: other beings die daily, in large numbers, so we can eat and exist. Rather than hiding from that fact (and buying our meat wrapped in cling film from the supermarket) we need to look that fact in the eyes and think again: *my very existence on this planet causes other beings to die!* Every child I birth will be entangled in this same dynamic. Every thought I think does not stay within the confines of my own head; it was last seen flying over London....

In our times we commonly speak of a carbon footprint and offsetting this (through donations, tree planting or voluntary work). The question I will now ask is: what is our "Wetiko Footprint"? How do we own this, address this and offset this?

The world is full of suffering. It is also full of overcoming it.
Helen Keller[10]

Reducing Suffering

(Tried-and-tested personal suggestions)

- One simple daily prayer that changed my life by cutting through all my "egoic waking-mind notions for my own life" was: "Spirit, lead me where you need me!"
- Radical Acceptance: whatever comes your way, try to accept that this is the right personalised soul lesson for you, at this time. Don't waste a lot of time or emotion ranting about "how unfair this is" or wondering "what have I done to deserve this" etc. Accept that *this is the lesson* and work out what learning is being presented on the level of soul. We can cause ourselves limitless suffering through mind-churning or obsessing on the themes of "should": this should never happen, the person should not do this etc. *It happened.* Or *the person did this*. Now how do you

move forward and extract the gold or gift?

- Make your peace with Death and make Death your ally and Lifelong Teacher. Once you truly accept that you will die one day and so will everyone you care about, death does not feel like a personal insult or grave injustice when it arrives. When our time comes, we need to be ready to go. When others go – we need to let them go, not entangle them in our own grief and excessive emotions (as that might hold them back and compromise their experience of death).
- Do your shadow-work in every moment – rather than endlessly seeing the faults in others and blaming them for things, endlessly accept that you find yourself in a Hall of Mirrors and find those things in yourself. That is where your power is found and this is also where the potential for change resides: *within you!*
- Forget completely about the notion of changing other people – the only person you can change IS YOU! Do not start relationships thinking the person will change. Do not stay in relationships where you see a person's potential, but they are not even working to realise it. Accept others just the way they are and see them for who they truly are. Make your circle of trusted close friends the people who see your authentic self and celebrate that – not people who try to make you the person they want you to be...
- Operate discernment, not judgment.
- Do your apology and forgiveness work. Even ask for forgiveness for things you *did not personally do* but your ancestors did, or someone did. I highly recommend that you read up on Hawaiian H'oponopono[11] and practice the four following simple statements (in any order):
    - *Thank you* (for coming to attention)
    - *I am sorry*
    - *Please forgive me*

  - *I love you*[8]
- Pay it forward: do not always ask "what is in this for me", practice active gratitude work for any blessings which others (or life, the gods) have bestowed on you and work out how you can bless others in turn. Pay it forward threefold.
- Commit random acts of kindness, just because you can or just because you happen to be the person standing in the right place on this planet.
- Set time aside daily for prayer, meditation, self-reflection and journaling. It does not matter exactly how you do this (different traditions and different people will do this in different ways) – it is the fast track to greater sanity and a spirit-led life.
- Keep a dream journal, track your daydreams as well, they may well contain vital clues and pointers. Is there a great yearning deep within you that has gone unanswered or that has been pushed aside by care responsibilities and commitments? Put some priority on life-long dreams that rise up from a deep inner well.
- Follow the coincidences. Try to trust that the Universe is not out to get us but actively holds and supports us. Form an active relationship with your god(s) or spirit(s) as you understand and perceive them.
- Attend some 12 Step Meetings and give the material a chance. Set a strong intention to heal your addictions – even the ones you have not yet admitted to yourself you have.
- No dying person ever wishes that "they had worked more" – make the distinction between "urgent" and "important".
- Spend time with children and allow your inner child to come out and play. Find and nourish the part of you that is timeless, fun-loving and life-enhancing.

Pain is inevitable. Suffering is optional.
Haruki Murakami [12]

Excess

Are these things really better than the things I already have? Or am I just trained to be dissatisfied with what I have now?
Chuck Palahniuk[13]

To live fully, we must learn to use things and love people, and not love things and use people.
John Powell[13]

The Master said, "If your conduct is determined solely by considerations of profit you will arouse great resentment.
Confucius[13]

Wetiko, terrorists, and criminal master minds all work through the human imagination. This causes diseases of the imagination but the anti-dote or cure is found in the human imagination too.

One key word that keeps cropping up in all these narratives is *excess:*

Wetiko works through the human craving for excess.

Imperialism and colonialism work through the principle of excess: wanting and annexing something that was not ours to take.

Serial killers go on to kill more people in ever more gruesome ways because there is something wrong with a feedback mechanism in their brain: they need the acceleration to achieve arousal or even to feel anything at all.

Consumerism is about excess: more-more-MORE! A better version, an even better one! A closely related issue is fixing broken things rather than replacing them. We need more "spare and repair centres", not more hypermarkets.

Many beings, including trees, oil reserves and crystals (not to mention child labour, unsafe conditions for seriously underpaid workers, exploitation of non-renewable resources etc.) pay for our greed, our yearning for ever-more.

It is time to question this and go full circle: do conservation work, human rights work, and also healing work and apology work.[14]

Activity#29: Hire the Inner FBI

Many years ago, a friend of mine applied for a job with the Police Force (in the Netherlands). He was asked whether he had ever stolen something. His answer was a wholehearted "yes!" He explained to me that it is unhinged to think you can go through life without ever stealing anything. Have you never stolen a pen, taken a glass from a hotel room, taking a cutting from a plant in someone's garden (without asking), quoted someone without giving the source of the words, left a shop and only discovered later that there was one item you didn't pay for (but not returned it) and forth?

In this activity we will hire the Inner FBI!

Go to a place where you can be undisturbed for a while. Bring a notepad and pen. Have a mirror ready. Get comfortable. Start by reading the instructions in full.

Drop into a state of daydreaming or active dreaming. Reflect on the fact that our minds are mysterious cavernous places where we hide things from ourselves.

Now set a strong intention to meet with the Inner FBI (they may look nothing like you'd expect the FBI to look! The investigators may appear as cartoons or in animal form!) Instruct them: ask them to find out where you are hiding information from yourself that needs retrieving now. Then let them do their job...

What did they dredge up? Did this surprise you? Does this change the (perhaps cherished) mental image you have of yourself? Does it increase your ability to feel more tolerance or compassion for others?

Is there anything else? – Write down your observations. Now use the mirror and really lock eyes with yourself. Who is looking back at you? Who are you? Can you accept this less-than-perfect person, to whom nothing human is alien, as YOU?

If you can do this, you will see others with new (less judgmental) eyes. Over the next few days meditate on the distinction between judgment and discernment.

Chapter 30

A Passionate Plea

In becoming intermediaries through which the divine creativity expresses itself and it made real in time, artists are participating in a re-creation of the eternal play of creation itself. Like alchemists, creative artists are liberating the creative spirit of the cosmos, an act they could only accomplish with the "blessing" of the very creative spirit they serve.
Paul Levy[1]

Evolution of the Imagination

Somewhere down the evolutionary track, human beings were granted the gift of imagination. Is this trait unique to human beings? I am writing this chapter the week that Koko[2], the famous gorilla who used sign language, died. There are debates as to how accurate and independent Koko's signing was. What we can safely say is that she mastered certain modified American Sign Language (ASL) signs to communicate effectively with her care givers. This is not the same thing as mastering sign language.

An eight-year-old juvenile chimpanzee named Kakama trudged along a path among the forest trees, following his pregnant mother. A scientist sat silently at a distance, watching Kakama pick up a log and carry it with him for hours. At one point, Kakama made a nest and placed the log in it, as if it were a small chimpanzee. Months later, two field assistants observed the same thing: Kakama was playing with a similar log, which they labelled "Kakama's toy baby."
Jason G. Goldman[3]

However, we humans have always enjoyed an upper hand whenever

> *it comes to handling complex situations and/or thinking in a creative manner. Humans have been blessed with a power to imagine the unseen, even the unreal. Moreover, we also possess the capacity to turn our imaginations into reality, as several examples have shown. Animals simply do not possess this ability of creative imagination. Or do they?*
>
> AnimalSake[4]

Dreaming involves the imagination. It has been demonstrated beyond doubt that most animals dream, meaning that they must use their imagination while doing so!

The BBC researchers studied the brain activity of rats, as the rodents were trying to learn to navigate through complex mazes, while awake. When the brain activity of the same rats was studied while they were asleep, the researchers got similar results as when the rats were awake. It was concluded that the rats were navigating through the mazes even while they were asleep, in their dreams.[4]

One study conducted by the BBC highlighted that animals can also pretend. (I would assume that most people, who have pets, will be aware of this! I vividly remember my parents' dog acting as if he was starving and near death's door, while we all knew that he had just been fed!)

This book represents a passionate plea for right use of the human imagination!

A Passionate Plea

I have started by explaining what the imagination is and how it operates.

I have offered a shamanic perspective on the imagination and shown, using examples from my own life and practice, that this "mental muscle" is more far-reaching and multi-dimensional than we commonly think.

I have explained that most people in western society never

receive training in using their imagination effectively, meaning that they are not aware of what outcomes they are actively feeding life force, or creating, in every waking moment. This means that all of us together are collectively creating very confused mixed outcomes (world peace remains elusive at the time of writing). The human imagination also "misfires": what did we learn from Berlin and China about walls? Yet, president Trump is now in all seriousness building a wall on the border between the US and Mexico (our youngest son reminds me that this project of erecting solid barriers was started well before his presidency)[5]. He is also separating children from their parents and retaining people in cages on the border. I am not the only person seeing ghostly and frightening pictures of the Holocaust in their mind's eye. This activates ancestral memories (and, I am convinced, memories of previous incarnations or lives lived on earth) for me and other "spiritual people".

I have given examples of how we need to use our imagination in order to do shadow work and take back the projections we commonly expect other to carry for us.

We have looked at the way human projections can be rather anthropomorphic or human-centred.

I have explored the close connection between our imagination and our capacity for self-healing. I have demonstrated how this is a very important (powerful and free) complement to mainstream medical care and treatments. Achieving and maintaining physical health and well-being requires a healthy (even vibrant) imagination.

We have ventured into non-Western cosmologies and belief systems.

We have examined the connection between the human imagination and the key qualities of empathy and compassion. We have moved beyond that and explored how we can use our imagination as an active cauldron or crucible for soul alchemy and transformation.

When we do not master this art, we may inadvertently remain stuck in perpetuating negative outcomes and imprints, set in motion a long time ago. The saying that *"if you are not part of the solution – you are part of the problem"* certainly applies here. For that reason, I have also examined how ancestral imprints shape the lives of all human beings and how we can engage imaginatively with unravelling and transmuting those (freeing and releasing our ancestors along the way).

We have made field trips into the most terrifying expressions of the human imagination: terrorists, serial killers and school shooters make very good use of their imagination too. For our personal and collective safety, and to counter this, we need to be more aware of the workings and dimensions of this.

We have faced up to the problems with our imagination: sins of commission and omission, curses, toxic thoughts and projections of unwanted shadow material.

The bottom line is that we cannot create what we cannot imagine -though we can unconsciously create things almost beyond the imagination. I have made a case for moving beyond this paradox, by becoming aware of what we dream, vision, create, attract and reinforce and bringing more focus and intention to this.

Another absolute bottom line is that shadow will not go away if we ignore it - shadow *is deeply wired into the human psyche and existence.* For that reason, it is our moral duty to find safe and acceptable expressions for our shadow selves and shadow material. We all have an inner Dr Jekyll and Mr Hyde. Horror movies are preferable to real life crimes…

We have looked at moral law and drawing moral lines and how the development of morality in human beings owes a lot to the imagination. The same thing is true for qualities such as empathy and compassion. To really understand those, we have also taken a close look at their opposites: narcissism and psychopathy. Those sadly have no cure, but we can use our imagination in countering them – and giving them a wide berth where possible. We can also work harder to find high octave expressions for the unique talents of people with personality disorders (such as psychopathy), who are able to observe our rules and laws. We can choose to heal our addictions and in doing so the larger human field becomes healthier for every person in recovery. We then start curbing excess in all its manifestations.

Excess is a key concept for many themes explored in this book. The human need for excess drives military expansion, imperialism, colonialism and any kind of advancement or again at the expense of other people and beings: more-more-more, me-me-me. Whales choking on plastic and observing the number of animal species reaching extinction, shows us where this mindset leads.

I have disclosed information about my family and personal history in the hope that it will invite others to heal long-standing patterns and imprints that stand in the way of leading a full and rewarding human life. I love my family dearly! They are the perfect family for the soul yearnings I came to manifest in this life. (Just as I hope and trust that my husband and I provide the right seedbed for the things our three sons need to manifest in life, through our love, efforts, mistakes and blind spots!) I have no doubt that my soul chose these circumstances with great attention to detail. For that reason, I do not wish to attract pity or be viewed as a "victim". I prefer to be perceived as a life-long learner in a rich process where every person I meet is a teacher for me. Thank you!

We have also looked at dreams, karma and expressions of the sacred feminine and masculine in a balanced human psyche.

I hope that, above all, I made the point that *we can have a lot of fun, adventures and moments of revelation doing all these things*!!

I see the human imagination as a very powerful muscle that needs regular exercise and using correctly for its intended purpose… Just like all "muscles" in a human body, it weakens and even atrophies when it is not used fully. The moment this happens our world of perception grows very small (no matter what our physical powers or limitations are).

A Passionate PS

This book opens with a beautiful Foreword from author, poet and piano tuner Anita Sullivan and I will close with a passionate plea from her. Anita introduced me to the concept of the The Sixth Extinction. This refers to a "biological annihilation" of wildlife amounting to the sixth mass extinction in Earth's history.[6]

Scientists have analysed both common and rare species and found that billions of regional or local populations have already been lost. They blame both human overpopulation and overconsumption for the crisis and warn that it threatens the survival of human civilisation, with just a short window of time in which to act. In this context please remember that the teenage Swedish activist Greta Thunberg speaks of "the house being on fire!"[7]

Previous studies have shown that species are becoming extinct at a significantly faster rate than for millions of years before, but even so extinctions remain relatively rare *giving the impression of a gradual loss of biodiversity*. Recent research instead takes a broader view, assessing many common species which are losing populations all over the world as their ranges shrink, but remain present elsewhere.

Damen Carrington[8], environment editor of The Guardian, writes: 'The study, published in the peer-reviewed journal Proceedings of the National Academy of Sciences, eschews the normally sober tone of scientific papers and calls the massive loss of wildlife a "biological annihilation" that represents a "frightening assault on the foundations of human civilisation". Prof Gerardo Ceballos, at the Universidad Nacional Autónoma de México, who led the work, said: "The situation has become so bad it would not be ethical not to use strong language.[9]"

The scientists found that a third of the thousands of species losing populations are not currently considered endangered and that up to 50% of all individual animals have been lost in recent decades. Detailed data is available for land mammals, and almost half of these have lost 80% of their range in the last century. The scientists found billions of populations of mammals, birds, reptiles and amphibians have been lost all over the planet, leading them to say a sixth mass extinction has already progressed further than was thought.'

In this book we have explored the work of Temple Grandin. One of her key teachings is that animals think in pictures. I learned this when I invited my colleague and friend Jill Hunter to teach the young people in my shamanic program for children (The Time Travellers in London) about animal healing work. One of the first techniques she introduced them to was using pictures (the sending and receiving of mental images) to communicate with animals.

Anita's private emails to me have made me wonder if our imagination does not contribute to the global catastrophe of mass extinction by us (well-meaningly, we need to be seriously worried at this point!) sending devastating mind pictures to animals. By doing so our imagination keep reinforcing the extinction outcome and the "it's too late to stop this" message.

A Possible Response to the Sixth Extinction

I'm suggesting that the power of all the sentient beings on Earth is immense. Together, all of us, down to the bacterial level (and that is a really powerful group!) we could simply decide: "No, we need not let this happen." An ongoing ceremony is already in place, I can hear it. It's happening at all three levels of reality: below, middle, and upper worlds. It's a background drone that swells and diminishes but does not stop. All creatures are ready and able to cast the extreme fullness of their energies into this work of staying alive. But this means accepting the possibility that the usual fatalism as a response to probable extinction – this time around – shall not be invoked. That this thing need not happen to us if we stay fully nourished; if we nourish one another, continuously, and far beyond what is normal for us. The collective imagination of the species on this Planet Earth is now called up for emergency duty. Only we can save us, by doing something that has never been done before. It is beyond hope, beyond expectation, but we do not know if it is beyond possibility. As Rilke says in the Duino Elegies, writing about the hero, "Time and again he takes off and charges into the changed constellation of his constant danger." The only thing that will save us now is for us to do something outrageously positive, and that means calling to action the entire collective imagination of every living being on Earth, at once and for as long as we can bear.

(Isn't this a fine job for shamans, to lead the way? I am already envisioning a way through the tree roots and water lilies, into the deep underground. We've gotta pile on our energies, make the drone so loud it cracks the sky).

Anita Sullivan[10]

On a related note award-winning shamanic teacher Sandra Ingerman[11] has taught for years that it is better to see the world and each other in their *divine perfection*, activating that outcome instead of the "seeing illness, seeing crisis" response.

Following on from The Sixth Extinction, I would also like to draw attention to the phenomenon of languages going extinct and words dropping out of dictionaries and (sooner or later) into oblivion.

Languages form over innumerable human generations and continue to change as new epistemologies are defined as important and incorporated into the culture. Each culture is a unique experiment in the human encounter with the nature of reality, an experiment carried out over extremely long lengths of time. The language

> *each culture develops encodes unique aspects of what they have experienced and found important as a culture. (And the loss of any language represents the loss of unique information about the nature of the Universe that took perhaps a hundred thousand years or more to gather).*
>
> Stephen Harrod Buhner[12]

I am trilingual: I speak three languages completely fluently. Additionally, I have studied (but not fully mastered) about fourteen other languages during this lifetime (ranging from Latin and Russian to Mandarin Chinese). Buhner explains in his book how people become a different person when they switch languages. When I first met my Swedish husband (and we spoke English), I wanted to be able to understand him speaking in his native tongue. I was nineteen years old and my gut instincts about language were sound!

When I get stuck thinking about something in one language I will often switch to another language. This unfailingly opens up new viewpoints and perspectives. Reality shape-shifts and becomes simultaneously more porous and multi-dimensional because one word rarely ever translates 100% into another language. Often there are additional (rare) meanings or the "foreign" word immediately shows the ancient history of that word. Just one example: in Swedish the word "bok" means both book and beech tree. That surely tells us something about the early days of book publishing!

Of the roughly 5,000 languages now spoken on Earth, only 150 or so are expected to survive to the year 2100, according to Buhner[12]. Robert MacFarlane[13], a leading nature writer, has been collecting unusual words for landscapes and natural phenomena for decades. He found himself on the island of Lewis while a new edition of the Oxford Junior Dictionary went to press. He noticed that there had been a culling of words related to nature. Broadband entered – bluebell was dropped:

> *Under pressure, Oxford University Press revealed a list of the entries it no longer felt to be relevant to a modern-day childhood. The deletions included* acorn, adder, ash, beech, bluebell, buttercup, catkin, conker, cowslip, cygnet, dandelion, fern, hazel, heather, heron, ivy, kingfisher, lark, mistletoe, nectar, newt, otter, pasture *and* willow. *The words taking their places in the new edition included* attachment, block-graph, blog, broadband, bullet-point, celebrity, chatroom, committee, cut-and-paste, MP3 player *and* voice-mail.
> Robert Macfarlane[13]

Macfarlane started building his own glossaries and compendia. He also published a beautiful book for children, beautifully illustrated by Jackie Morris: The Lost Words.[14] It is dedicated to the words that are so rapidly disappearing from our children's lives.

There is a close relationship between the human imagination and language. We use language to talk to ourselves and interpret events, to assign meaning to them, to communicate concepts and ideas to others. The moment our vocabulary becomes impoverished – our collective imagination also loses out. Language connects us to both land and our ancestors, to history and the unique wisdom of those who came before us. We lose far more than words alone, when we do not realise this!

Let's cherish our mother tongue and other languages. Let's give our imagination access to the richest possible vocabulary and the texture of words our ancestors used. Let's collects words for wind and write poetry inspired by the names of trees. Let's ask our friends from other cultures to teach us the most interesting words from their own language!

Lagom, (Swedish): exactly right, just enough (not too much and not too little)

Uitwaaien, (Dutch): going for a walk (or cycling trip) and

letting the wind clear your mind of stuck thoughts and old energy
Imelda Almqvist[15]

As if you could kill time without injuring eternity
Henry David Thoreau[16]

There is no remedy for love but to love more
Henry David Thoreau[17]

Activity #30: Everything Is Medicine

When my three sons were much younger, and the youngest one still in a pushchair, one day we were walking down the hill, at the end of a long day. Youngest son was crying and kicking his legs furiously. I had run out of ideas for calming him. I just wanted to reach our front door and get dinner on the table. At that point my eldest son picked three rubber bands off the pavement (London postmen are always dropping those bands everywhere!). He handed them to youngest son and showed him how you can stretch them and use them to make cat's cradle type shapes. Instant silence and relief from the screaming! Eldest son shrugged his shoulders and said: "Everything is medicine, often you just need to know what to pick up in the street..."

My son taught me a powerful lesson that day and I often think back to his wise words. They echo the wisdom of Native American peoples who speak of Bear Medicine, Big Medicine or The Medicine Way and they are not referring to medicine in the Western *medical* sense of the word.

For the final activity in this book I invite you to see the world through the eyes of my son's younger self for a day: assume that *everything is medicine!* As you go about your business, look at things you would not normally pay attention to, such as bottle tops, twigs, stones, autumn leaves, discarded envelopes, bottles in different colours, feathers, sea glass.... For every single item, try to conceive of a medicine purpose.

Rather than giving an old tee shirt to the charity shop (thrift shop or Goodwill in American English), spend a night making a rag doll for a child you know

If a piece of paper flutters around (even a flyer or junk mail) look for a sacred message. Make note of it or cut out it out and stick it in your journal for this book.

If you see twigs that have dropped into interesting patterns and formations, ask someone who knowns the runes to give you a reading on those shapes and their message. Take a photograph of this ephemeral gift.

If you are up for an additional task: reflect on words of uncommon beauty or power from your mother tongue and (only if this is an option) in any other languages you speak. Start keeping a glossary. Write an occasional poem about your discoveries!

Remember Max Weber's words[18]: *For one day choose to live in a world that remains an enchanted garden!*

This book is a passionate plea for the right use of the human imagination!

Notes

Chapter 1

1. https://en.wiktionary.org/wiki/medicine
2. https://en.wikipedia.org/wiki/History_of_medicine
3. https://en.wikipedia.org/wiki/Traditional_medicine
4. http://www.wpro.who.int/china/mediacentre/factsheets/traditional_medicine/en/
5. https://deskgram.net/explore/tags/millionmamasmovement
6. http://www.shamanicteachers.com/
7. https://www.verywellmind.com/what-is-art-therapy-2795755
8. https://en.wikipedia.org/wiki/Medicine_man
9. Foundation for Shamanic Studies, https://www.shamanism.org/
10. https://www.thoughtco.com/cultural-diffusion-definition-3026256
11. https://www.theguardian.com/world/2018/nov/28/india-body-john-allen-chau-missionary-killed-by-sentinelese-tribe
12. https://www.etymonline.com/word/shaman
13. http://freya.theladyofthelabyrinth.com/?page_id=35
14. *Türklerin* İnanç *Sistemi, Ibrahim Sari,* Noktaekitap, 2017, p.115
12. http://elensentier.co.uk/

Chapter 2

1. http://www.peterturchi.com/books/
2. https://www.etymonline.com/word/imagination
3. https://en.wikipedia.org/wiki/Fantasy_prone_personality
4. https://www.simplypsychology.org/psyche.html
5. Adapted from http://www.carl-jung.net
6. https://peterborough75.blogspot.com/2011/11/c804ebook-download-pdf-laws-of-healing.html
7. https://www.sheldrake.org/
8. https://www.learnreligions.com/as-above-so-below-occult-phrase-origin-4589922

Chapter 3

1. Quoted in "What Life Means to Einstein: An Interview by George Sylvester Viereck" in The Saturday Evening Post (26 October 1929)
2. https://www.youtube.com/watch?v=s2cixaL9H3U
3. http://www.coda-uk.org/
4. http://www.shaman-healer-painter.co.uk/info2.cfm?info_id=109559
5. *Owning Your Own Shadow, Understanding the Dark Side of the Psyche* by Robert A. Johnson, Bravo Ltd, 2009
6. https://en.wikipedia.org/wiki/The_Unbearable_Lightness_of_Being

Chapter 4

1. Thomas Moore quote from "Care of the Soul" featured by Travel Alchemy: http://www.travel-alchemy.com/knowing-your-shadow/
2. C. G Jung, The Philosophical Tree (1945), Collected Works 13: Alchemical Studies Paragraph 335
3. Susan Rossi, Open Channel Astrology, Access the Cosmos Within, openchannelastrology.com
4. https://en.wikipedia.org/wiki/John_Bauer_(illustrator)

Chapter 5

1. Read more at: https://www.brainyquote.com/topics/imagination
2. http://paganpages.org/content/2017/05/a-spiritual-toolkit-for-the-exam-period/
3. *Natural Born Shamans: A Spiritual Toolkit for Life* by Imelda Almqvist, 2016, Moon Books

Chapter 6

1. https://www.brainyquote.com/quotes/voltaire_100338
2. Adapted from: https://en.wikipedia.org/wiki/Allegory_of_the_Cave
3. https://www.youtube.com/watch?v=Nc5DSQnuh74
4. *The Seed of Yggdrasil: Deciphering the Hidden Messages in Old Norse*

Myths by Maria Kvilhaug, Whyte Tracks, 2017, http://freya.theladyofthelabyrinth.com/

5. *Lost Gods of England* by Brian Branston, Thames and Hudson Ltd, 1974
6. *Dawn Behind the Dawn: A Search for the Earthly Paradise* by Geoffrey Ashe, Henry Holt and Co, 1991
7. Abstract and review: https://www.kirkusreviews.com/book-reviews/geoffrey-ashe/dawn-before-the-dawn/
8. https://www.youtube.com/watch?v=UuDOS60twVU
9. https://marcelgomessweden.wordpress.com/2011/08/18/the-five-worlds-the-cosmology-of-lurianic-kabbalah/
10. Cosmos: http://www.shaman-healer-painter.co.uk/info2.cfm?info_id=224477
11. https://www.theguardian.com/artanddesign/2015/mar/25/iceland-construction-respect-elves-or-else
12. https://www.news.com.au/lifestyle/real-life/news-life/river-granted-person-status-and-legal-rights-its-strange-to-give-a-natural-resource-a-personality/news-story/cdba312497a141ce2880a4ca6d487563
13. https://buddhists.org/buddhist-symbols/samsara-in-buddhism/
14. https://www.friggasweb.org/renewal.html
15. http://www.betsybergstrom.com/
16. https://www.newspiritjournalonline.com/suicide-answering-the-call-for-symbolic-death-and-rebirth/
17. https://imeldaalmqvist.wordpress.com/2016/09/29/the-reverse-magic-of-worrying/
18. http://www.patheos.com/blogs/christiancrier/2015/12/21/what-did-jesus-say-or-teach-about-heaven/

Chapter 7

1. Personal email correspondence reproduced with permission, Friday 29 June 2018, with Susan Rossi, openchannelastrology.com
2. https://www.nytimes.com/2000/09/20/business/business-travel-apparent-case-air-rage-southwest-airlines-ends-what-later-ruled.

html
3. https://theurbanshaman.online/griefwalker-a-review-and-invitation-to-the-death-feast/
4. www.youtube.com/watch?v=nWmVQd7D0V0
5. https://www.youtube.com/watch?v=ALT8zbjnjkY
6. *The Smoke Gets in Your Eyes: And Other Lessons from The Crematorium* by Caitlin Doughty, Canongate Books, 2016
7. https://deathcafe.com/
8. *Sacred Art: A Hollow Bone for Spirit (Where Art Meets Shamanism)* by Imelda Almqvist, Moon Books, 2019
9. https://charlotteducann.blogspot.com/2013/02/52-flowers-morning-glory.html?m=0
9. *The Love Hall, Brendan's Travel Guide to the Best Places in the Spirit World*, Polar Bear & Cubs, 2014
10. https://www.grandmotherscouncil.org/our-mission/
11. Xeni Jardin, https://edition.cnn.com/2017/07/21/opinions/cancer-is-not-a-war-jardin-opinion/index.html
12. *The Love Hall, Brendan's Travel Guide to the Best Places in the Spirit World*, Polar Bear & Cubs, 2014
13. https://www.hinduwebsite.com/reincarnation.asp,
14. Holy Quran, http://corpus.quran.com/translation.jsp?chapter=4&verse=93
15. https://hods.org/pdf/Jewish%20Perspectives%20on%20Issu.pdf

Chapter 8

1. https://www.goodreads.com/quotes/406960-a-good-friend-will-help-you-move-but-a-true
2. https://www.goodreads.com/work/quotes/41392349-etched-in-bone
3. https://www.youtube.com/watch?v=gTZgfyOW-DA
4. http://www.ascensionsymptoms.com/
5. https://www.refinethemind.com/reality-tunnels-robert-anton-wilson/
6. https://en.wikipedia.org/wiki/Reality_tunnel

7. https://www.theguardian.com/world/2009/jan/15/women-developing-countries-die-childbirth
8. https://www.meaningfulhq.com/rising-strong.html

Chapter 9

1. https://creation.com/world-creation-stories
2. https://www.theguardian.com/science/2009/feb/17/evolution-versus-creationism-science
3. http://www.viralnova.com/killers-describe-killing/
4. https://www.murdermiletours.com/blog/motives-for-murder-why-do-serial-killers-kill
5. https://www.livescience.com/474-controversy-evolution-works.html
6. https://www.azquotes.com/quote/539128
7. https://nationalpost.com/opinion/john-robson-if-death-has-no-meaning-then-how-can-life
8. https://evolutionnews.org/2012/07/what_are_the_to_1/
9. http://www.dailyom.com/cgi-bin/display/librarydisplay.cgi?lid=3649
10. http://www.throughthewoodstherapy.com/the-story-im-telling-myself/
11. http://blogs.reuters.com/john-lloyd/2012/02/28/god-richard-dawkins-and-the-meaning-of-life/
12. *Beeld en Werkelijkheid,* van Ringelestein, Meulenhof, 1963
13. *The Lost Language of Plants: The Ecological Importance of Plant Medicine to Life on Earth,* Stephen Harrod Buhner, Chelsea Green Publishing, 2002, p.31
14. *The Lost Language of Plants: The Ecological Importance of Plant Medicine to Life on Earth,* Stephen Harrod Buhner, Chelsea Green Publishing, 2002, p.29
15. https://relevantmagazine.com/culture/10-cs-lewis-quotes-show-he-was-ahead-his-time/

Chapter 10

1. https://medium.com/@brian.cronin.3/proceed-with-caution-exploring-the-human-psyche-jung-nietzsche-8981f9d3449f
2. https://www.brainyquote.com/quotes/thomas_aquinas_166249
3. https://www.simplypsychology.org/abnormal-psychology.html
4. https://en.wikipedia.org/wiki/Toxicity
5. https://issuu.com/theempathmagazine/docs/the_empath_magazine_-_issue_2
6. http://bloggingdickinson.blogspot.com/2012/06/word-is-dead-when-it-is-said.html
7. Comment by long-term student Katharine Lucy Haworth, in closed Facebook group titled The Poison Mother, reproduced with permission, July 2018
8. Poetic Edda, Lokasenna: http://www.sacred-texts.com/neu/poe/poe10.htm
9. The Poison Mother, art video by Imelda Almqvist: https://www.youtube.com/watch?v=YpEfiuthtYo&t=112s?
10. On-line article by Peter Langman author of Why Kids Kill: Inside the Minds of School Shooters), https://ed.lehigh.edu/theory-to-practice/2013/school-shooters
11. *Natural Born Shamans: A Spiritual Toolkit for Life* by Imelda Almqvist, Moon Books 2016, p.109
12. https://www.psychologytoday.com/us/blog/how-do-life/201410/dangerous-personalities
13. https://www.azquotes.com/author/49903-Ramzi_Yousef
14. https://apjjf.org/-Yuki-Tanaka/1606/article.html
15. Video on UCTV: Explaining the Inexplicable: Suicide Bombers' Motivation as the Quest for Personal Significanc https://www.uctv.tv/shows/Explaining-the-Inexplicable-Suicide-Bombers-Motivation-as-the-Quest-for-Personal-Significance-15142
16. https://www.simplypsychology.org/abnormal-psychology.html
17. https://www.psychologytoday.com/us/basics/psychopathy
18. https://www.psychologytoday.com/intl/blog/the-superhuman-mind/201803/do-all-serial-killers-have-genetic-predisposition-kill

19. http://freya.theladyofthelabyrinth.com/?page_id=117
20. https://www.psychologytoday.com/intl/blog/darwins-subterranean-world/201802/the-psychopath-next-door
21. https://www.youtube.com/watch?v=g1EG8DJZ3os&t=67s
22. *Columbus and Other Cannibals: The Wetiko Disease of Exploitation, Imperialism and Terrorism* by Jack D. Forbes, Seven Stories Press, 2009, Acknowledgments p.xi
23. 2degreesoffreedom.blogspot.co.uk/2006/09/synergetics-by-r-buckminster-fuller.html
24. *Dispelling Wetiko: Breaking the Curse of Evil* by Paul Levy, North Atlantic Books, 2013, p.13
25. https://www.awakeninthedream.com/dispelling-wetiko-book-summary
26. http://jungcurrents.com/jung-collective-shadow-scapegoat-evil
27. https://www.goodreads.com/quotes/115992-your-mind-is-like-an-unsafe-neighborhood-don-t-go-there
28. https://en.wikipedia.org/wiki/Jacob_wrestling_with_the_angel
29. http://bodhi.sofiatopia.org/psychopathy.htm
30. https://www.psychologytoday.com/us/blog/here-there-and-everywhere/201701/11-warning-signs-gaslighting
31. http://archive.emilydickinson.org/correspondence/holland/l185.html
32. https://en.wikipedia.org/wiki/The_Stranger_Beside_Me
33. https://www.grunge.com/110562/traits-serial-killers-eerily-common/
34. https://en.wikiquote.org/wiki/Richard_Ramirez
35. https://thepsychologist.bps.org.uk/volume-30/july-2017/false-memories-childhood-abuse
36. https://en.wikipedia.org/wiki/David_Finkelhor
37. https://psmag.com/social-justice/dangerous-idea-mental-health-93325
38. https://psmag.com/social-justice/dangerous-idea-mental-health-93325, Book: *The Myth of Repressed Memories: False Memories and Allegations of Sexual Abuse*, Elizabeth Loftus, St. Martin's Press,

2000
39. https://www.crimetraveller.org/2019/01/talking-with-serial-killers/
40. *Talking with Serial Killers: The Most Evil People in the World Tell Their Own Stories,* Christopher Barry-Dee, John Blake, 2018

Chapter 11

1. http://jungcurrents.com/jung-shadow-darkness-conscious
2. *Sacred Art: A Hollow Bone for Spirit (Where Art Meets Shamanism),* Imelda Almqvist, Moon Books 2019, p.93
3. https://archive.org/stream/ManOfLightInIranianSufismByHenryCorbin/Man-of-Light-in-Iranian-Sufism-by-Henry-Corbin_djvu.txt
4. Kay Scarpetta is a fictional character and protagonist in a series of crime novels written by Patricia Cornwell, https://en.wikipedia.org/wiki/Kay_Scarpetta
5. https://sacredtrust.org/faculty/
6. https://www.vice.com/en_au/article/ypv58j/genetic-memory
7. *The Witches Ointment: The Secret History of Psychelic Magic,* Thomas Hatsis, Inner Traditions/Bear, 2015
8. https://www.youtube.com/watch?v=-0j_32U-Nes&t=37s
9. https://urbanbalance.com/the-story-of-two-wolves/
10. The Orlando Shooting: Blog About Shadow and Intuition https://imeldaalmqvist.wordpress.com/2016/06/12/the-orlando-shooting-blog-about-shadow-and-intuition/
11. http://paganpages.org/content/2018/03/never-again-school-shootings/
12. https://en.wikipedia.org/wiki/Bacchanalia
13. http://www.deadlysins.com/
14. http://www.bbc.co.uk/religion/religions/hinduism/concepts/concepts_1.shtml
13. http://www.buddhanet.net/cbp2_f7.htm and http://buddhismandthaiamulet.blogspot.com/2015/06/life-after-death.html
15. Quoted by Helga Kuhse and Peter Singer in the following article

in Bioethics: (Vol. 52, No. 3, Bioethics (AUTUMN 1985), pp. 505-542) https://www.jstor.org/stable/40970386?seq=1#page_scan_tab_contents

16. Three quotes takes from Beyond Good and Evil by Friedrich Nietzsche, https://www.nietzsche-quotes.com/beyond-good-and-evil

Chapter 12

1. https://www.merriam-webster.com/dictionary/moral%20law
2. http://www.jkevinbutcher.com/thomas-aquinas-on-injustice/
3. http://www.thetablet.co.uk/student-zone/ethics/ethics-and-religion/natural-moral-law
4. https://www.loebclassics.com/view/marcus_tullius_cicero de_re_publica/1928/pb_LCL213.211.xml?readMode=recto
5. https://www.biography.com/people/st-thomas-aquinas-9187231
6. Adapted from: https://www.slideshare.net/aquinas_rs/what-is-natural-moral-law
7. https://townhall.com/tipsheet/laurettabrown/2019/01/25/heres-a-list-of-states-that-permit-abortion-up-to-birth-for-any-reason-n2540247
8. Spirit Children, art video by Imelda Almqvist: https://www.youtube.com/watch?v=GpSLQLHN2B4&t=14s
9. http://www.dignitas.ch/?lang=en
10. https://www.youtube.com/watch?v=JJDqceiwR2U
11. *Quotes To Remember (Volume 2),* Dr. Purushothaman, Centre for Human Perfection, p.14
12. https://www.quora.com/Did-Einstein-really-say-Adversity-introduces-a-man-to-himself-If-so-where-and-when-did-he-say-this
13. https://www.thoughtco.com/moral-panic-3026420
14. *Folk Devils and Moral Panics,* by Stanley Cohen, Routledge, 2011

Chapter 13

1. http://www.planetofsuccess.com/blog/2011/developing-empathy-

walk-a-mile-in-someone's-shoes/

2. https://www.goodreads.com/quotes/613585-pain-is-inevitable-suffering-is-optional-say-you-re-running-and
3. https://vunela.com/compassion-is-better-than-empathy/
4. https://www.etymonline.com/word/compassion
5. https://philosophynow.org/issues/52/Empathy_and_Imagination
6. https://en.wikipedia.org/wiki/Suicide_attack)
7. https://apjjf.org/-Yuki-Tanaka/1606/article.html
8. https://blog.usejournal.com/beware-the-near-enemies-in-life-tech-9dcf31167bdc
9. http://reducing-suffering.org/short-introduction-reducing-suffering/
10. *Zeitgeist* by Todd Wiggins, Phoenix, 1997
11. http://www.autismtoolbox.co.uk/understanding-autism/social-imagination/
12. https://www.amazon.co.uk/George-Sam-Charlotte-Moore/dp/0241956609/ref=sr_1_1?s=books&ie=UTF8&qid=1525166577&sr=1-1&keywords=george+and+sam
13. *The Horse Boy: A Father's Miraculous Journey to Heal His Son* by Rupert Isaacson, Penguin 2009
14. *The Long Ride Home: The Extraordinary Journey of Healing That Changed a Child's Life*, Penguin, 2014
16. Temple Grandin, https://www.ted.com/speakers/temple_grandin)
16. Greta Thunberg, https://www.independent.co.uk/voices/davos-greta-thunberg-climate-change-global-warming-a8746536.html
17. http://www.jalderson.com/imagination-autism-irony-treatment/
18. v http://med.stanford.edu/news/all-news/2014/11/5-questions--temple-grandin-discusses-autism--animal-communicati.html.html
19. http://www.sandraingerman.com/
20. https://www.youtube.com/watch?v=YpEfiuthtYo
21. https://www.psychologytoday.com/us/blog/focus-forgiveness/201105/the-hawaiian-secret-forgiveness
22. *The Wisdom of Psychopaths: What Saints, Spies and Serial Killers Can Teach Us About Success* by Kevin Dutton, http://

wisdomofpsychopaths.com/

Chapter 14

1. *God and Diseases*, David Tacey, Routledge, 2012
2. *E.C. Krupp, Celestial Catechism, The History of Non-Western Culture,* John Wiley & Sons, 1999
3. https://www.britannica.com/topic/anthropomorphism
4. http://www.theoi.com/Daimon/Aidos.html
5. http://www.skepdic.com/pareidol.html
6. *Faces in the Clouds: A New Theory of Religion,* Stewart Elliott Guthrie, Oxford University Press, 1995, p.130
7. https://www.psychologytoday.com/intl/blog/singular-perspective/201801/see-the-world-through-patterns
8. The Creative Explosion: An Inquiry into the Origins of Art and Religion, John E. Pfeiffer, Harper and Row, 1982, p. 220
9. https://en.wikipedia.org/wiki/Moon_rabbit
10. https://www.psychologytoday.com/intl/blog/social-dilemmas/201508/the-surprising-power-conspiracy-theories
11. https://www.psychologytoday.com/gb/blog/hide-and-seek/201312/the-psychology-scapegoating
12. https://en.wikipedia.org/wiki/Displacement_(psychology)
13. https://theconversation.com/why-are-some-people-more-gullible-than-others-72412
14. http://www.bbc.com/future/story/20180124-the-enduring-appeal-of-conspiracy-theories
15. https://en.wikipedia.org/wiki/David_Grimes_(meteorologist)
16. https://www.sciencedirect.com/science/article/abs/pii/0375960184906674
17. https://positivepsychologyprogram.com/pollyanna-principle/
18. https://pdfs.semanticscholar.org/5bee/28cb402f342d2dbe1d79cf3267ec3338c061.pdf
19. https://psmag.com/social-justice/the-dangers-of-spiritual-amateurism-in-america
20. *A Death on Diamond Mountain: A True Story of Obsession, Madness*

and the Path to Enlightenment by Scott Carney, Gotham Books, 2015

21. *Natural Born Shamans: A Spiritual Toolkit for Life* (Using Shamanism Creatively with Young People), Moon Books, Imelda Almqvist, 2016

Chapter 15

1. From private email correspondence with Susan Rossi, 18 May 2018, quoted with permission
2. https://www.scientificamerican.com/article/how-are-traits-passed-on/

Chapter 16

1. https://www.mrmoneymustache.com/2011/10/22/what-is-hedonic-adaptation-and-how-can-it-turn-you-into-a-sukka/
2. http://astro.if.ufrgs.br/fis2008/TheHistoryofNon-WesternScience.pdf
3. https://www.independent.co.uk/life-style/health-and-families/happiness-behaviours-characteristics-science-relationships-kindness-a7843631.html

Chapter 17

1. *Sacred Art: A Hollow Bone for Spirit (Where Art Meets Shamanism)*, Moon Books, 2019, p.149
2. *The MD Emperor Has No Clothes: Everybody is Sick and I Know Why*, Peter Glidden, 2012
3. The Shamanic View of Mental Illness, Jason Gaddis interviews Malidoma Some in this online article: https://www.jaysongaddis.com/the-shamanic-view-of-mental-illness/
4. Independent: https://www.independent.co.uk/life-style/health-and-families/rd-laing-was-the-countercultures-favourite-psychiatrist-a-dangerous-renegade-or-a-true-visionary-a6755021.html
5. *Natural Born Shamans: A Spiritual Toolkit for Life* (Using shamanism creatively with young people of all ages) by Imelda Almqvist,

Moon Books, 2016, p. 70
6. Blog by Imelda Almqvist titled The Great Unmoveable Goddess Called Insomnia: https://imeldaalmqvist.wordpress.com/2016/09/06/the-great-unmoveable-goddess-called-insomnia/
7. https://www.kirkusreviews.com/book-reviews/kat-duff/the-alchemy-of-illness/
8. *The Alchemy of Illness,* Kat Duff, Harmony; Bell Tower ed. Edition, 2000, p. 33

Chapter 18

1. Cancer History, News Medical, (https://www.news-medical.net/health/Cancer-History.aspx)
2. https://medicalxpress.com/news/2016-03-holy-grail-cancer-treatment.html
3. https://www.stuff.co.nz/national/102115864/in-narrative-therapy-mori-creation-stories-are-being-used-to-heal
4. https://www.cancerquest.org/patients/what-cancer
5. Cell Division and Cancer, https://www.nature.com/scitable/topicpage/cell-division-and-cancer-14046590
6. https://www.news-medical.net/health/Cancer-History.aspx
7. https://www.nationalgeographic.com/magazine/2018/12/inequality-rich-poor-essay-jared-diamond/
8. https://www.amnesty.org/en/what-we-do/indigenous-peoples/
9. https://www.thedailystar.net/editorial/news/environmental-pollution-out-control-1635133
10. https://fitzvillafuerte.com/what-would-happen-if-we-redistribute-wealth-equally-to-everyone.html
11. https://history.state.gov/milestones/1989-1992/collapse-soviet-union
12. https://en.wikipedia.org/wiki/Chinese_Communist_Revolution
13. https://www.telegraph.co.uk/news/earth/earthnews/9815862/Humans-are-plague-on-Earth-Attenborough.html
14. http://www.theoi.com/Ther/DrakonHydra.html
15. https://www.change.org/p/cancer-sucks-so-let-s-rename-the-

zodiac-constellation-from-cancer-to-sebastian

16. Susan Rossi in private email correspondence, 18 May 2018, reproduced with permission, https://openchannelastrology.com/
17. https://www.psychologytoday.com/us/blog/how-the-mind-heals-the-body/201411/is-there-cancer-prone-personality
18. https://www.nature.com/articles/s41568-018-0004-9
19. http://archives.esf.org/coordinating-research/eurocores/news/ext-news-singleview/article/finding-a-cure-for-cancer-the-holy-grail-of-science-74.html
20. https://www.youtube.com/watch?v=klK2A-w9Qaw&t=103s
21. https://www.youtube.com/watch?v=zScMj14mUI8
22. https://www.khanacademy.org/science/biology/cellular-molecular-biology/stem-cells-and-cancer/a/cancer
23. https://www.sairasalmon.com/awakening-your-grail-wisdom/
24. https://onezero.medium.com/the-race-to-diagnose-cancer-with-a-simple-blood-test-6ec5d38eb1c9

Chapter 19

1. https://www.psychologytoday.com/us/blog/in-flux/201608/8-things-the-most-toxic-people-in-your-life-have-in-common
2. 88 https://issuu.com/theempathmagazine/docs/the_empath_magazine_-_issue_2
3. https://www.psychologytoday.com/gb/blog/the-web-violence/201806/what-is-dehumanization-anyway
4. *Modern Machiavelli, 13 Law of Power, Persuasion and Integrity,* Troy Bruner and Phil Eager, Changemakers Books, 2017, p. 122
5. http://mysticinvestigations.com/genies/
6. https://www.facinghistory.org/resource-library/decision-making-times-injustice/holocaust
7. https://www.history.com/topics/holocaust/what-is-genocide
8. https://io9.gizmodo.com/5791530/why-humans-all-much-more-related-than-you-think

Chapter 20

1. https://psychcentral.com/blog/narcissists-who-cry-the-other-side-of-the-ego/
2. https://www.healthyplace.com/personality-disorders/malignant-self-love/coping-with-the-narcissist-stalker
3. https://www.psychologytoday.com/intl/blog/hide-and-seek/201203/thinking-about-love-the-myth-narcissus
4. https://www.greekmythology.com/Myths/Mortals/Narcissus/narcissus.html
5. https://www.psychologytoday.com/us/blog/romance-redux/201306/5-early-warning-signs-youre-narcissist
6. https://www.huffpost.com/entry/sociopath-signs-is-your-e_n_3181512
7. https://en.wikipedia.org/wiki/Malignant_narcissism
8. https://newrepublic.com/article/116748/americanization-narcissism-author-elizabeth-lunbeck-interview
9. https://www.verywellmind.com/what-is-the-collective-unconscious-2671571
10. Blog: https://imeldaalmqvist.wordpress.com/2017/03/30/trumps-teachings/
11. Online article: https://io9.gizmodo.com/narcissism-is-one-of-the-most-misunderstood-psychologic-1588867730
12. https://www.psychologytoday.com/us/blog/lifetime-connections/201601/are-narcissists-born-or-made
13. *Dangerous Personalities: An FBI Profiler Shows You How to Identify and Protect Yourself from Harmful People* by Joe Navarro and Toni Sciarra Poynter, Rodale Books, 2018
14. *The Gift of Fear: Survival signals that protects us from violence,* by Gavin de Becker, Bloomsbury Publishing PLC, 2000
15. 'Why Do Narcissists Lose Popularity Over Time?' Online article by Scott Barry Kaufman: http://www.creativitypost.com/psychology/why-do-narcissists-lose-popularity-over-time
16. https://www.huffpost.com/entry/signs-of-narcissism_n_5a26cf6de4b069df71fa196b

17. https://www.sane.org/information-stories/the-sane-blog/mental-illness/is-narcissism-common-the-answer-may-surprise-you

Chapter 21

1. https://www.goodtherapy.org/blog/psychpedia/imagination
2. https://steemit.com/subculture/@lpfaust/deeper-dives-a-world-of-pure-imagination-my-float-through-the-altered-states-in-a-sensory-deprivation-tank
3. King, Paul. "What Happens in the Brain During Sensory Deprivation?" Quora. April 17, 2013.
4. http://psychologytomorrowmagazine.com/much-needed-rest-world-sensory-deprivation-tanks/
5. *Statistics of Mental Imagery, Francis Galton* (1880), First published in Mind, 5, 301-318, Classics in the History of Psychology, http://psychclassics.yorku.ca/Galton/imagery.htm
6. Mo Costandi, 'If you can't imagine things, how can you learn?' https://www.theguardian.com/education/2016/jun/04/aphantasia-no-visual-imagination-impact-learning
7. https://www.brainyquote.com/quotes/aldous_huxley_386509
8. Professor Martin Procházka, Dream, Imagination and Reality in Literature: An Introduction, https://www.pf.jcu.cz/stru/katedry/aj/doc/sbaas01-introduction.pdf

Chapter 22

1. https://www.psychologytoday.com/za/blog/transcending-the-past/201610/understand-your-dreams-using-jungs-active-imagination?amp
2. https://www.psychologytoday.com/za/blog/transcending-the-past/201610/understand-your-dreams-using-jungs-active-imagination?amp
3. https://www.scientificamerican.com/article/the-science-behind-dreaming/
4. Rose Cailola, blog, https://www.rewireme.com/roses-blog/dreaming/

5. https://plato.stanford.edu/entries/dreams-dreaming/
6. https://www.thesap.org.uk/resources/articles-on-jungian-psychology-2/carl-gustav-jung/dreams/
7. https://lindayaelschiller.com/ancient-practice-dream-incubation/
8. https://www.crosswalk.com/family/career/3-things-you-didn-t-know-about-joseph-in-the-bible.html
9. https://epages.wordpress.com/2012/02/12/deciphering-dreams-different-perspectives/
10. http://www.indigenousinstyle.com.au/aboriginal-culture/dreamtime/
11. http://www.beliefnet.com/columnists/dreamgates/2012/01/daydreams-of-science-the-benzene-ouroboros-and-the-clapham-omnibus.html
12. The Rainbow Serpent, https://www.didjshop.com/stories/rainbow.html
13. Robert Moss: https://mossdreams.com/
14. *Phantasy in Everyday Life: A Psychoanalytical Approach to Understanding Ourselves,* by Julia Segal, Routledge, 1991
15. Gods of Portals, Life Transitions and Liminal Spaces, presentation by Imelda Almqvist at Thresholds, the annual conference of The Gatekeeper Trust: https://www.youtube.com/watch?v=LzxmXAJiPLc&t=322s
16. https://www.space.com/32728-parallel-universes.html
17. http://www.spiritofmaat.com/archive/may3/moss.htm

Chapter 23

1. https://www.science20.com/sandygautam/the_faculty_of_imagination_neural_substrates_and_mechanisms
2. http://www.entelechyjournal.com/simonbaroncohen.htm
3. https://www.ncbi.nlm.nih.gov/pmc/articles/PMC6557866/
4. http://www.entelechyjournal.com/simonbaroncohen.htm
5. https://www.inspiredinquiries.com/
6. https://www.ncbi.nlm.nih.gov/pubmed/16773904
7. https://the-mouse-trap.com/2007/06/05/the-faculty-of-

imagination-neural-substrates-and-mechanisms/

8. *E. C, Krupp, 'Sky Tales and Why We Tell Them', Science Across Cultures: The History of Non-Western Science,* Volume 1 Astronomy Across Cultures, p.3
9. *Magical Tour of The Night Sky: Use the Planets and Stars for Personal and Sacred Discovery*, Renna Shesso, Weiser Books, 2012
10. https://www.psychologytoday.com/us/blog/the-athletes-way/201306/imagination-can-change-perceptions-reality
11. Christopher Bergland, https://www.psychologytoday.com/gb/blog/the-athletes-way/201411/imagination-and-reality-flow-conversely-through-your-brain
12. https://www.psychologytoday.com/intl/blog/the-athletes-way/201508/why-does-overthinking-sabotage-the-creative-process?amp
13. http://www.wired.co.uk/article/neuroscience-of-imagination
14. http://abc7news.com/archive/9441384/
15. http://www.wired.co.uk/article/false-memory-syndrome-false-confessions-memories. (Book: *The Memory Illusion: Remembering, Forgetting, and the Science of False Memory* by Dr Julia Shaw, Random House Books, 2017)
16. https://en.wikipedia.org/wiki/Valerie_F._Reyna
17. https://www.jjay.cuny.edu/faculty/deryn-strange
18. https://scienceblogs.com/neurophilosophy/2008/06/18/do-you-swear-to-tell-the-truth-or-whatever-you-remember
19. https://www.ranker.com/list/why-innocent-people-confess-to-crimes/lea-rose-emery?page=3
20. ttp://astro.if.ufrgs.br/fis2008/TheHistoryofNon-WesternScience.pdf

Chapter 24

1. https://www.huffingtonpost.com/judith-johnson/what-is-karma_b_1376246.html
2. https://openchannelastrology.com/
3. http://moon-books.net/blogs/moonbooks/karma-projections-fantasy-

and-delusion/
4. https://www.physicsclassroom.com/class/newtlaws/Lesson-4/Newton-s-Third-Law
5. https://www.psychologytoday.com/us/conditions/delusional-disorder

Chapter 25

1. https://www.stuff.co.nz/national/102115864/in-narrative-therapy-mori-creation-stories-are-being-used-to-heal
2. https://www.macmillandictionary.com/dictionary/british/whanau
3. https://www.facebook.com/groups/1902301606465391/
4. http://realscandinavia.com/st-lucia-day-in-sweden/
5. http://www.differencebetween.net/miscellaneous/difference-between-colonialism-and-imperialism/
6. Under the Korowai: https://www.youtube.com/watch?v=odo_-Vh2-fI
7. https://www.nytimes.com/2014/03/09/magazine/reaching-my-autistic-son-through-disney.html
8. https://www.desiringgod.org/articles/five-things-ive-learned-from-kids-with-autism
9. http://www.wou.edu/history/files/2015/08/Lucie-Johnson.pdf
10. https://imeldaalmqvist.wordpress.com/2017/04/07/the-gods-and-goddesses-of-the-future/

Chapter 26

1. https://www.youtube.com/watch?v=Z7bo3tYV8Go
2. https://www.biography.com/scholar/carl-jung
3. https://appliedjung.com/the-archetypes-of-the-anima-and-animus/
4. http://www.northernshamanism.org/ergi-the-way-of-the-third.html
5. https://www.gaia.com/article/divine-masculine-and-feminine
6. The Lay of Thrym, Poetic Edda, retold in English prose by D.L. Ashliman, 2009, https://www.pitt.edu/~dash/thrym.html

Chapter 27

1. https://en.wikipedia.org/wiki/Disenchantment
2. https://www.urbandictionary.com/define.php?term=Ableism
3. http://www.patheos.com/blogs/johnbeckett/2015/09/4-steps-to-re-enchant-the-world.html
4. http://www.science20.com/science-autism-spectrum-disorders/some-thoughts-parenting-and-then-research-based-blogging-culture-and-autism
5. http://college.cengage.com/early_childhood_education/course360/diverse_learners_1111829462/ebook/demelendez_1428376984_ch02.pdf
6. https://www.psychologynoteshq.com/bronfenbrenner-ecological-theory/
7. https://en.wikipedia.org/wiki/Disability-culture
8. https://www.thoughtco.com/acculturation-definition-3026039
9. https://pdfs.semanticscholar.org/73d0/2e1d99469f4fa16bffa04ef188a1ba2cd002.pdf
10. https://en.wikipedia.org/wiki/Lawrence-Kohlberg
11. https://www.simplypsychology.org/piaget.html
12. https://meganmeierfoundation.org/statistics
13. https://onlinelibrary.wiley.com/doi/abs/10.1080/00207590500345898
14. https://thepsychologist.bps.org.uk/volume-24/edition-2/aspergers-syndrome-—-difference-or-disorder
15. https://www.theguardian.com/science/blog/2015/jul/16/autism-doesnt-have-to-be-viewed-as-a-disability-or-disorder
16. https://network.crcna.org/disability-concerns/glamorizing-disability
17. https://innovativepublichealth.org/blog/self-harm-websites-and-teens-who-visit-them/

Chapter 28

1. http://www.wiseoldsayings.com/addiction-quotes/
2. https://www.addictioncenter.com/treatment/12-step-programs/

3. *Columbus and Other Cannibals: The Wetiko Disease of Exploitation, Imperialism and Terroris,* by Jack D. Forbes, Seven Stories Press, 2009, Acknowledgments p.xi
4. https://www.goodreads.com/work/quotes/26266149-dispelling-wetiko
5. http://jungcurrents.com/jung-collective-shadow-scapegoat-evil
6. *Dispelling Wetiko, Breaking the Curse of Evil,* North Atlantic Books, 2013, Paul Levy, p.33

Chapter 29

1. https://www.psychologytoday.com/intl/blog/imagine/201003/einstein-creative-thinking-music-and-the-intuitive-art-scientific-imagination
2. https://www.youtube.com/results?search_query=imelda+almqvist
3. Alissa Cook in 'Of Memory and Muses: The Wellsprings of Creativity', 2013, https://scholarworks.montana.edu/xmlui/handle/1/2988
4. https://www.greekmyths-greekmythology.com/nine-muses-in-greek-mythology/
5. https://en.wikipedia.org/wiki/Ontology
6. https://en.wikipedia.org/wiki/Epistemology
7. *Feeding Your Demons: Ancient Wisdom for Resolving Inner Conflict,* by Tsultrim Allione, Hay House, 2009
8. *Dark Side of the Light Chasers: Reclaiming your power, creativity, brilliance, and dreams,* Debbie Ford, Hodder Paperbacks, 2001
9. https://www.youtube.com/watch?v=B4U_zh7jr4s&t=54s
10. https://www.brainyquote.com/quotes/helen_keller_109208
11. https://www.hooponopono.org/
12. http://4urself.com/blog/2015/8/18/pain-is-inevitable-suffering-is-optional-haruki-murakami
13. https://www.brainyquote.com/topics/excess
14. The Global Apology Project: https://www.facebook.com/groups/1902301606465391/

Chapter 30

1. *Dispelling Wetiko: Breaking the Curse of Evil* by Paul Levy, North Atlantic Books, 2013, p.18
2. https://en.wikipedia.org/wiki/Koko_(gorilla)
3. http://www.bbc.com/future/story/20130207-can-animals-imagine
4. AnimalSake, https://animalsake.com/do-animals-have-imagination
5. https://www.bbc.com/news/world-us-canada-46824649
6. https://www.theguardian.com/environment/2017/jul/10/earths-sixth-mass-extinction-event-already-underway-scientists-warn
7. https://www.theguardian.com/environment/2019/jan/25/our-house-is-on-fire-greta-thunberg16-urges-leaders-to-act-on-climate
8. https://www.theguardian.com/environment/2018/oct/30/humanity-wiped-out-animals-since-1970-major-report-finds
9. https://timesofmalta.com/articles/view/the-end-of-civilisation.702216
10. Anita Sullivan, Manifesto, in private email correspondence, 29 July 2019, reproducted with permission
11. http://www.sandraingerman.com/tnoctober2016.html
12. *The Lost Language of Plants: The Ecological Importance of Plant Medicines to Life on Earth,* by Stephen Harrod Buhner, Chelsea Green Publishing, 2002, p.27
13. http://www.theguardian.com/books/2015/feb/27/robert-macfarlane-word-hoard-rewilding-landscape
14. *The Lost Words,* by Robert Macfarlane and Jackie Morris, Hamish Hamilton, 2017
15. http://www.shaman-healer-painter.co.uk/
16. https://www.brainyquote.com/quotes/henry_david_thoreau_379356
17. https://www.brainyquote.com/quotes/henry_david_thoreau_103440
18. https://en.wikiquote.org/wiki/Disenchantment

Acknowledgments

No book is ever written by one mind alone! Therefore, I would like to thank friends, colleagues, students and strangers!

I thank Anita Sullivan for writing the Foreword. Anita is both a poet and piano tuner – no one uses words quite the way that she does!

Lucya Starza (who edited my first book: Natural Born Shamans: A Spiritual Toolkit for Life) for the suggestion of adding an activity at the end of every chapter. She made this suggestion for my second book (Sacred Art: A Hollow Bone for Spirit) but the reactions I received from readers were so positive that I have decided to apply this to all my books!

My publisher: The Moon Books team for their continued faith in my unorthodox books and writing projects!

My sacred art students who faithfully show up for some of the most mysterious art retreats ever taught. I learn something from every single one of you, every time!

Jill Hunter and Susan Rossi for anchoring my professional and moral compass as well as being talented colleagues and friends.

Todd Wiggins for clarifying key concepts in Buddhism.

Nimue Brown for beta-reading and valuable early feedback.

Jessica Lempp for our discussions about *inner activism*!

The author of every book I have ever read. Our London house is like the Alexandrian Library rising from the ashes, we even keep books in our bathroom…

My husband and three sons: Ulric, Quinn, Elliott and Brendan Almqvist, for putting up with a "full time weird" (wyrd!) mother and a house full of students at regular intervals.

Last but not least: the spirits! You unfailingly set me tasks that fill me with trepidation and anxiety. Doing the work of Spirit often means walking "The Path of Panic Attacks". However, once

I drop into trust and engage with an open heart, you unfailingly bring me all the pieces that I need to complete the challenge. So here it is: another book you urged me to write! I hope that I did the task justice.

Author Biography

Imelda Almqvist is an international teacher of shamanism and sacred art. Her first book *Natural Born Shamans: A Spiritual Toolkit for Life (Using shamanism creatively with young people of all ages)* was published by Moon Books in 2016 and her second book Sacred Art: A Hollow Bone for Spirit (Where Art Meets Shamanism) was published in March 2019. She was a presenter on the Shamanism Global Summit in both 2016 and 2017 and a presenter on Year of Ceremony with Sounds True in 2018. She appears in a TV program made for the Smithsonian Channel (the series is called Mystic Britain) about the Mesolithic site Star Carr in Yorkshire talking about arctic deer shamanism! Imelda divides her time between the UK, Sweden and also teaches in the US. *"Medicine of the Imagination: Dwelling in Possibility"* is her third book and she is currently working on her fourth book *"Evolving Gods: The Sacred Marriage of Tradition and Innovation"*. It will focus on the Seidr and the wisdom teachings of the Northern European Tradition. She has recently started a fifth book about the ancient indigenous (non-Christian) spirituality of The Netherlands. Her website is: www.shaman-healer-painter.co.uk

From the Author

Thank you for purchasing this book! I hope that reading it was a much of an adventure as writing it was for me! May I ask you politely to take a moment to leave a review on your favourite on-line site. (Most people read reviews on amazon as part of the process of deciding to buy a book). If you would like to receive updates on courses I teach and events I participate in, I invite you to subscribe to my newsletter by contacting me through my website: www.shaman-healer-painter.co.uk. I will then add you to the relevant list.

You may also contact me about events, public speaking and

teaching in different locations. I love adventures, meeting new people and learning new things! I have (limited) availability for on-line consultations and supervision sessions for shamanic practitioners and sacred art practitioners.

Wild blessings! Imelda Almqvist

www.shaman-healer-painter.co.uk *(website)*
https://imeldaalmqvist.wordpress.com/ (blog)
https://www.youtube.com/results?search_query=imelda+almqvist
(YouTube channel: interviews, presentations and art videos)

PAGANISM & SHAMANISM

What is Paganism? A religion, a spirituality, an alternative belief system, nature worship? You can find support for all these definitions (and many more) in dictionaries, encyclopaedias, and text books of religion, but subscribe to any one and the truth will evade you. Above all Paganism is a creative pursuit, an encounter with reality, an exploration of meaning and an expression of the soul. Druids, Heathens, Wiccans and others, all contribute their insights and literary riches to the Pagan tradition. Moon Books invites you to begin or to deepen your own encounter, right here, right now.

If you have enjoyed this book, why not tell other readers by posting a review on your preferred book site.

Recent bestsellers from Moon Books are:

Journey to the Dark Goddess
How to Return to Your Soul
Jane Meredith
Discover the powerful secrets of the Dark Goddess and transform your depression, grief and pain into healing and integration.
Paperback: 978-1-84694-677-6 ebook: 978-1-78099-223-5

Shamanic Reiki
Expanded Ways of Working with Universal Life Force Energy
Llyn Roberts, Robert Levy
Shamanism and Reiki are each powerful ways of healing; together, their power multiplies. *Shamanic Reiki* introduces techniques to help healers and Reiki practitioners tap ancient healing wisdom.
Paperback: 978-1-84694-037-8 ebook: 978-1-84694-650-9

Pagan Portals – The Awen Alone
Walking the Path of the Solitary Druid
Joanna van der Hoeven
An introductory guide for the solitary Druid, *The Awen Alone* will accompany you as you explore, and seek out your own place within the natural world.
Paperback: 978-1-78279-547-6 ebook: 978-1-78279-546-9

A Kitchen Witch's World of Magical Herbs & Plants
Rachel Patterson
A journey into the magical world of herbs and plants, filled with magical uses, folklore, history and practical magic. By popular writer, blogger and kitchen witch, Tansy Firedragon.
Paperback: 978-1-78279-621-3 ebook: 978-1-78279-620-6

Medicine for the Soul

The Complete Book of Shamanic Healing

Ross Heaven

All you will ever need to know about shamanic healing and how to become your own shaman…

Paperback: 978-1-78099-419-2 ebook: 978-1-78099-420-8

Shaman Pathways – The Druid Shaman

Exploring the Celtic Otherworld

Danu Forest

A practical guide to Celtic shamanism with exercises and techniques as well as traditional lore for exploring the Celtic Otherworld.

Paperback: 978-1-78099-615-8 ebook: 978-1-78099-616-5

Traditional Witchcraft for the Woods and Forests

A Witch's Guide to the Woodland with Guided Meditations and Pathworking

Mélusine Draco

A Witch's guide to walking alone in the woods, with guided meditations and pathworking.

Paperback: 978-1-84694-803-9 ebook: 978-1-84694-804-6

Wild Earth, Wild Soul

A Manual for an Ecstatic Culture

Bill Pfeiffer

Imagine a nature-based culture so alive and so connected, spreading like wildfire. This book is the first flame…

Paperback: 978-1-78099-187-0 ebook: 978-1-78099-188-7

Naming the Goddess

Trevor Greenfield

Naming the Goddess is written by over eighty adherents and scholars of Goddess and Goddess Spirituality.

Paperback: 978-1-78279-476-9 ebook: 978-1-78279-475-2

Shapeshifting into Higher Consciousness

Heal and Transform Yourself and Our World with Ancient Shamanic and Modern Methods

Llyn Roberts

Ancient and modern methods that you can use every day to transform yourself and make a positive difference in the world.

Paperback: 978-1-84694-843-5 ebook: 978-1-84694-844-2

Readers of ebooks can buy or view any of these bestsellers by clicking on the live link in the title. Most titles are published in paperback and as an ebook. Paperbacks are available in traditional bookshops. Both print and ebook formats are available online.

Find more titles and sign up to our readers' newsletter at http://www.johnhuntpublishing.com/paganism
Follow us on Facebook at https://www.facebook.com/MoonBooks and Twitter at https://twitter.com/MoonBooksJHP